25
BICYCLE TOURS
in Vermont

Let Backcountry Guides Take You There

Our experienced backcountry authors will lead you to the finest trails, parks, and back roads in the following areas:

50 Hikes Series

50 Hikes in the Maine Mountains
50 Hikes in Southern and Coastal Maine
50 Hikes in Vermont
50 Hikes in the White Mountains
50 More Hikes in New Hampshire
50 Hikes in Connecticut
50 Hikes in Massachusetts
50 Hikes in the Hudson Valley
50 Hikes in the Adirondacks
50 Hikes in Central New York
50 Hikes in Western New York
50 Hikes in New Jersey
50 Hikes in Eastern Pennsylvania
50 Hikes in Central Pennsylvania
50 Hikes in Western Pennsylvania
50 Hikes in the Mountains of North Carolina
50 Hikes in Northern Virginia
50 Hikes in Ohio
50 Hikes in Michigan

Walks and Rambles Series

Walks and Rambles on Cape Cod and the
   Islands
Walks and Rambles in Rhode Island
More Walks and Rambles in Rhode Island
Walks and Rambles on the Delmarva
   Peninsula
Walks and Rambles in Southwestern Ohio
Walks and Rambles in Ohio's Western
   Reserve
Walks and Rambles in the Western
   Hudson Valley
Walks and Rambles on Long Island
Walks and Rambles in and around St. Louis

25 Bicycle Tours Series

25 Bicycle Tours in Maine
30 Bicycle Tours in New Hampshire
25 Bicycle Tours in Vermont
25 Mountain Bike Tours in Vermont
25 Bicycle Tours on Cape Cod and the Islands
25 Mountain Bike Tours in Massachusetts
30 Bicycle Tours in New Jersey
25 Bicycle Tours in the Adirondacks
25 Mountain Bike Tours in the Adirondacks
30 Bicycle Tours in the Finger Lakes Region
25 Bicycle Tours in the Hudson Valley
25 Bicycle Tours in the Twin Cities and
   Southeastern Minnesota
30 Bicycle Tours in Wisconsin
25 Mountain Bike Tours in the Hudson Valley
25 Bicycle Tours in Ohio's Western Reserve
25 Bicycle Tours in Maryland
25 Bicycle Tours on Delmarva
25 Bicycle Tours in and around
   Washington, D.C.
25 Bicycle Tours in Coastal Georgia and the
   Carolina Low Country
25 Bicycle Tours in the Texas Hill Country and
   West Texas

We offer many more books on hiking, fly-fishing, travel, nature, and other subjects. Our books are available at bookstores and outdoor stores everywhere. For more information or a free catalog, please call 1-800-245-4151 or write to us at The Countryman Press, PO Box 748, Woodstock, Vermont 05091. You can find us on the Web at www.countrymanpress.com

250

BICYCLE TOURS
in Vermont

John Freidin
Photographs by the author and others

3rd EDITION

Backcountry Publications
Woodstock · Vermont

An invitation to the reader

Although it is unlikely that the roads you cycle on these tours will change much with time, some road signs, landmarks, and other items may. If you find that such changes have occurred on these routes, please let the author and publisher know, so that corrections may be made in future editions. Other comments and suggestions are also welcome. Address all correspondence to:

Editor, 25 Bicycle Tours™ Series
Backcountry Guides
PO Box 748, Woodstock, VT 05091-0748

Backcountry Guides is an imprint of The Countryman Press.

Library of Congress Cataloging-in-Publication Data

Freidin, John S.
    25 bicycle tours in Vermont/ John S. Freidin; photographs by the author and others. —3rd ed.
        p.   cm.
    ISBN 0-88150-330-4 (alk. paper)
    1. Bicycle touring—Vermont—Guidebooks. 2. Vermont—Guidebooks. I. Title.
    GV1045.5.V5F73 1996
    796.6'4'09743—dc20   95-50661
                    CIP

10 9 8 7 6 5 4 3 2

Second Printing, updated, 1999

Printed in Canada

Text design by Sally Sherman

Cover design by Joanna Bodenweber

Cover photograph of the Jenne Farm in Reading by Bo Gibbs for Bike Vermont, Inc., Woodstock, VT

Interior photographs by the author except as noted

Maps by Dick Widhu, © 1996 The Countryman Press, Inc.

Published by The Countryman Press
PO Box 748, Woodstock, VT 05091-0748

Distributed by W. W. Norton & Company, Inc.
500 Fifth Avenue, New York, NY 10110

Acknowledgments for the New Edition

First I want to thank the many cyclists who have written me letters of appreciation, correction, and advice. Their words have spurred me on and, I hope, made this new book more accurate and useful.

Having not ridden most of these roads for nine years, it was a special pleasure to revisit them in 1995. The joy of cycling in Vermont is irrepressible. And, though increases in traffic led me to alter a few routes, I was delighted to find that Vermont's best cycling roads still have few motor vehicles. Vermont is indeed a cyclist's delight—in 1995 as it was when I first rode here in 1972!

Bruce Burgess was a source of great help on this edition. The new tours out of Middlebury and Alburg and the riding in Essex, New York, are largely based on his work. I also want to thank Bill Perry and Vermont Bicycle Touring for allowing me to use some of VBT's photographs. No one knows bicycling in Vermont like Vermont Bicycle Touring.

Neil Quinn and Betsy Bates of the West Hill Shop helped me sharpen the Putney–Westminster tour, and Allan Kalsmith of the Black Lantern Inn in Montgomery steered me to some sensational riding in Canada to make what was always my favorite ride—Montgomery to Richford—even better. Others who were especially kind to me are Sol Baumrind, Wes and Mary Ann Carlson, Paul Cillo, David Deen, Ann Seibert, Kelsey Woodward, and Deborah Young.

My research was helped by the earlier work of Christina Tree and Peter S. Jennison. Their book *Vermont: An Explorer's Guide* (The Countryman Press, 1994) is a wealth of information and a useful supplement to this one, as is *The Vermont Road Atlas and Guide,* second edition, published by Northern Cartographic of Burlington, Vermont.

Most of all, I want to thank Gail and Abe for their daily support of my efforts to make this the best bicycle touring guide possible.

New Haven, Vermont
November, 1995

Foreword

John Freidin has written a book for people who want to see my native Vermont without hurry. His knowledge and love of this beckoning state shine through his descriptions of its people, places, and history. And his clear instructions will guide you confidently along our backroads.

25 Bicycle Tours in Vermont is a guide for travelers who want to get off the beaten path. John has chosen those less-traveled roads that will make all the difference to the Vermont you will see while you are here and remember long afterwards.

So if you really want to see and breathe Vermont—heed John's advice. Use this book and take your time. You will discover why those of us who have lived here all our lives would never live anywhere else.

Patrick J. Leahy
US Senator, Middlesex, Vermont

When I think of bicycle touring, I think of Vermont. When I think of organized bicycle tours, I think of John Freidin. When I'm asked what is the standard of excellence for organized tours, I recommend John's outfit, Vermont Bicycle Touring.

Why I can recommend this book so highly is that I've worked with John for years and know he knows a great deal about selecting and road-testing tours. You can be assured that these tours, in terms of the diversity and beauty they offer, take you to the heart of Vermont. Moreover, in selecting the tours John has provided tours that can be modified in hundreds of ways to meet your particular cycling and recreational needs. In effect, you have hundreds of touring options in this book.

As an experienced cyclist, John has made sure that these tours take you to places that will add miles of pleasure to your recreational cycling. If you want to shop, swim, or rest during your tour, this book will show you how. Perhaps most important, *25 Bicycle Tours in Vermont* presents the essence of bicycle touring: traveling under your own power to beautiful places at a pace that suits you. That is the ultimate in independence.

James C. McCullagh
Editor & Publisher, Bicycling *Magazine*

*For my parents Doris and Jesse Freidin,
that we might have ridden
these roads together, and
for Gail, Abe, and Luke*

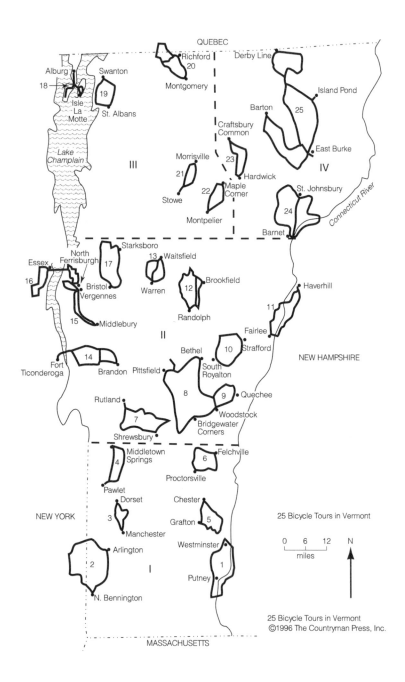

QUEBEC

Richford
20
Montgomery

Derby Line

Island Pond

Barton
25

Alburg
18
Isle
La
Motte

Swanton

19

St. Albans

Craftsbury
Common

East Burke

Lake
Champlain

III

Morrisville
23
21
Hardwick
Stowe
22
Maple
Corner

IV

St. Johnsbury

Connecticut River

24

Montpelier

Barnet

Starksboro

North
Ferrisburgh

Essex

16

17

13
Waitsfield

Warren

12

Brookfield

Bristol
Vergennes

Haverhill

15
Middlebury

Randolph

11

II

Fairlee

Bethel
10
Strafford

14
Fort
Ticonderoga

Brandon

Pittsfield

South
Royalton

NEW HAMPSHIRE

8

9
Quechee

Rutland

7

Woodstock
Bridgewater
Corners

Shrewsbury

Middletown
Springs

Felchville

4

6

Proctorsville

Pawlet

Dorset

Chester

NEW YORK

3

Grafton
5

Manchester

Westminster

25 Bicycle Tours in Vermont

Arlington

0   6   12   N

2

1

miles

N. Bennington

I

Putney

25 Bicycle Tours in Vermont
©1996 The Countryman Press, Inc.

MASSACHUSETTS

Contents

Introduction

Caterpillars and butterflies. On a ride one day, it struck me that bicyclists could be either one. The difference is their views of the terrain. To caterpillars every hill looks like a mountain, while to butterflies even mountains look level as they float over them. But given time every caterpillar grows into a butterfly. To me this is the greatest beauty of bicycling: that everyone in good health can become a good rider simply by doing it. Thanks to the efficiency of bicycles, most cycling requires only a little strength and no agility or speed.

This book is for both caterpillars and butterflies. Whether you have not ridden in years or cycle a thousand miles a season, *25 Bicycle Tours in Vermont* guides you to routes matching your ability in one of the most exquisite cycling environments imaginable. It enables you to find your way with confidence, it identifies the unpaved roads, and it alerts you to hills—both up and down. It suggests places to stay overnight so you can easily create your own vacation using a sumptuous inn, a charming bed & breakfast, or a riverside campground; it tells you about places to swim, find food, and get your bicycle repaired; it deepens your enjoyment of what you see by telling you a little about the history, architecture, geology, wildlife, and other curiosities along the way.

I selected the following 25 tours for their beauty and diversity. Each one had to be beautiful; and, as a group, they had to provide a breadth of choices wide enough to suit every level of cyclist and unveil as many facets of Vermont as possible. In length they range from 7 to 152 miles; in terrain from flat to very hilly. Some tours can be fully enjoyed on a three-speed bicycle; most are best ridden on a multigeared derailleur bicycle. The tours are dispersed throughout the state, but every tour ends where it begins. There are overnight tours and day trips, trips that visit handsome villages and trips through remote wonderlands, trips laden with history and trips that take you swimming, fishing, or bird-watching.

Many places are beautiful, but beauty alone does not satisfy bicyclists. Vermont is a cyclist's delight not merely because of its beauty, but also because of its scale and temperament. Here, where we still live in villages not cities, worship in churches not cathedrals, and travel on roads not highways, the environment is scaled to human proportions. Seldom do more than 10 miles separate general stores; rarely does a climb remain arduous for more than 2 miles. The pace of Vermont life more closely resembles the speed of a bicycle than that of an automobile, and the friendliness of the people is more like the cooperation of tandeming than the competitiveness of motoring. To bicycle is to steep yourself in an environment; to do so in Vermont is to fall in love with both the place and the pedaling.

Selecting a Tour

From the state map on page 8, see which tours fall in an area you find interesting or convenient. The tours are grouped into four regions. Next, look over the tours you are considering to see which suit you in terms of distance, terrain, and points of interest.

The 25 tours present far more than 25 choices. Many have side trips or shortcuts. And no tour is the same ridden in one season as it is in another, ridden with friends as ridden alone, ridden in the rain as ridden in the sunshine, ridden when leaves are on the trees or ridden when the trees are bare. Once you know a ride well in one direction, try it in the other.

The round-trip distance(s), number of any unpaved roads, and difficulty of the terrain are stated at the beginning of each tour. The terrain is rated according to the length, grade, and frequency of the hills you must climb. If you want to know the precise nature of the terrain, read the entire tour. But remember, since every tour completes a circle, every inch of climbing is matched by an inch of descent. Here are what my ratings mean:

- *Easy* terrain is generally level and never produces more than 1.5 miles of uphill riding every 25 miles. Easy terrain is suited to three-speed bicycling.
- *Easy-to-moderate* terrain is also generally level but requires 1.5 to 3 miles of climbing every 25 miles and brings some fast downhills. While some cyclists may enjoy this terrain on a three-speed bicycle, most will prefer it on a multigeared derailleur bicycle.
- *Moderate* terrain necessitates 3 to 6 miles of ascent for each 25 miles

Overlooking the Sugarbush Valley in Waitsfield

and is best ridden on a multigeared derailleur bicycle with a low gear in the mid-40s or lower.*

- *Moderate-to-difficult* terrain requires climbing 3 to 6 miles every 15 miles or so, and the grades are likely to be steeper than on moderate terrain. Gearing reaching into the 30s is helpful.
- *Difficult* terrain also requires 3 to 6 miles of climbing for each 15 miles of riding, but the hills are often steep. Gearing in the low or mid-30s is desirable.

Vermont terrain is never really level, and consequently bicycling here is more fun than in most other places. If you want to be cautious, just assume that I have slightly underestimated the difficulty of the terrain. But don't be timid!

Lodging

This edition of *25 Bicycle Tours in Vermont* differs from earlier editions in one key respect: Each tour now includes suggestions of inns, bed & breakfasts, and campgrounds. In this way I hope to make it easy for you to make the tour into an overnight vacation. Vermont has many campgrounds and lots of inns. They vary widely in character, cost, size, and location. I have listed places I would like to stay. Some are extraordinary, some are about all that is accessible; some are great bargains, others are pricey; some serve outstanding meals, others serve only a continental breakfast; some have private baths and designer sheets, others don't. I hope that you will write to tell me your opinions so the next edition of this book will be even better. You can easily uncover far more options than I have suggested by contacting the local chambers of commerce, whose addresses and telephone numbers are included at the end of each tour. They can provide comprehensive lists of places to stay.

Preparing for a Tour

The best way to get in shape for bicycling is to bicycle. Other sports (such as swimming and running) help, but they do not place identical

---

* To determine the lowest gear on your bicycle, count the teeth on the smaller front chain ring, divide that number by the number of teeth on the largest cog of the freewheel, and then multiply the quotient by the diameter, in inches, of the rear wheel.

demands on your body. To build your stamina, bicycle frequently and regularly—at least two or three times a week—and gradually increase the distance and speed you ride.

Several days before starting, read the entire tour. Decide what to carry—such as food and a bathing suit—and what to get along the way.

Make sure your bicycle is in good repair. Most need overhauling every 2000 miles or 2 years. When you ride, wear a helmet and carry a pump and equipment to repair flat tires.

Saddle soreness is common to cyclists. Within limits you grow accustomed to your perch, and proper cycling pants help. But the saddle itself makes a difference. Most cyclists, myself included, prefer one of the orthopedically designed saddles, made differently for women and men.

"A Vermont year is 9 months winter and 3 months damn poor sleddin'," goes the proverb. Although there are wonderful days for cycling in April and November, the principal bicycling season runs from May through October. I like May and June best, because the days are long and the landscape is brilliantly green and strewn with wildflowers. July and August are great for swimming and rarely too hot or humid to be uncomfortable. Fall foliage season, covering roughly 5 weeks from mid-September to mid-October, turns the trees into a riot of color, but the discomfort of cold or wet days is greater. Vermont weather is extremely volatile. From May through August daytime temperatures can range from 40 to 90 degrees F (4–33 C). During September and October they can go from 30 to 80 F (-1–27 C). Prepare yourself for a variety of temperatures by dressing in layers.

Select brightly colored clothing that breathes as well as insulates. Your muscles should be kept warm, especially your legs and knees, and your skin should be kept dry except on the hottest days.

Carry water and a little food. Drink before you are thirsty and eat before you are hungry to keep your strength and spirits up. You need little protein but lots of fluid and carbohydrates.

Doing a Tour

Read the tour before you start. Each one includes a sketch map that is best used in conjunction with an official Vermont road map, available free from the Vermont Travel Division, 134 State Street, Montpelier, VT 05602 (802-828-3236).

When you are riding, pause at each turn to read the directions for the next turn, for it may come immediately. All roads are paved unless noted otherwise. The text also describes the most prominent grades.

The tours are presented in a regular pattern. Beside each of the cumulative mileages are the directions to follow to stay on the route. Notes about the terrain, road surface, and subjects of interest follow.

Vermont law stipulates that "every person riding a bicycle is granted all rights and is subject to all of the duties applicable to operators of vehicles, except . . . those provisions which by their very nature can have no application." It also says that cyclists "shall ride as near to the right side of the roadway as practicable." Several regulations govern bicycling after dark, which it is best not to do at all. Violations of Vermont bicycle laws are punishable by fine.

To these laws I would add the following recommendations: Wear a helmet; ride single file; do not turn to look behind you while you are riding; do not bicycle across railroad tracks; and never make a left turn while you are riding. Stop, get off your bicycle, look, and then walk across, please. Although the text mentions many potential dangers, it must not be relied upon as the final word, for road and traffic conditions constantly change. Rely only on yourself for your safety.

Very few cyclists can conquer every hill. But before walking, try this trick. When you reach your lowest gear and can no longer turn the pedals, stop and stand by your bicycle for a minute. Then get back aboard and continue on your way until you need to take another of these "granny stops." They truly relieve your pain and allow your body to gather enough energy to resume pedaling. You can climb nearly any hill more quickly and easily by taking "granny stops" than by pushing your bicycle.

Now, go and enjoy yourself.

SOUTHERN VERMONT

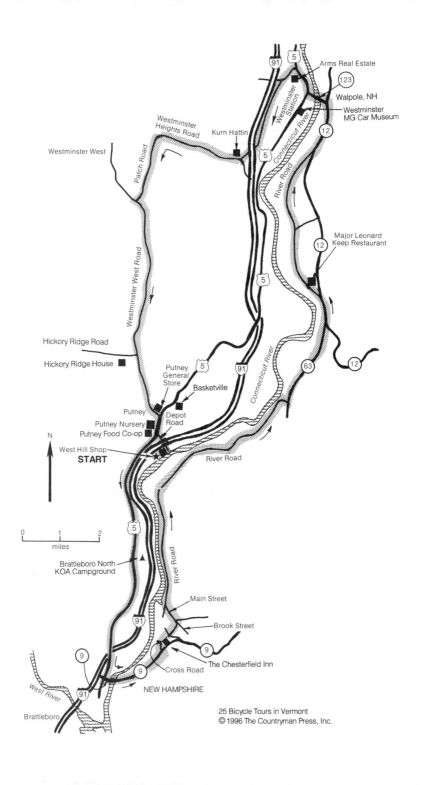

91
5
Arms Real Estate
123
Walpole, NH
Westminster
MG Car Museum
Westminster Station
Connecticut River
Westminster Heights Road
Kurn Hattin
Westminster West
5
River Road
Patch Road
12
Major Leonard
Keep Restaurant
12
Westminster West Road
5
Hickory Ridge Road
Hickory Ridge House
5
91
Connecticut River
63
12
Putney General Store
Basketville
Putney
Depot Road
Putney Nursery
Putney Food Co-op
N
West Hill Shop
START
River Road
0   1   2
miles
5
Brattleboro North
KOA Campground
River Road
91
Main Street
Brook Street
9
9
The Chesterfield Inn
9
9
Cross Road
NEW HAMPSHIRE
West River
91
Brattleboro

25 Bicycle Tours in Vermont
© 1996 The Countryman Press, Inc.

1
Putney–Westminster

Moderate terrain; 41.5 miles

The Putney region abounds with activity and beauty. This tour focuses on the splendidly rural Connecticut River valley and offers superb diversity of water scenes, farmland, orchards, and dense woods. The first 30 miles are generally easy, but there's a good bit of climbing near the end, and so the terrain should be considered moderate.

For years Putney has attracted skilled weavers, blacksmiths, cabinetmakers, and other craftspeople; many, such as Green Mountain Spinnery, have studios in or near the village. The Putney Nursery grows the largest selection of wildflowers in the eastern United States. And on the first weekend in October, oarsmen and -women from far and wide convene in Putney for a major rowing regatta.

This tour owes much to my special friends Betsy Bates and Neil Quinn. Betsy led tours for Vermont Bicycle Touring for 15 years, and she and Neil run one of Vermont's finest bicycle/ski shops. So it's appropriate to start the tour at their West Hill Shop, which has a large parking area as well as a superlative staff and complete inventory. The West Hill Shop, which is open 7 days a week, sits at the end of a long driveway that opens onto Depot Road opposite the Putney Inn, just over 0.1 mile east of exit 4 off Interstate 91.

0.0   *Turn left out of the driveway of the West Hill Shop onto Depot Road, which is unsigned here, and ride uphill over I-91 toward US 5 and Putney Village.*

Just before you turn onto Depot Road, you are facing the Putney Inn and a local information booth. Consider stopping to get the latest news about local events.

The communes that flourished in Putney and throughout Vermont during the 1960s and early 1970s had forebears in Putney 130 years earlier. As Ralph Waldo Emerson commented at that

19

time: "The ancient manners were giving way. There grew a certain tenderness on the people, not before remarked. It seemed a war between intellect and affection . . . The key to the period appeared to be that the mind had become aware of itself."

One hundred thirty years ago in Putney, John Humphrey Noyes, the son of an upstanding family, decided that humankind was no longer corrupted by original sin. Instead, like the children of the '60s, Noyes believed all persons might achieve perfection on earth and so created a community to sustain his beliefs. His followers practiced Bible Communism: the sharing of all labor and property. "All mine thine, and all thine mine."

Noyes's permissive views of sexuality differentiated him from other Christian socialists of his time. He saw little distinction between owning property and owning persons: "The same spirit which abolished exclusiveness in regard to money, would abolish. . . exclusiveness in regard to women and children." Noyes's community practiced "multiple marriage," whereby adults shared sexual intimacy and child care alike.

Eventually, even Putney could not tolerate Noyes's views, so he and his followers fled to Oneida, New York, where their religious and social concerns were transmuted into the aesthetic and commercial concerns of the famous silver-plate company they founded.

Looking back on his father's Putney community, one of Noyes's sons recalled a quality of life strikingly similar to the communal life of the 1960s: "The relation between our grown folks had a quality intimate and personal, a quality that made life romantic. Unquestionably the sexual relations of the members under the Community inspired a lively interest in each other, but I believe that the opportunity for romantic friendships also played a part in rendering life more colorful than elsewhere."

0.2 At the stop sign at the top of the hill, turn left onto US 5 South toward Brattleboro. Beware of traffic.

Directly across US 5 from this stop sign is the Putney Food Co-op, where you can buy some good food to carry along.

Putney is widely known for apples (a tenth of Vermont's crop), athletes (Olympians Bill Koch, Tim Caldwell, and Eric Evans), artists (Jim Dine), authors (John Irving and John Caldwell), and, of course, Aiken—the Honorable George—governor, senator, and horticulturist. Putney is known even more widely for the Putney School (established in 1935), an innovative private coeducational boarding high school for 165 students. Life at the Putney School carefully integrates college preparation with work on the school and its small farm: "We harvest our own vegetables, sing Bach together, and live close to the land."

US 5 has considerable traffic, but a nice wide shoulder. The first 2 miles go downhill; thereafter it rolls more down than up.

In 3 miles you reach the entrance (on your left) to the Brattleboro North KOA Campground. And 0.1 mile farther is the Walker Farm (also on your left), a great source of fresh local produce, fruit, and cold drinks.

6.0 *At the traffic light, continue straight on Putney Road (US 5 South). Do not turn onto Old Ferry Road; it will not take you across the Connecticut River.*

6.7 *At the traffic light, turn left onto Route 9 East toward Keene, New Hampshire. Beware of traffic on VT 9; the road does not always have a good shoulder.*

In 0.25 mile, you cross the Connecticut River and enter New Hampshire. The Connecticut rises at the conjunction of the Vermont, New Hampshire, and Canadian borders and flows 412 miles southward into Long Island Sound at Old Saybrook. It is New England's longest river and separates Vermont and New Hampshire for the 235 miles of their common border.

There are 13 dams along the Vermont–New Hampshire section of the river. Most are owned by New England Power Company and generate electricity during times of high demand. As a result the water level changes as much as 12 feet at places, which can be hard on wildlife.

After you cross the river, which is the lowest point on the tour, you climb uphill for 0.5 mile.

8.7 *At the crossroad, turn left onto Cross Road. Be careful of traffic on NH 9 as you turn.*

If you were to continue for another tenth of a mile on NH 9 East beyond Cross Road, you would reach the Chesterfield Inn on your left.

9.1 *At the stop sign at the crossroads, go straight to continue on Cross Road.*

In 0.25 mile, Cross Road dives down a winding, steep hill. Ride cautiously.

9.6 *At the stop sign, turn left onto Brook Street.*

9.7 *At the next stop sign, turn left onto Main Street, which becomes River Road.*

Main Street goes down another winding, steep hill.

10.1 *At the intersection, where Main Street turns 90 degrees to the left, go straight toward River Road.*

River Road is quiet, shaded, and winding. You'll ride up and down several short hills, a couple of which will probably make you puff, but most of the way is easy.

In a half mile the Connecticut River is on your left. In the early spring (April through mid-May), thousands of waterfowl migrate up the river. Take time to look and you may see Canada geese, snow geese, black ducks, wood ducks, scoters, horned grebes, ring-necked ducks, mergansers, herring gulls, and common golden-eyes.

A half mile farther on, you pass a marker commemorating the spot where in 1761 Moses Smith built the first house in Chesterfield.

17.1 *At the intersection with Partridge Brook Road, continue straight on River Road.*

17.9 *At the T, turn left onto NH 63 North. Thereafter, stay on NH 63, which is the main road; do not turn onto the side roads.*

NH 63 rolls over two half-mile hills.

20.2 *At the stop sign, turn left onto NH 12 North toward Walpole.*

Beware of the traffic at this intersection.

20.8 *Just before you would pass Major Leonard Keep Restaurant on your left, turn left off NH 12 onto River Road, which goes downhill.*

Cross NH 12 very cautiously.

As you approach the next intersection, you will be riding downhill, around a curve that bends sharply to your right. Go very

22

slowly, for the road is often littered with sand and gravel.

22.7 *Turn left to continue on River Road, which is unsigned.*

25.1 *At the stop sign, turn left onto NH 12 North, which is unsigned here. Thereafter, stay on NH 12, which is the main road; do not turn onto the side roads.*

25.9 *At the blinking light, continue straight on NH 12 North.*

26.6 *At the second blinking light, turn left onto NH 123 North toward Westminster, Vermont, and ride back across the Connecticut River.*

27.0 *At the T just after you pass through the underpass (in West-minster Station), turn right toward Bellows Falls and US 5, and ride 25 yards up a short hill to the stop sign. There, bear right onto US 5 North.*

If you enjoy antique automobiles, don't turn right onto US 5 North. Instead, turn left and follow US 5 South 0.4 mile to the Westminster MG Car Museum on your left. It houses a 30-car collection of the classic British sportscar and is open Saturday and Sunday, noon to 5 PM. Admission is charged. After your visit head north on US 5 to the turn described at mile 27.7 below.

In 1775 Westminster witnessed one of the first outbreaks of violence between the New York colonial authorities and the people living in the area we now know as Vermont. The Yorkers claimed jurisdiction over all land between Lake Champlain and the Connecticut River, and so did New Hampshire. Neither would honor land grants made by the other. In order to preserve their right to land granted them by both authorities, Vermonters convened in Westminster on January 16, 1777, and declared their independence of both New York and New Hampshire. This step soon led to Vermont's separate nationhood and subsequent refusal to join the original 13 colonies when they formed the United States. Not until 1791 did Vermont agree to become the 14th state.

27.7 *Just beyond Arms Real Estate (on your left), turn left toward Kurn Hattin Homes onto the unsigned road toward I-91.*

If you reach Allen Brothers Farm Store on your left, you have ridden 150 yards beyond your turn. But if you're hungry, stop at the farm; it offers a tempting selection of fresh fruit and cold drinks.

28.3 *At the first left (just before I-91), turn left onto Westminster Heights Road toward Kurn Hattin and Westminster West. Thereafter, continue to follow the signs for Kurn Hattin and Westminster West; do not turn onto the side roads. After about 5 miles this road is called Patch Road.*

The first 1.5 miles are easy, but then you begin to climb. First there's a hard 3-mile pull that gets steep at the top. Then, after a 0.75-mile downhill, you climb another half mile and then descend a steep and winding hill, half a mile long, that carries you to your next turn.

Along the way you'll ride through the campus of Kurn Hattin, a private, nonprofit residential school for about 100 children, grades one through eight. For more than a century, Kurn Hattin has been providing structure, support, and education for boys and girls who are not able to live successfully at home. The children come from a variety of socioeconomic backgrounds and live in this bucolic setting, which includes a small farm.

34.9 *At the yield sign (near Westminster West), turn sharply left toward Putney onto Westminster West Road, which is unsigned here.*

Immediately you start uphill again; this time for a mile, the last half of which may feel like a wall. But then your work is truly over. The next 4 miles head gaily downhill nearly all the way to Putney.

After you've ridden 3.9 miles on Westminster West Road, you reach Hickory Ridge Road on your right. If you turn right there, Hickory Ridge House, a bed & breakfast inn, will be on your left in 0.3 mile, slightly uphill.

40.6 *At the stop sign in Putney, bear right onto US 5 South.*

As you arrive at this stop sign, the Putney General Store will be on your left. It's a good place to get a sandwich, ice cream, or coffee.

A quarter of a mile north, on the right side of US 5, is Basketville, a family business that has been making baskets of Vermont white ash for 150 years. Call 802-387-5509 for a schedule of times for tours of the factory workshop. Or just ride there. Basketville also sells a barnful of home furnishings from candles to furniture.

As you ride down the main street of Putney, consider stopping at Heartstone Books on your right. Owners Rosemary Ladd and John Smith have a good selection of new and used books.

41.1 Beside the Putney Food Co-op on your right, turn left toward I-91 onto Depot Road, which is unsigned here.

41.5 Turn right into the entrance to the West Hill Shop, where you began.

For general information on lodging, restaurants, attractions, and special events, contact the Brattleboro Area Chamber of Commerce, 180 Main Street, Brattleboro, VT 05301 (802-254-4565).

Where to Stay

Chesterfield Inn, NH 9, PO Box 155, Chesterfield, NH 03443 (603-256-3211 or 800-365-5515), has grown up from a 1787 tavern and farm. Set on attractive grounds with lovely flower gardens, the inn is now a place of comfortable elegance. Innkeepers Judy and Phil Hueber have built spacious guest rooms with every modern convenience. The inn has a fine chef and serves breakfast, lunch, and dinner. If you're sensitive to road noise, ask for a room that faces away from NH 9.

Hickory Ridge House, Hickory Ridge Road, RD 3, Box 1410, Putney, VT 05346 (802-387-5709), is a wonderful circa-1808, brick Federal house, listed in the National Register of Historic Places. The rooms are delightfully decorated; I'm especially fond of the Blue and Yellow Rooms. Innkeepers Jacquie Walker and Steve Anderson serve an elegant, hearty breakfast with the inn's own preserves, baked goods, and eggs, plus local maple syrup.

Brattleboro North KOA Campground, US 5, RD 2, Box 560, Putney, VT 05346, is a small, clean campground of 42 sites and 5 motel cottages. Each site is set on a level lawn with a shade tree, picnic table, and charcoal grill. There's also a sparkling swimming pool, outdoor playground, and indoor recreation area with games and television.

Bicycle Repair Services

Andy's, 165 Winchester Street, Keene, NH (603-352-3410)

Banana's Cycling Company, 82 Main Street, Keene, NH (603-357-2331)

Brattleboro Bicycle Shop, 178 Main Street, Brattleboro, VT (802-254-8644)

Norm's Ski & Bike Shop, Martel Court, Keene, NH (603-352-1404)

Specialized Sports, Putney Road, Brattleboro, VT (802-257-1017)

West Hill Shop, Depot Road, Putney, VT (802-387-5718)

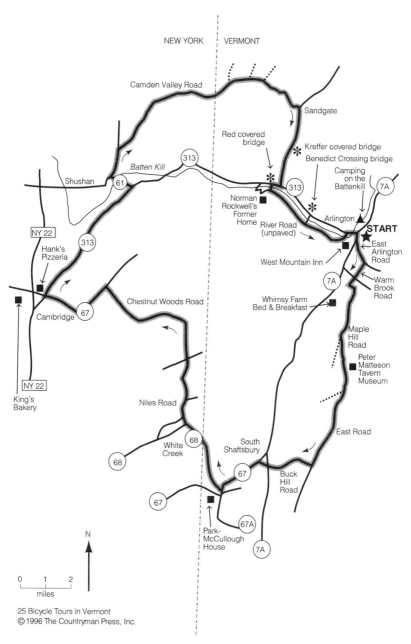

NEW YORK | VERMONT

Camden Valley Road

Sandgate

Red covered bridge

Kreffer covered bridge

Benedict Crossing bridge

313

Camping on the Battenkill

7A

Batten Kill

61

Shushan

Norman Rockwell's Former Home

313

Arlington

START

NY 22

Hank's Pizzeria

313

River Road (unpaved)

East Arlington Road

West Mountain Inn

67

Cambridge

Chestnut Woods Road

7A

Warm Brook Road

Whimsy Farm Bed & Breakfast

Maple Hill Road

NY 22

King's Bakery

Peter Matteson Tavern Museum

Niles Road

68

68

White Creek

South Shaftsbury

East Road

67

67

Buck Hill Road

67A

Park-McCullough House

7A

N

0   1   2
miles

25 Bicycle Tours in Vermont
© 1996 The Countryman Press, Inc.

28

2
Arlington–North Bennington

Moderate terrain; 50.7 miles (11.7 unpaved)

Southwestern Vermont and adjacent New York are Norman Rockwell country. This tour, which avoids the region's busy highways and follows unpaved roads almost a quarter of the way, is especially fun to ride on a mountain bike. But it does not require such a bicycle; I've enjoyed it many times on a normal touring bicycle with narrow tires. Following wooded lanes and lush valleys between ridges of the Green and Taconic Mountains, the route offers many fine views—from the intimate to the panoramic. If you have time and a fishing license, you can try your luck in some of the greatest trout water in the country, because for 10 miles you cycle along the famous Batten Kill. Or you can swim in that river beneath a red covered bridge by the house where Norman Rockwell lived. The tour also takes you to a 130-year-old Victorian mansion, now open as a museum.

0.0 **From the intersection of VT 7A and VT 313 in Arlington, follow VT 7A South 200 yards and then turn left onto East Arlington Road toward East Arlington.**

Just before you turn, you pass the Norman Rockwell Gallery on your left. Rockwell lived in West Arlington from 1939 to 1953, and this is where he did most of his illustrations of small-town American life. Describing his life here, Rockwell wrote: "Vermont is inspiration to my work. Moving to Arlington had given my work a terrific boost . . . Now my pictures grew out of the world around me, the everyday life of my neighbors . . . I just painted the things I saw." The gallery is located in an old white church and displays many of Rockwell's *Saturday Evening Post* covers. Admission is charged.

Arlington was also the home of Dorothy Canfield Fisher, the immensely popular chronicler of Vermont life.

Connecticut Anglicans settled Arlington in 1763 so they might enjoy the amenities permitted by their faith in a more tolerant climate than puritanical Connecticut. Under their influence Arlington became the first Vermont town to take such liberties as raising maypoles and decorating Christmas trees.

The St. James Cemetery in Arlington bears witness to the early presence of these Episcopalians. One of Vermont's oldest burial grounds, the cemetery contains many curious headstones. Called Tory Hollow during Revolutionary times, Arlington was a Loyalist stronghold but was also briefly the residence of Ethan Allen, whose two children and first wife, Mary Brownson, are buried in St. James Cemetery.

There will be no other places to buy food for the next 12 miles, so you may want to stop at Cullinan's Store, which faces East Arlington Road on the left 100 yards after you cross VT 7A.

1.0 *Turn right onto Warm Brook Road.*

1.7 *At the stop sign, go straight to continue on Warm Brook Road.*

2.1 *Turn left onto Maple Hill Road. (At its southern end, in South Shaftsbury, this road is called East Road.)*

In 75 yards Maple Hill Road becomes unpaved for 5.5 miles. After a level quarter mile, Maple Hill Road goes gently but steadily uphill for 1.5 miles and then flattens out and descends.

5.0 *At the fork, bear left to stay on Maple Hill Road, which is still unpaved and goes downhill.*

In 0.4 mile—by the first sign for East Road—you start up a hill that lasts a half mile.

As the slope of the hill tapers off, you reach on your left the Peter Matteson Tavern, now owned by the Bennington Museum. Records from 1784 indicate that this building served as a public house as well as the homestead of a 200-acre farm. Although fire destroyed most of the original structure in 1976, it has been rebuilt and furnished with early American antiques. The museum is not open on a regular basis, but it is a pretty place to stop and rest.

Beyond the museum, the road climbs for 0.5 mile more and then descends until the next turn.

10.0 *At the first paved road on your right, turn right onto Buck Hill*

Road. (There is probably no road sign at this corner.)

Buck Hill Road tilts sharply upward for 150 yards and then runs rapidly downhill to South Shaftsbury, dropping from a height of 1200 feet to 740 feet in less than 2 miles.

12.0 *At the stop sign in South Shaftsbury, go straight across Main Street (also VT 7A) onto Church Street, the sign for which is on the far side of VT 7A.*

12.3 *Just after crossing the railroad tracks, bear left onto VT 67 West, called Eagle Street here.*

14.0 *At the stop sign, turn left to continue on VT 67 West (also Upper Main Street).*

14.3 *At the intersection beside the redbrick Merchant's Bank (on the right) in North Bennington, turn right to continue on VT 67 West, called Bank Street here.*

It is well worth detouring here to visit the Victorian mansion that was home to two of Vermont's governors: Instead of turning right, go straight across the intersection and ride 1 block to West Street. Turn right onto West Street and follow it uphill 75 yards to the Park-McCullough House at the corner of West and Park Streets. Built in 1865, this gracious 35-room mansion exemplifies the extravagant tastes and lifestyle of the Gilded Age: opulent rooms with 14-foot ceilings, a grand stairway, the stained-glass skylight, marble mantels, parquet floors, Persian rugs, outdoor sculptures, period carriages, an outstanding collection of antique toys and dolls, and formal gardens. Tours begin daily on the hour 10–3, mid-May through October. Admission is charged. After your visit, return to the intersection at the Merchant's Bank and ride west on VT 67.

14.5 *At the fork, bear right off VT 67 onto the road toward White Creek, New York. (In New York this road is called County Road 68.)*

In 1.25 miles, you cross the state line into New York.

18.1 *At the 90-degree left curve, go straight—off County Road 68 onto Niles Road, though there may be no street sign there.*

18.3 *At the T, turn right to continue on Niles Road.*

19.5 *At the crossroad, go straight onto Chestnut Woods Road, which*

The Kreffer covered bridge in West Arlington

at its end in 5 miles is called Chestnut Hill Road.

In a half mile you begin climbing for a mile. The first half is steep; the second half is gradual. The grade then turns downward and is often quite fast.

24.5 *At the stop sign, turn left onto Ash Grove Road (NY 67 West).*

26.9 *At the stop sign in Cambridge, New York, turn right onto Maple Street (NY 313 East).*

Hank's Pizzeria at the Corner Store, directly in front of you at this stop sign, treats bicyclists generously and makes good pizza, calzone, and subs. If you ride past Hank's so you pass the front steps on your right and continue straight across Route 22 for a half mile into the village of Cambridge, you will find King's Bakery on your left. Their confections are a treat.

33.5 *Turn left off NY 313 onto County Road 61.*

33.9 *At the stop sign, turn right, away from Shushan, onto the unsigned road.*

34.7 *At the fork beside a white house with a stone retaining wall (on your left), bear right onto Camden Valley Road. Follow the signs for Sandgate and Camden Valley Road for the next 8 miles.*

In 3.25 miles the pavement ends. Camden Valley Road is then unpaved but well packed for 2.5 miles, which slope gently uphill. A quarter mile after the surface becomes paved again, the road shoots sharply downhill through a series of tight S-curves usually littered with loose gravel. These conditions last 0.75 mile and must be ridden cautiously. After the curves, the road continues moderately downhill for 1.25 miles more.

42.8 *At the T in Sandgate, which is merely an intersection, turn right toward West Arlington onto Sandgate Road, though there may not be a street sign there.*

For the next 3 miles you descend gently, almost without pause, back to the Batten Kill. About halfway down you pass the Kreffer covered bridge on your left. In 1977 designer Susan DePeyster and carpenter William Skidmore converted an open-planked bridge spanning the Green River here into this short covered bridge.

45.9 *At the stop sign in West Arlington, which is little more than this intersection, turn right onto VT 313 West.*

46.3 *At the red covered bridge on your left, turn left onto the unsigned and unpaved road that goes through the bridge.*

The bridge, built in 1852, stretches 80 feet across the Batten Kill. The swimming is excellent; access is best from the shore at the far end of the bridge.

46.4 *At the stop sign, turn left onto River Road, which is unpaved.*

As you approach this T, the house to your right is the one where Norman Rockwell lived between 1943 and 1954. It is now the Inn at Covered Bridge Green.

47.9 *At the first bridge (Benedict Crossing), turn right onto the unpaved and unsigned road. In 1.75 miles, just before you cross the Batten Kill, the road becomes paved.*

Just before you cross the river, you'll find the driveway on your right that leads 0.2 mile uphill to the West Mountain Inn.

50.0 At the stop sign, turn right onto Battenkill Drive, which is also VT 313 East.

50.7 At the stop sign, you are back in Arlington at the intersection of VT 313 and VT 7A, where you began.

For general information on lodging, restaurants, attractions, and special events, contact the the Arlington Chamber of Commerce, PO Box 245, Arlington, VT 05250 (802-375-2800) or the Bennington Area Chamber of Commerce, Veterans Memorial Drive, Bennington, VT 05201 (802-447-1163).

Where to Stay

West Mountain Inn, River Road, Arlington, VT 05250 (802-375-6516), means superb hospitality and stately comfort. Set on 150 hillside acres, the inn provides 18 individually decorated rooms with delightful special touches. Llamas and lop-eared rabbits graze in the pasture; exotic goldfish swim in the garden pool. The food and wine list are excellent. Innkeepers Wes and Mary Ann Carlson are superb hosts.

Whimsy Farm Bed & Breakfast, Box 507, Arlington, VT 05250 (802-375-6654), is a lovely converted farmhouse. Run by the O'Dea family, this B&B features beautiful lodging with skylights, exposed beams, a sun deck, and private baths. The generous country breakfasts feature eggs fresh from the henhouse.

Camping on the Battenkill, VT 7A, Arlington, VT 05250 (802-375-6663), is a perfectly sited campground, just 7.5 miles south of Manchester. Its 103 sites are spread out over 35 acres and divided between the woods and open fields. All are close to the Batten Kill, where the swimming and trout fishing are superb.

Bicycle Repair Services

Battenkill Sports, VT 11 and VT 30, Manchester Center, VT (802-362-2734)

Bike Barn, 205½ Northside Drive, Bennington, VT (802-442-4645)

Cutting Edge Mountain Outfitters, 160 Benmont Avenue, Bennington, VT (802-442-8664)

Mountain Bike Peddler, 954 E. Main Street, Bennington, VT (802-447-7968)

3
Dorset–Manchester

Easy terrain; 19.2 or 23.8 miles

For more than a century, the genteel colonial and Victorian residences that grace Dorset and Manchester have served as summer, and more recently winter, retreats for cosmopolitan easterners. Both old and new homes are beautiful and immaculately maintained. The lands that surround them are as striking for their gardens and lawns as for their sugar maples and weathered barns.

Although most roads in the area have become congested, this tour avoids both the traffic and the numerous factory-outlet stores. Following shaded back roads past magnificent homes and then skirting open fields at the bases of Mount Equinox (elevation 3816 feet) and Mother Myrick Mountain (elevation 3290 feet), the route leads to many distinctive shops, eateries, outstanding golf courses, and cultural attractions, such as the Southern Vermont Art Center and the Dorset Playhouse. Well-groomed farms where horses and cattle are raised nestle beneath the mountains along the valley where this tour follows the Batten Kill. Marvelous swimming awaits you at the old marble quarry in Dorset. The tour begins and ends by the village green in Dorset.

0.0 *Leave Dorset on Church Street, which runs westward from Route 30 between the village green and the Dorset Inn (1796), Vermont's oldest continuously operated inn. If you are looking for food, you can buy a sandwich and choose from a wide selection of other items at Peltier's General Store, directly across the green from the Dorset Inn.*

Originally a center of trade and finance for local farmers, Dorset has grown over the last hundred years into a community of seasonal residents, retired persons, and other exurbanites. They have meticulously preserved the town's architecture and brought to Dorset a cultural vitality that supports a summer theater, many

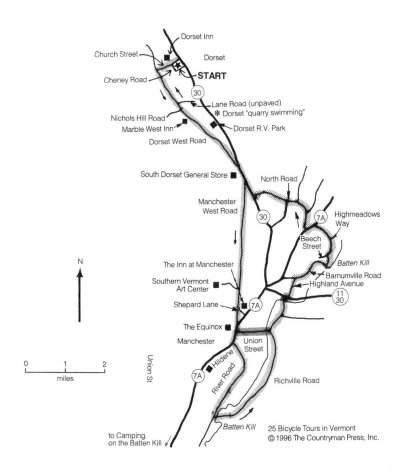

restaurants, and several galleries of antiques and art.

The United Church of Dorset and East Rupert (1912), on your left as you leave town, is built of Dorset marble and decorated with stained-glass windows that depict local pastoral scenes. It's worth a visit. The Dorset Playhouse can be found on Cheney Road 1 block south of the church. Call ahead (802-867-5777) for the schedule and reservations.

0.6   *At the stop sign, turn left onto West Road.*

In 1.25 miles, at the corner of West and Nichols Hill Roads, you pass on your right a state historical plaque marking the site of the Cephas Kent Tavern. There, in 1776, Ethan Allen's Green Mountain Boys proclaimed Vermont's independence of New Hampshire and New York. From 1777 until 1791, when it became the 14th state, Vermont was an independent nation.

The Marble West Inn is on your right just 0.1 mile beyond the plaque for Kent Tavern.

3.7 *At the stop sign, turn right onto VT 30 South, which is unsigned here. Beware of traffic on VT 30.*

4.3 *Just beyond the South Dorset General Store (on your right), turn right onto Manchester West Road.*

Within 0.5 mile, you begin climbing the toughest hill on this tour. It rises gradually for 1.75 miles. After a plateau at the top, you ride downhill nearly 2 miles to Manchester.

Halfway down on your right is the entrance to the Southern Vermont Art Center. The driveway, nearly a mile long, goes uphill all the way, but the effort is well rewarded. The center offers exhibitions of paintings, sculpture, and photography; concerts; and a botany trail of unusual ferns and wildflowers. The Garden Café, which overlooks the center's sculpture garden, serves lunch 11:30–3. For reservations, which are advised, call 802-362-4220. The Southern Vermont Art Center is open from late May through October, 10–5, Tuesday through Saturday, and noon–5 on Sunday. Admission is charged. For information about concerts and exhibitions, call 802-362-1405.

On your left, about a mile past the entrance to the Southern Vermont Art Center, is Shepard Lane. If you turn left there, you'll reach the Inn at Manchester in a third of a mile.

7.7 *At the stop sign in Manchester, go straight onto VT 7A (Main Street) South.*

FOR THE 19.2-MILE RIDE: Ride just 50 yards on VT 7A (Main Street) to The Equinox (on your right), and then walk across VT 7A to Union Street. Follow Union Street 1 mile downhill to the stop sign. Beware of the railroad tracks at the bottom. At the stop sign, turn left onto Richville Road, which may be unsigned, and ride 0.5 mile to the small concrete bridge. Then proceed from Mile 13.9 below.

Immediately on your right is the American Fly Fishing Museum, which displays hundreds of handmade bamboo rods, including some owned by Daniel Webster, Ernest Hemingway, Herbert Hoover, and other well-known Americans. The museum is open daily 10–4, May through October. There is no admission fee, but contributions are encouraged.

Just beyond the museum, behind a marble sidewalk, stands the magnificent, columned Equinox. In the 19th century, this hotel provided its Victorian guests with stables and horse-carriage service to and from the railroad station in Manchester Depot.

In 1991 The Equinox was refurbished and is now a four-star, 2300-acre resort hotel. It is a spectacular establishment—especially for Vermont. Golfers will find the 65-year-old Walter Travis golf course irresistible. It was recently rebuilt to conform with its original Scottish tradition by golf course architect Rees Jones.

Across the way from The Equinox is the Manchester gallery of the Vermont State Craft Center at Frog Hollow. It features superb contemporary and traditional arts and crafts by some of Vermont's finest artisans.

From The Equinox it's only a mile—straight south on VT 7A—to Hildene, the grand Georgian Revival mansion built in 1904 for Robert Todd Lincoln, son of the president. This 24-room monument to turn-of-the-century wealth and exclusiveness has been carefully restored and authentically furnished and is now open to the public. Tours include a brief demonstration of the 1000-pipe organ, which can be played manually or with one of the 240 player rolls. Hildene is open 9:30–5:30 daily, mid-May through October. Allow yourself at least an hour and a half for the tour. There is a fee for the tour and a smaller charge if you just visit the grounds. Among the formal gardens and paths that lead to the Batten Kill, you're sure to find a delightful place to picnic and walk. Hildene also hosts many special events; call 802-362-1788 for information.

8.2 Just beyond the sign on your left for the Ekwanok Country Club, turn left onto River Road.

River Road begins with a fast, curving descent that grows gentle after a half mile and lasts 2 miles.

The Dorset Playhouse

10.4 *Just beyond the pictorial duck-crossing sign and a large white house (on your right), turn left onto Richville Road, which is the first possible left turn off River Road. There may be no street sign at this intersection.*

You immediately cross a bridge over the Batten Kill, one of Vermont's most famous wild trout streams.

13.9 *Just after crossing a small concrete bridge, bear left to stay on Richville Road, which may be unsigned.*

14.2 *At the stop sign in Manchester Depot, turn right onto VT 30 North (also VT 11 West and Depot Street). Beware of traffic.*

If you were to turn left instead of right, you would quickly find yourself in a mile-long strip of factory-outlet stores. The area is so congested that it is not an appropriate place to bicycle, so don't attempt to ride there. You can walk to the shops and lock your bicycle when you get to them.

14.3 *Turn left onto Highland Avenue.*

14.4   At the stop sign, go straight up the hill to continue on Highland Avenue, which leads through a residential section of
Manchester and avoids the congestion of the village center.

14.8   At the stop sign, turn right onto Barnumville Road, which is unsigned here.

Barnumville Road goes up for a half mile and then rolls down into
a pastoral setting that overlooks the nearby mountains.

16.2   At the stop sign just before the railroad tracks, turn left to
continue on Barnumville Road, which is unsigned here.

16.4   At the T at the intersection of Beech Street, turn right onto
Highmeadows Way, which immediately goes uphill. There may
not be a street sign there.

The climb lasts a half mile and then heads down a steep hill,
which ends suddenly, in 0.3 mile, at a stop sign. Go slowly.

17.2   At the stop sign, turn left very carefully onto US 7 South,
though there may not be a route marker there.

Fortunately, there is a wide shoulder to ride on, for US 7 is a major
highway.

17.5   Turn right onto North Road.

After an easy half mile, North Road turns upward for a quarter
mile and then downward for nearly a mile.

19.2   At the stop sign, turn right onto VT 30 North, which is unsigned here. Beware of traffic.

20.1   At 0.4 mile beyond the South Dorset General Store (on your
left), turn left very carefully onto Dorset West Road.

In 1.9 miles you reach the Marble West Inn on your left. If you
enjoy swimming, a special opportunity lies ahead at an old marble
quarry. Just 0.2 mile beyond the Marble West Inn, turn right onto
Lane Road, which is unpaved, and ride 0.6 mile to the stop sign.
There, turn right onto VT 30 South and ride very carefully 0.5
mile until you see a single-story white building on your right.
Directly across VT 30 a path leads to the Dorset quarry, now filled
with spring water that makes for delicious swimming. Actually
there are two quarries—one within 20 yards of the road and a sec-

ond, popular with skinny-dippers, about 100 yards beyond the first. Both are open for unsupervised swimming. In 1758 Vermont settlers established America's first commercial marble quarry here. Dorset marble has been used for public buildings in Vermont and throughout the country. No mining has taken place here for years, however.

23.2 *Turn right onto Church Street.*

23.8 *You are back at Peltier's Store in Dorset across from the Dorset Inn, where this tour began.*

For general information on lodging, restaurants, attractions, and special events, contact the Manchester Chamber of Commerce, RD 2, Box 3451, Manchester Center, VT 05255 (802-362-2100).

Where to Stay

Marble West Inn, Dorset West Road, Dorset, VT 05251 (802-867-4155), overlooks a flower-filled meadow directly on the bicycle route about 2 miles from the Dorset green. This small, rather elegant inn has eight guest rooms, all with private bath. Each of the two common rooms has a marble fireplace; one also has a baby grand piano, the other a library. Innkeepers June and Wayne Erla serve a hearty breakfast and fine dinners. Children 12 and older are welcome.

The Inn at Manchester, Main Street, Manchester, VT 05254 (802-362-1793), has been a favorite stopping place for cyclists since the late 1970s. This gracious inn exudes a homey, understated elegance. Six fireplaces, a charming mixture of antique furniture and contemporary art posters, an expansive front porch just made for rocking, and a swimming pool quickly put you at ease. Innkeepers Stan, Harriet, and Amy Rosenberg are ideal hosts and serve delicious breakfasts with flair. Many restaurants are within easy walking distance.

Dorset R.V. Park, Dorset, VT 05251 (802-867-5754), is a small campground located off VT 30, midway between Dorset and Manchester. There are 40 shaded, level sites and a separate tenting area with picnic tables and fire rings set among the pine trees. There is also a recreation hall and laundry.

Bicycle Repair Services

Battenkill Sports, VT 11 and 30, Manchester Center, VT (802-362-2734)

Great Outdoors Trading Company, 41 Center Street, Rutland, VT (802-775-6531)

Green Mountain Schwinn Cyclery, 133 Strongs Avenue, Rutland, VT (802-775-0869)

Marble City Bicycles, 1 Scale Avenue, Rutland, VT (802-747-1471)

Mountain Tread-n-Shred, 150½ Woodstock Avenue, Rutland, VT (802-747-7080)

Sports Peddler, 158 North Main Street (US 7), Rutland, VT (802-775-0101)

4
Middletown Springs–Pawlet

Moderate-to-difficult terrain; 28.5 miles, plus 2.6-mile side trip

On the western edge of Vermont, not far from Rutland and Manchester, is a quiet, pristine region of exquisite land and charming villages. This tour explores that region. The route carves a winding path along the edge of hillsides, overlooking small streams, orderly farms, and the maple-covered flanks of the Green and Taconic Mountains. The terrain is alternately challenging, exhilarating, and blissful; the landscape is always beautiful. The tour starts in Middletown Springs, a quiet, remote village of mostly Victorian homes. In addition to two lovely inns—both on the National Register of Historic Places—Middletown Springs has three antiques shops: one specializing in fine American and European clocks, another in old oil lamps, and a third in 19th-century formal furniture and accessories. A century ago ladies and gentlemen traveled here to bathe in the healing waters of the iron and sulfur springs. Though that opportunity no longer exists, you can still arrange through your innkeeper to get a therapeutic massage. And during your tour you can visit two fine potters, an alpaca farm, and a restored railroad station in Pawlet.

0.0 *From the Middletown Springs green, follow VT 140 East, which here is also East Street and VT 133 North.*

Over the next 5.5 miles, you ride from an elevation of 887 feet at Middletown Springs to 1263 feet at Tinmouth. After a mile of gently rolling terrain, you climb a substantial grade for a half mile. You may want to get some food to carry along, since the only other opportunity is in Pawlet on the side trip, nearly 20 miles away. You can buy a snack at either Grant's Store on East Street or the Middletown Market and Deli on South Street.

In 1772 Native Americans showed local colonists the springs along the Poultney River, and soon thereafter legends of the springs' medicinal benefits began to grow. Although the springs played lit-

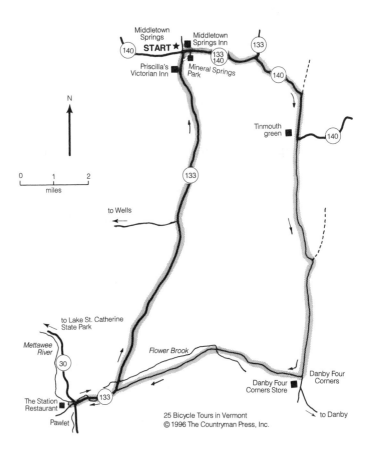

Middletown
Springs
START ★
140
Middletown
Springs Inn
133
133
140
Priscilla's
Victorian Inn
Mineral Springs
Park
140
N
Tinmouth
green
140
133
0   1   2
miles
to Wells
to Lake St. Catherine
State Park
Mettawee
River
30
Flower Brook
Danby Four
Corners
Danby Four
Corners Store
The Station
Restaurant
133
Pawlet
to Danby

25 Bicycle Tours in Vermont
© 1996 The Countryman Press, Inc.

tle role in the town's development, by 1810 the population had grown to 1207, the highest it would ever reach. Middletown Springs had four forges, two distilleries, two clothiers, a tannery, five gristmills, and two cider mills. But the following year, a great flood forced the Poultney River out of its course, and the springs were buried. When a second flood again rerouted the river and uncovered the springs in 1868, a local entrepreneur, A.W. Gray, was there to seize the opportunity. Gray, the successful manufacturer of treadmills using horses or dogs to generate power, began bottling the waters and then assembled the capital to build the Monvert Hotel, where 250 city folk could come to "take the waters."

Between 1871 and 1906, guests arrived at the Monvert by horse-drawn carriage from the Poultney railroad depot. Once at the hotel, these fortunate visitors dined on caviar and lobster while listening to a string orchestra. They played tennis, croquet, and other lawn games, but mostly came to drink and bathe in the waters, which the Monvert claimed could cure "obesity, anemia, nervous dyspepsia, insomnia, diabetes, rheumatism, gout, and nervous troubles." "Nothing," promised the hotel's brochure, "can be more refreshing and exhilarating after a hard ride on the wheel than one of the aforementioned baths and a rubdown by the attendant." What cyclist could argue with that!

The hotel gradually lost its following as travelers opted for baths, such as those at Saratoga Springs, New York, that could be reached directly by railroad coach. And in 1927 another flood reburied the springs. Then, in 1970 local volunteers dug out the old spring boxes and built a replica of the Victorian springhouse. The site is charming, if barely suggestive of the grand attention focused upon it a hundred years ago. The stream is too shallow for swimming but makes a delightful place to cool off and relax.

To get to Mineral Springs Park, turn right onto Burdock Avenue, which is diagonally across VT 140 from the Middletown Springs Inn.

2.4   Turn right to continue on VT 140 East.

The first mile goes dramatically uphill, and the second goes equally dramatically down.

5.6   Beside the Tinmouth green on your right, where VT 140 turns to the left, go straight toward Danby Corners onto the unsigned road.

The first mile takes you nicely downhill again. Thereafter, the terrain is generally easy.

Between the 1780s and 1837, Tinmouth was a small iron-manufacturing center with its own furnace and forges. Now small farms and a few summer homes dominate the town.

9.2   At the stop sign, turn right onto the unsigned road. You immediately start up a 1-mile climb.

12.5 **At the stop sign in Danby Four Corners, turn right onto another unsigned road. Look carefully for this turn to avoid riding to Danby, which lies 4 miles downhill off the route.**

You can get a snack and cold drink here at the Danby Four Corners Store. Just beyond Danby Four Corners you must pedal uphill for about 1.5 miles, but then you begin a long, beautiful descent that extends nearly without interruption to the next instruction.

18.4 **At the stop sign, turn right onto VT 133 North.**

Within a mile the road turns uphill for 1.5 miles. It then levels off for 2.5 miles and then climbs up another 0.5 mile.

2.6-MILE SIDE TRIP TO PAWLET: If you want to get something to eat or just extend your ride with some pretty cycling and a visit to a small village with several interesting shops and artists, do not turn right. Instead, continue straight onto VT 133 South, which is unsigned here, and ride 1.3 miles to the next stop sign, which is in Pawlet. In this direction VT 133 is tipped just far enough downhill to make a nice difference.

Set at the convergence of Flower Brook and the Mettawee River, Pawlet prospered as a mill town 150 years ago. Now it is home to some 900 Vermonters and about 30 dairy farms.

At the falls in the center of this tiny village stands a handsome, though idle, waterwheel, 27 feet in diameter and 4 feet wide. Johnny Mach built the wheel during the Depression to supply his general store and home with electricity. Flower Brook offers excellent swimming just upstream of Johnny Mach's old waterwheel. It is easiest to reach the water from the north side of the river, by the post office. While you are in Pawlet, be sure to stop in Mach's General Store to take a look through the viewing box.

My first stop in Pawlet is always the studio of potter Marion McChesney, opposite the Station Restaurant. She is a delightful source of information about Pawlet, and her gracious manner makes every visit a real treat. Ask to see her sea stones, her contemporary porcelain in pastel glazes, and her recycled roadkills, which every cyclist can relate to. At Flower Brook Pottery, you can visit Georgeanna Alexopoulos, who creates whimsical handmade, handpainted work. And if you're curious about alpacas,

The Station Restaurant in Pawlet

call Hunter Callen at Mettowee Valley Farm (802-325-3039). It's an exquisite site, where the Callen family raises multihued, registered alpacas about a mile out of town. Finally, visit the Station Restaurant for a Wilcox rum and ginger cone—or coffee and a sandwich—at the converted train station decorated with railroading memorabilia.

After your visit, retrace your way back up VT 133 North to the intersection where your side trip to Pawlet began. As you know, it is gently uphill all the way. When you reach the intersection, bear left to continue on Route 133 North to Middletown Springs.

23.6 Go straight to continue on VT 133 North; do not turn left toward Wells.

The road continues uphill for 0.25 mile and then rolls the rest of the way to Middletown Springs.

28.5 At the stop sign, you are back in front of the green in Middletown Springs, where you began.

For general information on lodging, restaurants, attractions, and special events, contact the Rutland Region Chamber of Commerce, 256 North Main Street, Rutland, VT 05701 (802-773-2772), or Manchester and the Mountains Chamber of Commerce, RD 2, Box 3451, Manchester Center, VT 05255 (802-362-2100).

Where to Stay

Middletown Springs Inn, 4 Park Avenue, Middletown Springs, VT 05757 (802-235-2531), sits directly on the town green. Built in 1879 in Italianate Victorian style, the inn remains true to that tradition. It features a striking walnut spiral staircase with grain painting, a rich assortment of period furnishings, and an antique pump organ in the library. Talented innkeepers Jackie and Steve Mott have created a comfortable and charming place. I recommend the Ethan Allen room, with its cannonball four-poster bed, or the Moses Vail room, with its mauve walls. Steve is a violin maker and fine furniture builder, and his work is scattered about the inn. The Motts serve a full country breakfast and—on weekends—dinner by candlelight with china and crystal. On other days, dinner is available if arranged in advance.

Priscilla's Victorian Inn, 52 South Street, Middletown Springs, VT 05757 (802-235-2299) is a spectacular 1870s Italianate Victorian mansion, set on 12 acres of gardens, lawns, mowed fields, and walking paths. Oriental carpets, five marbleized fireplaces, and a spiral staircase create a visual feast. In the living room there is a Steinway baby grand player piano, and in the basement game room several old (free) pinball machines, a Wurlitzer jukebox with 78s, and Foosball. The tone is one of elegance and good fun thanks to sparkling innkeeper Priscilla Lane. She enjoys herself, her guests, and her memorable inn. My favorite rooms are #1, which faces South Street, and #6, which overlooks the English Garden. Priscilla loves to cook and serves delicious breakfasts in her sunny dining room or on the broad back porch, and dinner by prior arrangement.

Lake St. Catherine State Park, RD 2, Box 1775, Poultney, VT 05764 (802-287-9158), sits on 117 acres on the shore of Lake St. Catherine. There are trails, a beach, boat rentals, and fishing as well as 51 camping sites and 10 lean-tos. All sites have fireplaces and picnic tables, but there are no hookups.

Bicycle Repair Services

Battenkill Sports, VT 11 and 30, Manchester Center, VT (802-362-2734)

Great Outdoors Trading Company, 41 Center Street, Rutland, VT (802-775-6531)

Green Mountain Schwinn Cyclery, 133 Strongs Avenue, Rutland, VT (802-775-0869)

Marble City Bicycles, 1 Scale Avenue, Rutland, VT (802-747-1471)

Mountain Tread-n-Shred, 150½ Woodstock Avenue, Rutland, VT (802-747-7080)

Sports Peddler, 158 North Main Street (US 7), Rutland, VT (802-775-0101)

Chester–Grafton

Easy-to-moderate terrain; 26.9 miles (4.6 unpaved)

Starting by the long, slender green along Main Street in Chester, this tour follows maple-shaded roads and streams through rolling countryside to some of Vermont's most beautiful architecture. For the cyclist interested in antiques, this tour is hard to beat. There are extraordinary shops all along the way—in Chester, Saxtons River, and Grafton.

The route uses nearly 5 miles of remote, unpaved roads—which are great fun—to avoid a busy highway and to find some wonderful buildings and two covered bridges. Many cyclists will enjoy this part of the tour best on a mountain bicycle, but really any bicycle will do.

Following small roads along the Williams River, the route comes to an 18th-century burial ground and provides delightful views of small farms and rolling hills. It then turns south along a winding stagecoach road through the woods; you are drawn into the pastoral scene as if no road existed at all. Finally, the tour reaches Grafton, a lovingly restored 19th-century village.

0.0   *Standing with your back to the front door of the Inn at Long Last on the Chester green, turn right to follow VT 11 East, also called Main Street.*

In the early part of the 19th century, a family of masons named Clark settled in Chester and turned its talents to building stone houses. These gracious homes constructed of locally quarried gray-green mica schist make Chester a special place. Often a full 2½ stories high, many contain secret rooms where before the Civil War blacks seeking freedom from slavery hid as they fled northward on the underground railway. Most of the stone houses face VT 103, both north and south of its intersection with VT 11.

If you like maps, do not miss the National Survey Company, headquartered in Chester. The company's excellent maps are sold

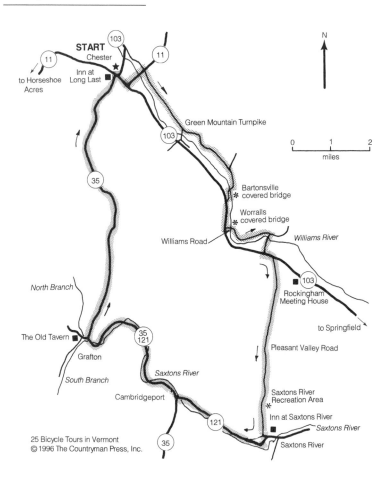

and displayed in its office on School Street, just around the corner from the green. Chester has several restaurants and a general store, although you need not carry much food along since you can shop or eat at restaurants in Saxtons River and Grafton.

0.2   *At the intersection, continue straight onto VT 11 East and VT 103 South toward Springfield.*

0.7   *Turn left onto VT 11 East.*

SIDE TRIP: If you object to cycling on unpaved roads, do not turn left. Instead, continue straight, off VT 11 East onto VT 103 South, the Calvin Coolidge Memorial Highway. Follow VT 103 South for 6.3 miles to the sign for Saxtons River on your right. From there, continue from Mile 7.9 below. VT 103 has a wide shoulder, but a lot of high-speed traffic. The unpaved roads are much more fun. They are shaded much of the way, lead past beautiful old homes, cross two covered bridges, and have very little traffic.

Regardless of which path you follow, you ride roughly parallel to a route developed by Native Americans as a footpath and later used by American colonists as a bridle path and military road. In 1849 the Rutland Railroad Company laid tracks over that path to link Rutland with Boston, thereby creating a new market for Vermont dairy products.

1.2   *At the crossroad, turn right onto Green Mountain Turnpike, which is unsigned and becomes unpaved in 20 yards.*

Over the next 1.5 miles, the road creeps very gently uphill; the surface is generally hard and smooth.

3.0   *Turn left toward Bartonsville and continue to follow unpaved Green Mountain Turnpike, though it is unsigned here. (If you miss this turn, you will reach a railroad-track crossing in 30 yards.)*

4.3   *At the intersection with the unpaved road on your left, continue straight to follow unpaved Green Mountain Turnpike, though it is still unsigned here.*

The road becomes paved in 0.2 mile.

4.5   *Go straight to continue on Green Mountain Turnpike, which is now paved and signed. It's still a very small road.*

In 0.6 mile, you ride through the Bartonsville covered bridge (1870), and just beyond it you must cross a set of railroad tracks, so ride very cautiously here. The Bartonsville bridge crosses the Williams River and is 151 feet long. It was built by Sanford Granger in the Town lattice style.

5.5   At the stop sign, turn left onto VT 103 South, which is unsigned here. (Because of high-speed traffic on VT 103, you might want to walk across.)

5.7   Turn left onto Williams Road, which becomes unpaved in 0.2 mile. (Because of high-speed traffic on VT 103, you might want to walk across.)

The surface of Williams Road is occasionally soft and has some loose rocks on it. You will enjoy it most on a fat-tire bicycle, but you can ride it with any bicycle; it will just require quite a bit of attention. You can bypass Williams Road—but you will miss a lovely little piece of Vermont—by just continuing south 1.8 miles on VT 103 until the sign on your right for Saxtons River and then continuing from Mile 7.9 below.

In 0.2 mile after the road becomes unpaved, you ride through the unspoiled Worralls covered bridge. Like the earlier covered bridge, this one was also built by Sanford Granger in Town lattice style. It is 87 feet long and also crosses the Williams River. This bridge is remarkable for its pristine condition, lack of signage, and wooden ramp.

7.2   At the intersection with Gaskill Road/Town Highway 16 on your left, continue straight on the unsigned road, which becomes paved in 20 yards.

7.3   Turn right onto the paved, unsigned road. You immediately cross the Williams River and then a set of railroad tracks.

7.7   At the stop sign, turn left onto VT 103 South, which is unsigned here. (Because of high-speed traffic on VT 103, you might want to walk across.)

7.9   Turn right toward Saxtons River onto Pleasant Valley Road, which is unsigned here.

Pleasant Valley Road climbs uphill for 0.75 mile and then runs downhill off and on for 2.5 miles. In just over 4 miles, you reach the Saxtons River Recreation Area on your left, where you can swim in a nice pond.

Instead of turning right toward Saxtons River, you may enjoy riding another 1.5 miles south on VT 103 to see the Rockingham Meeting House (1787). It sits on a high knoll on your right, just off

VT 103. This two-story clapboard structure is one of the best examples of Federal-style church architecture in New England. Inside are a high pulpit and box pews, each accommodating 10 to 15 people, some of whom must sit facing away from the pulpit. In back of the church lies an old cemetery, which contains some of the most interesting gravestone carvings in Vermont. The carvings are delicately etched on fragile, weathered slate.

12.6 At the stop sign on the outskirts of Saxtons River, turn sharply right onto VT 121 West, which is unsigned here.

If you're hungry, turn left onto VT 121 East and ride 0.5 mile into Saxtons River, where there are a grocery, pizza parlor, and the Inn at Saxtons River, which serves lunch.

VT 121 is narrow and winding; it was once a stagecoach road. On the curves, ride carefully close to the edge of the pavement, because the bends in the road may prevent motorists from seeing you.

Before leaving Saxtons River you might enjoy visiting the two antiques shops and looking at the 19th-century kitchen and parlor and excellent early photographs maintained by the Saxtons River Historical Society at the former Congregational Church (1836) on Main Street. The collection is open afternoons from Memorial Day through mid-October on Saturdays, Sundays, and holidays.

15.5 At the yield sign at the T, in Cambridgeport, turn right to continue toward Grafton on VT 121 West, which here joins VT 35 North.

19.4 At Grafton, turn right onto VT 35 North toward Chester.

The unique story of Grafton bears telling. Surrounded by low-lying hills at the confluence of the Saxtons River's two branches, Grafton has ridden the crests of prosperity and the troughs of depression. In the 1820s nearly 1500 people lived there and thrived on the profits of 13 soapstone quarries and many water-powered mills, including 2 that loomed the fleece of some 10,000 sheep pastured on the surrounding hillsides. As Grafton flourished, its people built not only churches and private homes of fine design and workmanship, but also a magnificent inn, now called the Old Tavern. With this facility Grafton became a town of distinction, hosting over the years such prominent guests as Ralph Waldo Emerson, Ulysses Grant, Theodore Roosevelt, Woodrow Wilson, and Rudyard Kipling.

One of the many stone houses in Chester

Near the end of the century, decline set in. Sheep farmers moved west in search of fresh grazing land, and woolen mills moved south in search of cheap labor. One by one the industries that had produced Grafton's wealth disappeared. By the end of the Great Depression, fewer than 400 people called Grafton home, and nearly all 80 houses in the village were up for sale at rock-bottom prices.

Then, in 1963, thanks to the great foresight and generosity of Dean Mathey, Pauline Dean Fiske, and Matthew Hall, the Windham Foundation was born. The purpose of Vermont's largest foundation is threefold: "to restore buildings and economic vitality in the village of Grafton; to provide financial support for education and private charities; and to develop projects that will benefit the general welfare of Vermont and Vermonters."

Over the past 30 years the foundation has bought and rehabilitated many buildings, including the Old Tavern, the Village Store, a dairy farm, a blacksmith's shop, and nearly half of the buildings in the central village. To bolster the town's economy, the foundation created the Grafton Village Cheese Company, and to protect open lands, it has gradually acquired 1900 acres around the village. That land is maintained for wildlife conservation, hiking, and cross-country skiing. This continuing effort has brought Grafton out of a long sleep into a new, but different, life. New jobs have been created, but the success of the foundation has pushed the price of real estate beyond the reach of many former residents. Newcomers have moved in, and some old-timers have left.

Still, Grafton is no museum town. It is a lively place where people live and work and govern themselves by town meeting. Most of the buildings are not open to the public because they are privately occupied. But much of interest is visible from the outside, and several buildings can be visited. Information and maps are available at the front desk of the Old Tavern. Along the side streets you can find several art galleries and antiques shops, a museum, and two covered bridges. The Village Store extends a warm welcome to bicyclists and sells fine sandwiches as well as a good selection of fresh fruit, wines, Grafton cheese, and fudge.

Upon leaving Grafton on VT 35 North, you climb a steep, heart-pumping hill. After a half mile the slope tapers off to a moderate grade lasting 1.5 miles. Then, after passing through woods, the road turns a corner and descends 2.5 miles into Chester.

26.7 At the stop sign, turn left onto VT 11 West.

26.9 You are back in Chester beside the green, where you began.

Misty Valley Books, on the green in Chester, is a delightful place to find a good read. You may also enjoy the Court Gallery Coffee House for coffee, food, and art; Raspberries and Thyme for lunch or ice cream; and the Chester Art Guild. All face the green.

For general information about lodging, restaurants, attractions, and special events, contact the Great Falls Regional Chamber of Commerce, PO Box 554, Bellows Falls, VT 05101 (802-463-4280); the Chester Chamber of Commerce, PO Box 623, Chester, VT 05143 (802-875-2939); or the Springfield Chamber of Commerce, 14 Clinton Street, Springfield, VT 05156 (802-885-2779).

Where to Stay

Inn at Long Last, Main Street, Box 589, Chester, VT 05143 (802-875-2444), is well known for its cooking, 2500-volume library, two tennis courts, and innkeeper Jack Coleman. Coleman was president of Haverford College before putting his energy into this classic Vermont village inn. He has also worked at blue-collar jobs such as collecting garbage, and he once undertook to learn about prison life by admitting himself as a prisoner. Guests are encouraged to roam about the spacious inn and select their rooms by looking over what's available. The Grand Opera Room is especially nice.

Inn at Saxtons River, Route 121, Saxtons River, VT 05154 (802-869-2110). This gracious Victorian clapboard building was built in 1903 as a hotel but then served as a private home before being imaginatively reconverted to an inn in 1974. My favorite rooms are #1 and #2; each has a queen-sized bed, private bath, and porch overlooking Main Street. The public rooms are gracious and include a tiny Victorian pub. Innkeepers Jeremy Burrell and Steven Griffiths provide good service.

Horseshoe Acres, RD 1, Box 206, Andover, VT 05143 (802-875-2960), is a fully equipped family campground. It has 20 tent sites and 90 sites with electricity and water. You can swim in either a pool or a pond, play softball, volleyball, or horseshoes, or enjoy the indoor game room.

Bicycle Repair Services

Barney's Bike Shop, VT 103, Chester Depot, VT (802-875-3517)

Bike Pedlar, 76 Main Street, Charlestown, NH (603-826-4757)

Equipe Sport, VT 30, Rawsonville, VT (802-297-2847)

Lane Road Cycle Shop, Lovers Lane Road, Charlestown, NH (603-826-4435)

Mountain Cycology, Lamere Square, Ludlow, VT (802-228-2722)

6
Proctorsville–Felchville

Moderate terrain; 27.2 miles (3.2 unpaved)

Starting in the old mill town of Proctorsville, this tour carves a beautiful circle through hardwood forests and quiet farmlands. The route is very special for the quiet beauty of the countryside and the blend of a hearty climb followed immediately by an exhilarating, 6-mile descent. The tour's difficult stretch—3.5 miles uphill along an unpaved road—comes at the beginning and is amply rewarded by delightful views of a peaceful valley and the charm of a road shaded by a canopy of trees. In fact, the abundance of trees makes this an especially appealing route during fall foliage, approximately September 20 to October 20 in this area. You bicycle nearly the entire way within sight of rivers or streams, and you twice have good places to swim. Though the tour is well suited to a narrow-tire bicycle, it is also good fun on a mountain bike, since 3.2 miles are unpaved.

0.0 *From the US Post Office on VT 131 in Proctorsville, follow VT 131 East, which is unsigned here.*

Before setting out, walk over to the Baba à Louis Bakery at the corner of VT 131 and Depot Street to pick up a little sustenance. The door to the bakery faces Depot Street.

0.3 *Turn left onto Twenty Mile Stream Road, which is Town Highway 3. Thereafter, follow Twenty Mile Stream Road straight; do not turn onto any of the side roads.*

Twenty Mile Stream Road immediately starts gradually uphill. In 0.5 mile, the grade turns steep for a half mile and then rolls up and down for 3 miles more. The road surface then becomes unpaved at the intersection with Chapman Road on your left.

Whitney Brook Bed & Breakfast is on your left 2.5 miles from the beginning of Twenty Mile Stream Road.

A half mile beyond Chapman Road, the grade again turns up-

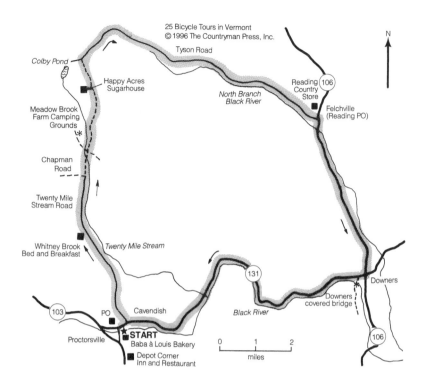

hill. It remains moderate until the last mile, which is steep. Although the road surface is well packed, loose rocks and washboardlike bumps may occasionally slow you down.

At the crossroads, a mile after the surface becomes unpaved, you can get to the Meadow Brook Farm Camping Grounds by turning left onto Meadow Brook Farm Road. The office is in a white house on your left across from a mailbox for "Spaulding." It's 0.3 mile, easy riding to the campground.

A mile and a half beyond the Meadow Brook Farm crossroads, you reach Jim and Sandy Peplau's Happy Acres Sugarhouse on your left. This is an opportune place to take a rest. The Peplaus are well known for their graciousness to bicyclists and will gladly explain how maple syrup is made and graded. They sell excellent syrup as well as hand-braided rugs and homespun wool. The studio of Porcupine Designs is also located at the Peplaus' farmhouse.

Philip Lightbear and Joanna Moonflower make Native American ceremonial pieces and rattles from natural materials such as turtle shells and moose ribs.

7.3 *At the T, turn right onto Tyson Road, which is paved.*

For 0.75 mile, Tyson Road goes uphill. Then it turns sharply down-hill and carries you along one of Vermont's most exhilarating descents. Slow down, and you can pick your own swimming hole in the North Branch of the Black River. On your way downhill you can see Mount Ascutney (elevation 3144 feet) on your right.

14.2 *At the stop sign in Felchville (Reading PO), turn right onto VT 106 South, which is unsigned here.*

Before leaving Felchville, if you are the least bit hungry, go into the Reading Country Store, on your left when you reach this stop sign. The store, which has cheered up more than one cold or wet rider, makes generous sandwiches to your specifications and has good selections of fresh fruit and other groceries. You can picnic on the lawn of the town hall across the street from the store or by the Black River.

The Reading Historical Society Museum, beside the town library on Route 106, contains old furniture, clothing, paintings, photographs, and unusual collections of advertising cards and old music. The museum is open by appointment only. Call Walter Mendoza at 802-484-7271.

18.4 *At the blinking light in Downers, turn right onto VT 131 West toward Cavendish.*

In 0.4 mile, if you turn left onto Upper Falls Road, which is un-paved and slightly hidden, you can ride 200 yards to the Downers covered bridge, built around 1840. Below the bridge lies a shallow, pleasant swimming hole in the Black River.

Nearly 7 miles west of Downers, just after you have ridden up a short rise that is the only significant incline on VT 131, you come into the small town of Cavendish. Cavendish has several ginger-bread houses, an old stone meetinghouse, and two general stores that face VT 131. Between 1974 and 1994 Alexander Solzhenitsyn and his family were Cavendish's most renowned residents.

27.2 *You are back in Proctorsville, where this tour began.*

> Down Depot Street on your left are Baba à Louis Bakery and, 0.1 mile farther, the Depot Corner Inn and Restaurant.

For general information about lodging, restaurants, attractions, and special events, contact the Ludlow Area Chamber of Commerce, Lemere Square, PO Box 333, Ludlow, VT 05149, or the Cavendish Chamber of Commerce, PO Box 625, Cavendish, VT 05142 (802-226-7560).

Where to Stay

Depot Corner Inn and Restaurant, Depot Street, PO Box 78, Proctorsville, VT 05153 (802-226-7970), is a disguised jewel. From the outside, this lovely inn is plain, but inside the decor is an ingenious mix of hand-stenciling, antiques, and clever wall hangings—very cheerful, comfortable, and friendly. Delightful hosts John and Deborah Davis run a fine kitchen that draws on their years of experience in the restaurant business in Santa Fe. They have a library full of magazines and games, and a lounge with five beers on tap.

Whitney Brook Bed & Breakfast, Twenty Mile Stream Road, RD 1, Box 28, Proctorsville, VT 05153 (802-226-7460), is an 1870 farmhouse with expansive lawns, colorful flower gardens, stone walls, and two small streams. The Green Room is my favorite, with its large hooked rug and hand-stenciling. There's a large living room with a fireplace, and an upstairs sitting area. Innkeepers Ellen and Jim Parrish serve a full breakfast that includes their own blueberry, strawberry, or blackberry preserves.

Meadow Brook Farm Camping Grounds, Twenty Mile Stream Road, RD 1, Box 44, Proctorsville, VT 05153 (802-226-7755), is a wonderfully private campground. Each campsite is partially shaded and has its own picnic table, fireplace, and grill. There's a large pond for swimming and a trout-stocked brook for fishing.

Bicycle Repair Service

Mountain Cycology, VT 103, Ludlow, VT (802-228-2722)

CENTRAL VERMONT

7

Rutland–North Shrewsbury

Difficult terrain; 24 miles (1.4 unpaved)

This tour dramatizes the remarkable spaciousness and pastoral nature of most of Vermont. Though it starts near the center of our second-largest city, the tour follows main roads for only 1 mile. The remainder of the tour lies in remote hills quilted with stands of birches, sugar maples, and evergreens. Views of some of the Green Mountains' highest peaks are stupendous. Often you can hear the Cold River bubbling alongside the road, and two covered bridges, each more than a century old, are on the fringe of the route. At the tour's end, though you are merely a mile from the tiny Rutland Airport, you have little sense of its presence as you follow a quiet farming valley that looks across hilltops to the sunset.

Consider doing the Rutland–North Shrewsbury tour in two directions. As I have written it, you climb to North Shrewsbury on the more gradual, but longer, approach. Try that one in the spring; then return in autumn—if you wait until the leaves have fallen, the views are even more spectacular—and tackle the climb from the shorter, but steeper, side.

0.0 ***From the traffic light on US 7 by the Green Mountain Plaza (Ames and Grand Union), 1.75 miles south of the center of Rutland, turn left onto US 7 North.***

US 7 is the main north-south artery in western Vermont. Fortunately, in this area, the highway has a shoulder suitable for cycling.

With a population of about 19,000, Rutland ranks as Vermont's second-largest city. Though it lacks the vigor and luster of Burlington—the state's largest city, and its medical, cultural, and commercial center—Rutland has its share of attractions. Early Victorian mansions evoke images of rural 19th-century prosperity, when Rutland was known as "the marble city." That epithet derives from the great marble deposits stretching from Rutland southward. The first commercial marble quarry in America was established just 30

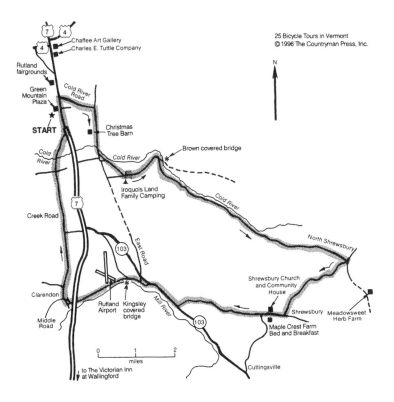

25 Bicycle Tours in Vermont
© 1996 The Countryman Press, Inc.

miles away in Dorset in 1758; see the Dorset–Manchester tour. The Vermont Marble Exhibit on Main Street in Proctor, just 6 miles northwest of the center of Rutland, is the world's largest presentation of the story of marble from quarry to sculpture. The exhibit is open daily, mid-May to late October, 9–5:30. Admission is charged.

Rutland takes justifiable pride in being the home of the state's oldest and finest newspaper, the *Rutland Herald* (established in 1794). Now in its third century, the *Herald* provides exceptional national and international news coverage for a rural daily and carries many *New York Times* features. One of New England's largest and most interesting traders in used and rare books, Charles E. Tuttle Company, faces the city park at 28 South Main Street (US 7). Four doors north, at 16 South Main, is the Chaffee Art Gallery, which is listed in the National Register of Historic Places. It displays both permanent and changing exhibitions of painting, sculpture, photography, and crafts. The gallery is open 10–5, Monday, Wednesday, Thursday, Friday, and Saturday; on Sunday it's open noon–4. For information on exhibitions and classes, call 802-775-0356.

If you seek more frenetic entertainment, try the Vermont State Fair, which runs one week a year beginning on the Saturday before Labor Day. The fair, which has its own fairgrounds on US 7 three-quarters of a mile north of where this tour starts, features daredevil and rodeo events, carnival booths, and harness racing, as well as livestock and agricultural exhibits. Rutland is also the "gateway city" to the immense skiing operation at Killington and the smaller one at Pico. For further information about continuing and special events, stop at the marble information booth in the park on South Main Street.

0.3   At the traffic light, turn right onto Cold River Road.

You cross a set of railroad tracks in 0.3 mile.

A major climb lies ahead. From 550 feet at Rutland, you pedal up to 1758 feet at North Shrewsbury. The grade is gentle to moderate most of the way, but several stretches are steep.

1.2   At the stop sign, turn right to continue on Cold River Road, which is unsigned here. Thereafter, follow the main road and signs for Meadowsweet Herb Farm.

In 0.75 mile, you reach the Christmas Tree Barn on your right. For more than 25 years, Gail Mills Buck and her family have been growing annuals and perennials to make wreaths. Using an ancient, noisy machine and a designer's eye, she creates wreaths of striking beauty and wonderful scents. She also sells a marvelous assortment of ornaments and potpourri. A visit to her 175-year-old barn is as stimulating to your sense of smell as it is to your nostalgia for an old-fashioned Christmas. The barn is open Thursday through Saturday 10–4 and by chance.

Two and a quarter miles farther on, by a yellow sign on the left that reads 8'11", an unpaved road forks to your left and passes through a charming covered bridge in a quarter mile. Built in Town lattice style in 1880, the Brown covered bridge sits in a romantic wooded hollow over the Cold River.

10.3 *At the fork in North Shrewsbury, bear right toward Cuttingsville.*

Don't pass W. E. Pierce General Store (on your left as soon as you turn) without taking a look. Founded in 1918, Pierce's was family-run until 1994, when it closed. Until the very end it was one of the most authentically old-fashioned stores in Vermont.

10.4 *Just 75 yards beyond W. E. Pierce General Store, bear right onto the unsigned road that goes downhill.*

Consider detouring here to visit Meadowsweet Herb Farm, just a mile away. To get to the farm, turn left here and follow the road 1 mile, gently downhill; the last 0.3 mile is unpaved.

Since 1978, Polly Haynes and her compatriots have been busy raising more than 200 herbs and scented geraniums and crafting them into herb wreaths, potpourri, and culinary blends. You can follow a map about the farm and discover gardens devoted exclusively to herbs having to do with the kitchen, the Bible, healing, weddings, and much more. Or you may prefer to take a well-earned rest on the lawn overlooking a still woodland pond, where two Chinese geese named Jack and Jill preside. The farm runs workshops on gardening and cooking and sells an unusual variety of spices, herbs, and cooking stuffs. From May through October Meadowsweet Herb Farm is open daily 1–5. Call 802-492-3565 for information about workshops. After your visit, return to the intersection and head downhill away from Pierce's Store.

The road immediately descends steeply for a half mile, turns sharply uphill for the next mile, and then finishes with a merry descent all the way to the next turn.

13.5 *A quarter mile beyond the Shrewsbury Community Church and Meeting House (1804) on your right, go straight onto the un-signed road. Do not turn left toward Cuttingsville.*

Directly across the road from the church is the Maple Crest Farm Bed & Breakfast, an enormous redbrick house with two front porches.

You now descend steeply through the woods for 3 miles. Keep your speed fully under control and be prepared to stop, for the road ends suddenly at a stop sign.

15.8 *At the stop sign, turn right onto VT 103 North, which may be unsigned here.*

In a half mile you cross the Long Trail, which runs 261 miles up the middle of Vermont from Massachusetts to Canada. It was built by the Green Mountain Club between 1910 and 1929.

17.0 *Turn left off VT 103 onto Airport Road toward the airport.*

17.1 *At the T, bear right to follow the main road.*

17.4 *At the fork, bear left down the hill.*

Just 50 yards after you bear left, a side road, called East Street, leads leftward to the Kingsley covered bridge on the Mill River. It's 120 feet long and was built by T. K. Norton in 1836.

Your road becomes unpaved in 100 yards and remains unpaved for 1.3 miles until just before the next direction. It goes gently downhill through the woods.

18.9 *At each of the three stop signs, go straight in order to cross four-laned US 7 onto Middle Road. The street sign is on the far side of US 7.*

In 0.4 mile you pass the Old Brick Clarendon Congregational Church (1824) on the right. You are now at an elevation of 600 feet, just 50 feet higher than you were in Rutland.

19.5 *At the fork, bear right onto Creek Road, which may be unsigned here.*

22.6 *At the stop sign at the crossroad, go straight to continue on Creek Road, which may be unsigned.*

23.4 *At the traffic light, turn left onto US 7 North.*

24.2 *At the traffic light, you are across from Green Mountain Plaza, where the tour began.*

For general information on lodging, restaurants, attractions, and special events, contact the Rutland Region Chamber of Commerce, 256 North Main Street, Rutland, VT 05701 (802-773-2772).

Where to Stay

Maple Crest Farm Bed & Breakfast, PO Box 120, Cuttingsville, VT 05738 (802-492-3367), is located in Shrewsbury, halfway through the tour at its highest elevation. The inn is tucked into a quintessential Vermont village—tiny, isolated, and high in the hills, far from every-

Cycling along scenic backroads

thing commercial. Built in 1808 as a tavern and stagecoach stop, Maple Crest Farm has large airy rooms, antique furnishings, and lots of country charm. My favorite guest rooms are the Gray Room and the Tavern Room. Breakfast features homemade buttermilk pancakes and award-winning maple syrup, made by innkeepers Donna, William, and Russell Smith. From Shrewsbury it's a 20-minute drive for dinner in Rutland or at the Victorian Inn at Wallingford, described below.

The Victorian Inn at Wallingford, 9 North Main Street, Wallingford, VT 05773 (802-446-2099), faces US 7 ten miles south of Rutland. Innkeeper-chef Konstantin Schonbachler provides cheerful and spacious guest rooms and serves outstanding dinners, prepared in regional American style. Konstantin and his young family have carefully created their inn from an elaborate three-story Victorian mansion, built in 1877 in the French Second Empire style. Dinner is served Tuesday through Saturday from 5:30. Sunday brunch is 10–3. You may dine indoors or on the flagstone patio outside.

Iroquois Land Family Camping, East Road, North Clarendon, VT 05759 (802-773-2832), has 45 open and wooded sites for tents and campers. The view is beautiful, and the campground has its own swimming pool.

Bicycle Repair Services

Great Outdoors Trading Company, 41 Center Street, Rutland, VT (802-775-6531)

Green Mountain Schwinn Cyclery, 133 Strongs Avenue, Rutland, VT (802-775-0869)

Marble City Bicycles, 1 Scale Avenue, Rutland, VT (802-747-1471)

Mountain Tread-n-Shred, 150½ Woodstock Avenue, Rutland, VT (802-747-7080)

Sports Peddler, 158 North Main Street (US 7), Rutland, VT (802-775-0101)

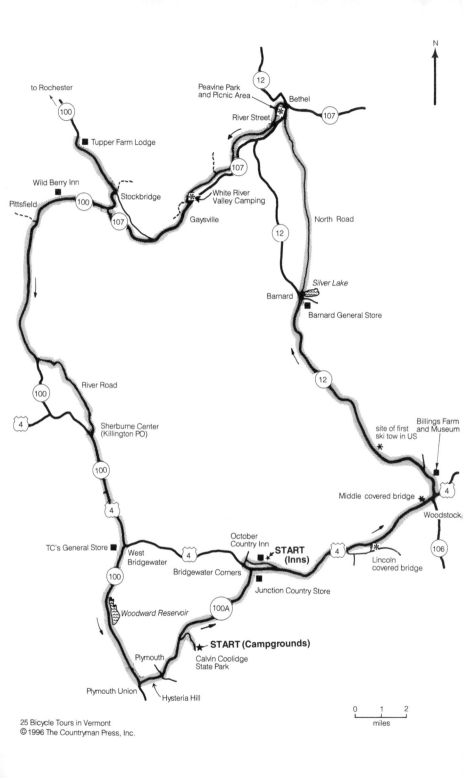

N

to Rochester

100

12

Peavine Park
and Picnic Area

Bethel

River Street

107

107

Tupper Farm Lodge

Wild Berry Inn

White River
Valley Camping

100

Stockbridge

North Road

Pittsfield

107

Gaysville

12

Silver Lake

Barnard

Barnard General Store

100

River Road

12

4

Sherburne Center
(Killington PO)

100

site of first
ski tow in US

Billings Farm
and Museum

4

Middle covered bridge

Woodstock

TC's General Store

4

October
Country Inn

START
(Inns)

4

106

West
Bridgewater

100

Bridgewater Corners

Junction Country Store

Lincoln
covered bridge

Woodward Reservoir

100A

START (Campgrounds)

Plymouth

Calvin Coolidge
State Park

Plymouth Union

Hysteria Hill

0   1   2
miles

25 Bicycle Tours in Vermont
© 1996 The Countryman Press, Inc.

8

Rivers of Central Vermont: A Two-day Tour

Moderate terrain; inn-to-inn: 73.7 miles (7.6 unpaved), or camping: 66 miles (7.6 unpaved)

The distance of each day's ride is given at the beginning of its directions.

This tour offers fine rural bicycling, as well as exceptional opportunities to fish, swim, and visit a nearly perfect hillside hamlet and a wonderful Vermont village. The ride follows streams and rivers most of the way and takes you to many sites of historical and architectural interest. I have written the tour so that it starts in Bridgewater Corners at the October Country Inn, because that is one of my favorite places. With the exception of 13 miles on US 4 and 4 miles on VT 107, which can be moderately busy, you follow lightly traveled roads.

On the first day you visit the exquisite village of Woodstock, where the architecture of early Vermont is carefully preserved. On the second day you bicycle into the hill town of Plymouth, where Calvin Coolidge spent his boyhood and took his oath as president. Words that Coolidge wrote about Plymouth in his autobiography in 1929 still fit that hamlet and most of the countryside along this tour: "As I look back on it I constantly think how clean it was. There was little that was artificial. It was all close to nature and in accordance with the ways of nature. The streams ran clear. The roads, the woods, the fields, the people—all were clean. Even when I try to divest it of the halo which I know always surrounds the past, I am unable to create any other impression than it was fresh and clean."

The tour is designed to suit both cyclists who like to camp and those who prefer to stay at country inns. Regardless of which accommodations you use, you will probably find it convenient to sleep at the trail's head the night before you begin riding. If you camp, you will save time and eat better by bringing most of your food from home. But whichever way you go, do not set out until you have contacted the places you intend to stay at night, for you cannot rely on their being prepared for you without notice.

Mileages for the inn-to-inn version are in parentheses; mileages for the camping version are not.

DAY I

Plymouth to Gaysville (campgrounds): *moderate terrain; 36.7 miles (5.0 unpaved)*

Bridgewater Corners to Rochester (inns): *moderate terrain; 39.7 miles (5.0 unpaved)*

0.0 *At the exit from Calvin Coolidge State Park, turn right onto VT 100A North.*

VT 100A runs downhill along Broad Brook for 4 miles and then flattens out for a mile before Bridgewater Corners.

5.0 *(0.0) With your back to the October Country Inn, turn right onto the unpaved road; ride 0.1 mile to the T. At the T, turn left onto the paved but unsigned road, and ride 25 yards to the stop sign. At the stop sign, turn left onto US 4 East.*

At the intersection of US 4 and VT 100A, you can pick up supplies at the Junction Country Store (on your right).

During the 1850s placer gold was discovered in Broad Brook above Bridgewater Corners. Something of a gold rush ensued, and there was a lot of panning and digging, but little gold turned up.

For the next 8 miles you follow the Ottauquechee River, a good trout stream. Beware of traffic on US 4; it is least bothersome early in the morning.

9.4 *(4.4) Turn right off US 4 onto the green metal bridge and ride carefully—you may want to walk—across the Ottauquechee River.*

9.5 *(4.5) At the fork, bear left onto the unpaved, unsigned road.*

9.6 *(4.6) At the intersection, continue straight on the unpaved, unsigned road so you keep the Ottauquechee River on your left.*

10.5 *(5.5) Turn left and ride or walk carefully through the Lincoln covered bridge.*

The Lincoln covered bridge stretches 136 feet across the Ottau-quechee River. Constructed in 1877, this bridge remains Vermont's only example of a Pratt-type truss.

10.6 *(5.6) At the T, turn right onto US 4.*

Beware of traffic on US 4.

13.3 *(8.3) At the intersection in the center of Woodstock, turn left onto VT 12 North.*

Woodstock possesses a wealth of early 19th-century architectural grace. Features of this attractive town, including the Billings Farm and Museum, which sponsors many special events, are described at length in Tour 9.

Along VT 12, about 2 miles beyond the museum, you pass a state historical sign marking a spot of enormous significance to Vermont. In 1934, on a sloping sheep pasture here, two ingenious Yankees hitched a rope to the engine of a Model T Ford to create the first ski tow in America. Now 20 ski areas operate in Vermont and accommodate in a single season about seven or eight times the state's population. Just beyond the site of the tow, you cross the Appalachian Trail, which runs from Maine to Georgia. VT 12 then turns uphill, presenting a long and sometimes arduous climb. A level respite of half a mile divides the winding grade into two parts, each 1.75 miles long. The first ascent remains gradual; the second, ending by a room-sized quartz boulder on the right, starts gently, but quickly grows steep. Over the 4 miles you gain roughly 850 feet in elevation. But with that climb you complete the hard work of the day and descend rapidly 2 miles into Barnard.

23.4 *(18.4) At Barnard, do not curve left to follow VT 12 North; instead go straight, off VT 12 onto North Road.*

Barnard makes an ideal place to picnic and swim. The Barnard General Store stocks an ample selection of food, runs a lunch counter where you can get hot soup and sandwiches, and also makes sandwiches to order at its deli counter. Across from the store, a lawn by the shore of Silver Lake provides a perfect place to stretch out, have lunch, and enter the water for a swim. If you are headed for the campground, the Barnard Store is a reliable place to get supplies.

During the 1930s, Sinclair Lewis and Dorothy Thompson lived in Barnard, and Thompson is buried in the cemetery here.

North Road runs past the southern tip of Silver Lake, up a short hill and then along a plateau from which you can catch glimpses of the Green Mountains to your left. About 3 miles from Barnard, the road begins to tilt downhill, getting progressively steeper as it approaches Bethel. The last mile—beginning 0.2 mile beyond a "35 MPH" sign—is very fast and requires your complete attention. By the time you reach Bethel, you have descended more than 700 feet.

30.3 *(25.3) At the stop sign outside Bethel, turn right onto VT 107 East.*
Bethel was the first town chartered by the Republic of Vermont during its 14 years as an independent nation, 1777–91.

30.7 *(25.7) After crossing a bridge and just before VT 107 goes beneath an overpass, turn left toward Peavine Park onto River Street, which may be unsigned here.*
In 0.4 mile you reach Peavine Park and Picnic Area on your left. It's an excellent place to stop; there's even a gazebo to shield you from bad weather. In 1.5 miles River Street becomes unpaved for 4 miles. The surface is hard and smooth most of the way.

35.0 *(30.0) At the fork, where the road is still unpaved, bear left so you cross a very small bridge.*
In 1.3 miles, the road becomes paved.

36.5 *(31.5) One-quarter mile after the pavement resumes, at the bottom of a short hill, turn left and cross the green iron bridge into Gaysville, which consists of a church and a tiny post office.*
The day's second superb swimming spot lies directly below this bridge in the White River. One of the principal tributaries of the Connecticut River, the White runs approximately 60 miles from Battell Mountain (elevation 3471 feet), west of Granville, to White River Junction. Its wonderfully clear waters provide not only exceptional swimming, but also fine cover for trout—especially rainbows and browns—and excellent, though strenuous, white-water canoeing.

36.7 *(31.7) The driveway to White River Valley Camping begins on your left immediately after the green bridge.*

(31.8) At the stop sign just beyond the Gaysville Post Office

(on your right), turn right onto VT 107 West.

Beware of traffic on VT 107. In 3 miles VT 107 runs uphill for a half mile.

(36.1) At the intersection of VT 107 and VT 100, turn right onto VT 100 North. If you are headed for the Wild Berry Inn, do not turn right. Instead, turn left onto VT 100 South and ride 1.5 miles. The Wild Berry Inn will be on your right.

(37.3) At the blinking light in Stockbridge, turn left to continue north on VT 100.

(39.7) Tupper Farm Lodge stands on your right facing VT 100.

DAY 2

Gaysville to Plymouth (campgrounds): *moderate terrain; 29.3 miles (2.6 unpaved)*

Rochester to Bridgewater Corners (inns): *moderate terrain; 34.0 miles (2.6 unpaved)*

0.0   *From White River Valley Camping, turn left out of the driveway onto the unsigned road.*

0.1   *At the stop sign, just beyond the Gaysville Post Office (on the right), turn right onto VT 107 West.*

      Beware of traffic on VT 107. In 3 miles VT 107 runs uphill for a half mile.

      (0.0) From Tupper Farm Lodge, turn left onto VT 100 South.

      (2.4) At the blinking light in Stockbridge, turn right to continue south on VT 100.

4.5   *(3.5) At the intersection of VT 107 and VT 100, go straight onto VT 100 South. Beware of traffic.*

      On a clear day you can catch a glimpse of Killington Peak directly ahead of you. Four miles south of the village of Pittsfield you begin climbing a relentless grade, which in 2 miles takes you up 550 feet in elevation. It is definitely the hardest part of the day.

13.1   *(12.1) Beside a large yellow traffic arrow that points to the*

right, turn left off VT 100 onto River Road, which is unpaved for the first 2.6 miles. There is a small green road sign 100 feet down River Road.

The surface of River Road is hard and generally free of rocks, but ride very cautiously on the downhill sections. River Road is far preferable to VT 100, because of the traffic on the latter.

17.0 *(16.0) At the yield sign, bear left onto the unsigned road and cross the small concrete bridge.*

17.1 *(16.1) At the stop sign in Sherburne Center (Killington PO), turn left onto VT 100 South, which here runs concurrently with US 4 East.*

Over the next 4 miles you encounter more traffic than you have seen since leaving Woodstock. But the road is wide, straight, and most of the way offers a shoulder suitable for cycling. For the final mile before your next turn, VT 100 dives downhill into West Bridgewater.

21.5 *(20.5) At the blinking light in West Bridgewater, turn right toward Plymouth Union onto VT 100 South.*

TC's General Store, to your right at this intersection, makes sandwiches, sells all you need for a picnic, and welcomes bicyclists to use the lavatories and refill their water bottles. A half mile south of the store, VT 100 starts up a gradual grade that grows steeper before ending in 1.5 miles at the foot of Woodward Reservoir.

27.0 *(26.0) Turn left onto VT 100A North toward Plymouth.*

Immediately upon making this turn, you face one of Vermont's most formidable short ascents. Fondly and not-so-fondly called Hysteria Hill by many bicyclists, this climb, though barely 0.5 mile long, tests the stamina and will of all who try it. But doubtless it merits the effort, for it brings an unspoiled downhill run of more than 5 miles. Of course, if you began this tour at Coolidge State Park, you already benefited from 4 of those 5 miles.

28.0 *(27.0) In 0.4 mile beyond the crest of Hysteria Hill and just past a pond on your right, turn left off VT 100A and ride 0.25 mile to Plymouth.*

Plymouth is a great source of aesthetic and historical pleasure.

Consisting only of a few trim 19th-century clapboard buildings and surrounded by hills, this tiny hamlet radiates peacefulness and security. Here, at 3 o'clock on an August morning in 1923, Vice President Calvin Coolidge was awakened to be told that President Harding had died. Then, by the glow of a kerosene lamp, Coolidge took the presidential oath from his father, a notary public. Fifty-one years earlier on Independence Day, Coolidge was born here in a weathered cottage beside the church where his family worshiped.

Now a state historic district, Plymouth merits a leisurely visit. The Coolidge family home, where the vice president was vacationing when Harding died, has been painstakingly restored to its condition on that eventful night. In like manner the room where Coolidge was born has been refurbished as the 19th-century borning room that it was. Perhaps most impressive is the Summer White House of 1924. You get there by climbing a narrow wooden staircase to the vaulted room above the general store. The floorboards are still unfinished as they were, no doubt, in August 1924, when Coolidge worked here. Though in great need of rest, he was not able to ignore all his presidential duties. So this space, which was usually used for town dances and Grange meetings, was wired for telegraph and two telephones. The president worked at a table made from plain wooden trusses and large boards. It stands there today.

Still more can be learned about those times by visiting the Wilder Barn, which exhibits a collection of 19th-century farm implements and horse-drawn vehicles. This collection dramatically illustrates the hardships farm families endured and the ingenious ways they accomplished with animal and human power tasks now performed by electricity and internal combustion engines. From late May till mid-October these buildings are open to the public daily 9:30–5:30. Admission is charged to all except the Summer White House.

Plymouth's Union Christian Church (1840), originally Congregational, illustrates the blending of mid- and late-19th-century architecture. The exterior remains unchanged since its construction and resembles that of other clapboard meetinghouses around the state. But in 1890 the congregation decided to replace the original box pews with a more up-to-date arrangement. Accordingly they

The house where President Calvin Coolidge was born in 1872, as seen through the window of the Union Christian Church in Plymouth

hired a master carpenter who refashioned the interior out of rare hard pine in a style known as Carpenter Gothic. This style achieves in wood the Gothic forms usually shaped by masonry. The church holds Sunday services from June through October at 11 AM.

The Calvin Coolidge Visitors Center (1972) houses a collection of Coolidge memorabilia, including many old photographs captioned with excerpts from his autobiography. The Plymouth Cheese Corporation at the northern end of the village makes a unique, granular curd cheese. Sometimes you can watch the process, and every day of the week you can sample the cheese and buy it. Before leaving Plymouth, you may enjoy seeing the simple grave where the former president is buried. Ask anyone for directions.

28.5 *(27.5) Retrace your way out of Plymouth to the stop sign and turn left onto VT 100A toward Woodstock.*

29.3 *(30.3) The entrance to Coolidge State Park is on your right, where, if you have been camping, you started the tour.*

(33.6) At the stop sign in Bridgewater Corners, turn left onto US 4 West, ride 0.2 mile, and turn right toward Bridgewater Center. Go 25 yards and then turn right onto the unpaved, unsigned road and ride 0.1 mile.

On your left, just before you turn off US 4, is the home of Mountain Brewers, one of Vermont's four micro-breweries. Widely known for its fine beers and ales, sold under the Long Trail name, Mountain Brewers uses all natural ingredients, no preservatives or pasteurization, and describes its beers as "truly handcrafted in small batches." Tours are offered daily noon–5.

(34.0) October Country Inn is on your left.

For general information on lodging, restaurants, attractions, and special events, contact the Woodstock Chamber of Commerce, 18 Central Street, Woodstock, VT 05091 (802-457-3555), and the Killington-Pico Area Association, PO Box 114, Killington, VT 05751.

Where to Stay

October Country Inn, Box 66F, Bridgewater Corners, VT 05035 (802-672-3412), is a cozy, cheerful, marvelously inviting place. Fashioned from a 19-century farmhouse, the inn is informal, but gracious. Delightful, talented innkeepers Richard Sims and Patrick Runkel specialize in ethnic cooking.

Tupper Farm Lodge, Route 100, Box 149F, Rochester, VT 05767 (802-767-4243), has something marvelous about it, something that makes every guest feel wonderful but that cannot be fully explained even by its delicious, bountiful meals, comfortable country accommodations, and superb swimming hole in the White River. Innkeepers extraordinaire Ann and Roger Verme have created their inn from an 1820 farmhouse.

Wild Berry Inn, Route 100, Stockbridge, VT 05772 (802-746-8141), is a 1780 post-and-beam farmhouse, now made over into a bed & breakfast. A combination of country antiques and contemporary furnishings creates a cheerful atmosphere. Innkeepers Barbara Havelka and Janet Heider gladly provide bicyclists with shuttle service to a nearby restaurant for dinner.

Calvin Coolidge State Park, Plymouth, VT 05056 (802-672-3612), is open from the Friday before Memorial Day to mid-October. There are tent sites and lean-tos, and several sites are in designated primitive areas accessible only by foot trail. Hot showers and flush toilets are provided. Vermont state parks do not accept reservations for fewer than two days.

White River Valley Camping, Box 106, Gaysville, VT 05746 (802-234-9115), is a member of VAPCOO. Owners Dan, Skip, and Inger Harrington have 100 spacious wooded, open, and river sites with cooking pits. They gladly accept reservations for a single night and are open May 1 through October 15. Flush toilets, hot showers, whirlpool, a laundromat, firewood, and ice as well as a nearby store are available.

Bicycle Repair Services

The Cyclery Plus, US 4, West Woodstock, VT (802-457-3377)

First Stop Bike Shop, US 4, West Bridgewater, VT (802-422-9050)

Green Mountain Bicycles, Route 100, Rochester, VT (802-767-4464)

Woodstock Sports, 30 Central Street, Woodstock, VT (802-457-1568)

9
Woodstock–Quechee

Moderate terrain; 24.9 miles (2.3 unpaved), plus 1.8-mile side trip

This tour takes you to Vermont's most elegant village and the magnificent horse and dairy farms that surround it. The landscape is exquisite and, by Vermont standards, rather pampered. The villages of Woodstock and Quechee offer lots to see and do. The tour starts in Woodstock, where Vermont's most stately architecture has been meticulously preserved. One Woodstock native, US Senator Jacob Collamer, liked to boast that "the good people of Woodstock have less incentive than others to yearn for heaven." Although the village often bustles with traffic and pedestrians by late morning, this route neatly avoids that commotion by following rarely used roads through the quiet countryside north and east of town. I've selected an exceptional inn overlooking a covered bridge on a side road 4 miles away from Woodstock. Except for two difficult climbs, the tour is not demanding and features one of Vermont's finest downhill runs, nearly 7 miles long. Slightly more than 2 miles at the tour's end are not paved, but they suit two-wheel travel well.

0.0 **From the intersection of US 4 and Route 12 (Elm Street) in Woodstock, follow VT 12 North toward Barnard.**

Before leaving, take at least a quick ride or walk along the side streets of the village. Many of Vermont's most distinguished 19th-century Federal homes line Woodstock's oval green and shaded residential streets. Since 1786 the shire town of Windsor County, Woodstock has always managed to be a center of wealth and gracious living. Though local manufacturing businesses developed along the rivers and streams around Woodstock during its first hundred years, industry waned when the railroad made the nation's goods accessible here in the mid-19th century. Finance and commerce, not manufacturing, have kept this town both prosperous and beautiful. Perhaps its former wealthy residents shielded

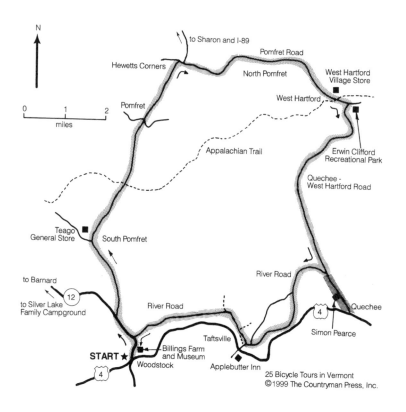

25 Bicycle Tours in Vermont
©1999 The Countryman Press, Inc.

Woodstock from change; certainly its most recent residents have tried. Telephone and electrical wires are buried; signs are kept to a minimum. In 1969, when a new bridge was needed to cross the Ottauquechee River, the town built a covered bridge in authentic Town lattice style, using only wooden pegs to hold it together.

Despite a year-round stream of visitors, Woodstock has little of the garishness that plagues some popular towns. Reserved, urbane, and exclusive, Woodstock's appeal derives from the pristine charm of its homes and the tastefulness of its shops and galleries. Four churches—the First Congregational (1807); St. James Episcopal

(1907); the Universalist (1835); and the Masonic Temple, formerly Christian Church (1827)—still ring bells cast by Paul Revere.

The Woodstock Historical Society (802-457-1822), housed in a former 1807 Federal-style home, exhibits early-19th-century antiques, including locally made furniture, portraits, silver, farm implements, quilts, doll houses, and etchings by John Taylor Arms. Behind the house a well-landscaped garden stretches to the Ottauquechee River. The Society is located at 26 Elm Street and is open from mid-May through October, Monday through Saturday 10–5 and Sunday 2–5. Admission is free.

During the warm weather the area hosts many special events, including a hot air balloon festival, polo matches, craft exhibits, and noontime concerts every Thursday on the library lawn. The Woodstock Chamber of Commerce (802-457-3555) publishes an annotated map of the village. You can get one free from the Information Booth on the green or at the chamber's office at 4 Central Street. Before leaving town, you might enjoy stopping at F. H. Gillingham & Sons (16 Elm Street). Founded in 1886 as a general store and now selling gourmet foods and hardware, Gillingham's offers a selection that will tempt the most weight-conscious cyclist.

Lots happens also in Quechee, at the other end of the tour. Call the Quechee Chamber of Commerce for information: 802-295-7900.

Just a half mile down VT 12, you pass the Billings Farm and Museum on your right, described at Mile 21.3 below.

1.1 **At a fork in the road, bear right off VT 12 onto the unsigned road toward South Pomfret.**

Over the next 2 miles the road climbs almost imperceptibly, but nevertheless steadily, as it follows Barnard Brook uphill through an exquisite landscape of gentle(wo)men's farms. The fields are tilled to the tops of the hills and down the sides.

3.1 **At the intersection by the Teago General Store in South Pomfret, bear right onto the unsigned road so you pass Teago's on your left.**

The Teago General Store sells beverages, cold cuts, cheeses, and breads. Near the store stands the redbrick Abbott Memorial Library, which contains a museum of local historical memorabilia.

About a mile and a half from South Pomfret, and later near West Hartford, you cross the Appalachian Trail, which runs through southeastern Vermont on its way from Georgia to Maine.

South Pomfret sits at an elevation of 736 feet above sea level. Over the next 3 miles you climb nearly 500 feet—sometimes quite steeply—before reaching Pomfret at 1200 feet. This hill presents the most difficult ascent of the tour. From Pomfret you glide downhill 7 miles to West Hartford, which lies at an elevation of 420 feet on the banks of the White River.

7.9 *At Hewetts Corners, continue straight onto Pomfret Road, which is unsigned here. Do not turn toward Sharon. (Maps of the intersection are deceptive. The road you follow through North Pomfret to West Hartford is a continuation of the road from Pomfret, while the road to Sharon branches off to your left and goes toward I-89. Some maps make it appear as though the road to West Hartford requires a right turn in Hewetts Corners, but it does not.)*

13.0 *At the stop sign by the bridge (on your left) outside West Hartford, turn right onto Quechee–West Hartford Road, which is unsigned here.*

If you are hungry, turn left and ride 0.1 mile across the bridge over the White River to the stop sign at VT 14. There, turn left onto VT 14 North and ride 100 yards to the West Hartford Village Store on your right.

If you would like to take a swim, the White River is the best place. From the stop sign at Mile 13.0, turn right onto Quechee–West Hartford Road and ride 0.1 mile uphill. Then turn left onto Westfield Drive and ride 0.2 mile. Turn left onto Recreation Drive and ride 150 yards downhill to Erwin Clifford Recreational Park. Ride cautiously, for the last half is unpaved and quite steep. There are picnic tables and toilet facilities at the park, as well as swimming access to the river.

Over the next 3 miles, the Quechee–West Hartford Road climbs out of the White River Valley, so be prepared for the second and final climb of the tour. About 2 miles before the next turn, the road turns downhill.

18.1 *At 0.1 mile after the inverted-Y road sign (on your right), turn sharply right onto River Road. Approach this turn cautiously, for when you reach it, you are going downhill.*

At 0.6 mile after turning onto River Road, you pass the Quechee Club on your left. This modern clubhouse on the edge of a new golf course belongs to a major development of opulent condominiums and recreational facilities.

> FOR THE 1.8-MILE SIDE TRIP TO QUECHEE: Instead of turning sharply right onto River Road at Mile 18.1, continue straight on Quechee–West Hartford Road for 0.9 mile more. The Simon Pearce Mill will then be on your right. Here you can watch master glassblowers turn molten glass into fine crystal. The 200-year-old former woolen mill, with its high brick walls, huge windows, and maple floors, provides a splendid site. Glassblowing requires enormous amounts of heat; the Ottauquechee River powers the 50-year-old turbine that generates all the power used in the building and a little extra. An elegant little restaurant at Simon Pearce serves lunch and dinner overlooking the falls.

19.2 *Do not turn right onto Hillside Road.*

21.3 *Within sight of, but before entering, the red Taftsville covered bridge (1836), turn right onto River Road, which is unpaved and unsigned. From this turn to the next, find your way by following the roads that keep the Ottauquechee River on your left.*

River Road is smooth, but unpaved, for 2.25 miles.

While you could return to Woodstock on US 4, it would be a foolish thing to do because of the high volume of traffic, narrow road width, and lack of beauty. Although the unpaved road demands attention, it is quiet, shaded, and provides a delightful view of the Ottauquechee.

To bicycle to the Applebutter Inn, do not turn right onto River Road. Instead, continue straight through the Taftsville covered bridge. Proceed cautiously, for the bridge is narrow, dark, and quite long; you may want to walk your bicycle. At the T on the other side of the bridge, turn right and ride 30 yards to the stop sign. At the stop sign, walk across US 4 toward the Taftsville Country Store and resume riding on Happy Valley Road. The Applebutter Inn is on your left on Happy Valley Road in 0.1 mile.

In 3 miles, just before you come to your next turn, you reach the entrance to the Billings Farm and Museum on your left. This premier agricultural museum sustains the spirit of late-19th-century Vermont agriculture. The farm milks championship Jersey cows, raises Southdown sheep, and uses draft horses and oxen for field chores. In the late 19th century, manufactured goods were displacing hand-crafted ones, and the railroad was tying local farmers to the markets and manners of the urban Northeast. The Billings Farm reveals the richness and sophistication of Vermont farm life as well as its ordinary details. Explore the barns at milking time, the farmlife exhibits, and the award-winning 1890 Farm House. During the early 19th century, Billings Farm was the home of the family of George Perkins Marsh, whose book *Man and Nature* (1864) became the bible of the early-20th-century conservation movement. The museum, as well as the Marsh-Billings-Rockefeller National Historic Park across the street at their former mansion, are the creations of Laurence and Mary Rockefeller; Mary's grandfather, Frederick Billings, purchased the farm in 1869. It is open daily 10–5, May through October. Admission is charged.

24.4 *At the stop sign, turn left onto Route 12 South.*

24.7 *Just beyond the "Bad Intersection" sign, turn left to continue on Route 12 South toward US 4.*

24.9 *You are back in Woodstock where the tour began.*

When you reach Woodstock, consider stretching your legs with a walk along one of the town's short nature trails, either Faulkner or Mount Peg. Maps of both are available free from the chamber of commerce.

For general information on lodging, restaurants, attractions, and special events, contact the Woodstock Chamber of Commerce, 18 Central Street, Woodstock, VT 05091 (802-457-3555), and the Quechee Chamber of Commerce, PO Box 106, Quechee, VT (802-295-7900).

Where to Stay

Applebutter Inn, Happy Valley Road, Taftsville, VT 05073 (802-457-4158), is an 1840 Federal home made over into an inn. It combines country elegance with congeniality at a site overlooking the Taftsville covered bridge. Innkeepers Bev and Andy Cook are delightful hosts.

Silver Lake Family Campground, Box 111, Barnard, VT 05031 (802-234-9974), is 10 miles north of Woodstock on Silver Lake. The campground has its own beach, hot showers, both wooded and open campsites, and rustic cabin rentals.

Bicycle Repair Services

The Cyclery Plus, US 4, West Woodstock, VT (802-457-3377)

Woodstock Sports, 30 Central Street, Woodstock, VT (802-457-1568)

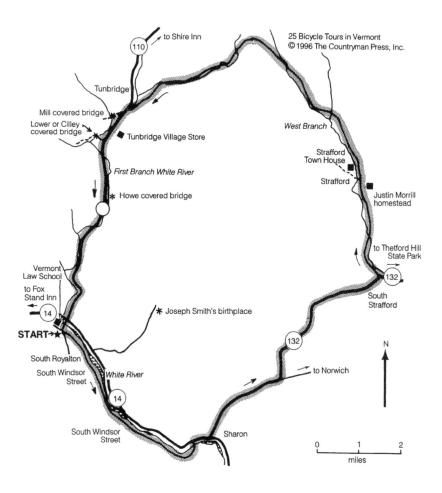

25 Bicycle Tours in Vermont
© 1996 The Countryman Press, Inc.

(110) → to Shire Inn

Tunbridge

Mill covered bridge

Lower or Cilley
covered bridge

■ Tunbridge Village Store

First Branch White River

* Howe covered bridge

West Branch

Strafford
Town House ■

Strafford

■ Justin Morrill
homestead

to Thetford Hill
State Park

(132)

South
Strafford

Vermont
Law School

to Fox
Stand Inn

(14)

* Joseph Smith's birthplace

(132)

START→★

South Royalton

to Norwich

South Windsor
Street

White River

(14)

South Windsor
Street

Sharon

N

0   1   2
miles

10
South Royalton–Strafford

Moderate-to-difficult terrain; 27.9 miles

With the exception of the Northeast Kingdom, 60 miles farther north, Orange County may be Vermont's most unspoiled region. It has no ski areas, large lakes, cities, or major mountains. Even Vermont's two interstate highways, 89 and 91, which enclose this unspoiled county on its south, east, and west, seem to funnel the traffic by, rather than draw it in. Yet Orange County is a wonderland of wooded hills and winding river valleys, ideal for bicycling. This tour follows untrafficked roads along the First and West Branches of the White River and across the ridges that separate them. Carving a circle through the tiny villages of South Strafford, Strafford, and Tunbridge, the tour brings excellent views down the valleys and across the rounded hills that feed their streams into the rivers below. Though the route is emphatically pastoral, the architecture is superb: three covered bridges, the outstanding Gothic Revival home of Senator Justin Morrill, and the exquisite village of Strafford, a cohesive unit of Greek Revival (1800–1840) residences and public buildings devoid of intruding modern structures. If you make the tour in mid-September, you can also join the spirited whirl of the Tunbridge World's Fair.

0.0   *Leave South Royalton by riding east on South Windsor Street, which runs down the northern side of the village green. Do not turn onto any of the side roads that come into South Windsor Street. Just keep the White River on your left until you see the "Narrow Bridge" sign.*

South Royalton is the home of Vermont Law School; there are many small restaurants in town.

Founded in 1972, Vermont Law School, the state's first and only, is a private, independent institution that enrolls approximately 520 men and women from throughout the United States and several other nations. The law school offers the J.D. and a Master of Science in Environmental Law. According to the school's catalog, its character is rooted in Vermont: "Traditionally, Vermont's culture has been dominated by the village and small-town way of life. This culture has given rise to a strong set of values which are still prevalent here: emphasis on individual rights and responsibilities; concern for the community and one's neighbors; appreciation of a clean environment as well as a viable economy. The law school espouses such values, integrating them into its course offerings and extracurricular activities. VLS expects its students to want to do good as much as to do well."

In Vermont an aspiring lawyer may also gain admission to the bar by reading law with a practicing attorney and then taking the state bar examination.

During the summer on Thursday evenings the South Royalton Band performs on the green. South Windsor Street parallels the White River, which along this stretch offers good swimming and excellent fishing for brown and rainbow trout.

4.7 **At the stop sign—just after you cross the narrow iron bridge over the White River outside Sharon—turn right onto VT 14 South, which is unsigned here.**

5.1 **In Sharon, turn left onto VT 132 East toward Strafford and South Strafford.**

Within a quarter mile, VT 132 tips steeply uphill for a mile, levels to a moderate grade for 2 miles, and then rises steeply again for just over a mile. It's a challenging climb. From the top, you start immediately down a glorious 2-mile descent. Initially the slope is an extremely steep 13 degrees, so take it cautiously and enjoy the views.

Joseph Smith, founder of the Church of Jesus Christ of Latter-day Saints, the Mormons, was born in 1805 on an outlying Sharon farm. Smith lived there until he was 10 and received his first visitation 4 years later in New York. About 5 miles from this intersection, at the end of a 2-mile climb up an unpaved road off VT 14, a quiet retreat has been built at Smith's birthplace. A monolith of Barre granite, 38½ feet high, weighing 39 tons—purportedly the world's largest—marks the site.

Home of US Senator Justin Morrill (1848) in Strafford

Each foot of the obelisk represents a year in the life of the prophet, who was lynched by a mob in the Carthage, Illinois, jail in 1844. Had it not been for the organizational genius of another Vermonter, Brigham Young, born in Whitingham, Mormonism might have died with Smith.

7.4 *Bear left to stay on VT 132. Do not go toward Norwich.*

11.5 *At the stop sign in South Strafford, turn left off Route 132 toward Strafford.*

If you're hungry, get food here. The next opportunity, which is a meager one, is 11 sometimes-challenging miles away. If you turn right instead of left at the stop sign and ride 0.25 mile, you can eat at the South Strafford Café or buy groceries at Coburns' General Store. Both will be on your left. Since the Justin Morrill homestead, a perfect spot to picnic, is less than 2 miles away, consider carrying your lunch there.

In between the café and the general store is a wonderful shop, Patricia Owens Raiments and Adornments. Patricia Owens is an engaging woman with a sharp and joyful eye for clothing. Her shop offers an eclectic mix of mostly used clothes for women, men, and children. Nearly everything is special and interesting, much of it cheerfully nostalgic. She loves cyclists and is glad to refill your water bottle. The shop is open every day in the fall, and afternoons otherwise. To be sure of the hours, call ahead (802-765-4335).

As you approach Strafford, you reach the rosy pink, Romantic Gothic homestead of Justin S. Morrill. It's on your right in 2.1 miles. This is the extraordinary home of an extraordinary American. Take some time for a visit; it's an opportunity you will not want to miss.

The principal building is an outstanding example of a Gothic Revival cottage. Accordingly, the elaborate shapes of Gothic design, originally cut from stone, are here rendered in wood. Finials crown the peaks of the steeply pitched gable roofs; bargeboards hang like icicles from the eaves. The interior is as fanciful as the exterior and includes novel solutions to contemporary problems such as airflow, heat, and protecting food from flies. Don't miss the hand-painted screens that cover the downstairs windows. From outside, you will see the romantic depictions of European landscapes but nothing of the interior of the house; from inside the screens look clear.

Morrill himself designed this 17-room cottage, its outbuildings, and the landscaping. The house was built between 1848 and 1851. It is now a National Historic Landmark and Vermont Historic Site open to the public 11–5 Wednesday through Sunday, mid-May through mid-October. Admission is charged.

Morrill was born in Strafford in 1810 and buried here in 1898. He was the son of a blacksmith and could not afford to attend college. Instead, he left school at 15 and made his way as a clerk and then the owner of several general stores. His financial success enabled him to retire in 1848 after just 17 years in local commerce. During the next 6 years, he built this home, studied the books he had been acquiring, married, and had the first of his two sons. In 1854 he was persuaded to run for the US Congress. Though he won his first election by just 59 votes, he was reelected to the

House five times and then elected US Senator six times. Forty-three years of service under 11 presidents!

He is known best for the Morrill Acts, passed during the Civil War and in 1890. Both grew from his own disappointment at not being able to afford college and from his vision that college must provide opportunities for "farmers, mechanics, and all those who must win their bread by labor," as well as those who enter the refined professions.

The Land Grant Act of 1862, signed into law by President Abraham Lincoln, granted each loyal state vast tracts of federal land for the support of colleges that would teach agriculture and the mechanic arts. Under this act and its successors, states received 17,400,000 acres of land—nearly three times the area of Vermont—and 69 land-grant colleges were established. The Morrill Act underwrote the first major practical and technical programs of study in American higher education, previously the exclusive bastion of classical studies in arts, sciences, and languages.

A quarter mile beyond the Morrill homestead, the magnificent Strafford Town House—some call it the Chartres of Vermont—stands directly in front of you on a rise at the far end of the village green. This splendid meetinghouse was built in 1799 by a subscription of pews and a special town tax levy. The Strafford Town House is not only the architectural center of the village, it is also the site of town meetings, weddings, concerts, and many other local events. One of the most interesting is the Strafford Town House Series. Sponsored by the Strafford Democrats, the series is designed to "provoke some critical thinking and discussions about current issues." Since its beginning in 1989, it has featured such nationally prominent speakers as John Kenneth Galbraith, Arthur Miller, William Sloane Coffin, Madeleine Kunin, and Tom Wicker. The series takes place Wednesday evenings in August at 7:30.

13.9 *As you approach the green in Strafford, bear right toward Chelsea and Tunbridge so you pass the green and Strafford Town House on your left.*

Just beyond Strafford you start uphill. The grade is gradual but steady for the first 2 miles. It then increases to moderate for 1.25 miles and ends with a mile that's just plain steep. For most of the

The Strafford Town House (1799)

4.25-mile climb, trees shade the road. At the top you have a panoramic view of the Green Mountains. Then the road drops steeply into a fast 4-mile run into Tunbridge.

22.2 *At the stop sign in Tunbridge, turn left onto VT 110 South. Make this turn very cautiously, for your visibility northward (to your right) is limited.*

VT 110 slopes slightly downward nearly the entire way, as it follows the First Branch of the White River 5.5 miles to South Royalton.

For more than a century Tunbridge has been celebrating the World's Fair of the Union Agricultural Society in mid-September. Sometimes drawing 15,000 people a day, the four-day festival blends the exuberant spirit of a carnival with the exhibits and competitions of an agricultural fair. Folklore says that in years past all sober persons were herded off the grounds at 3 in the afternoon as undesirables. Others say the bacchanalian tradition continues. In any case, if you arrive during the fair, judge for yourself and watch the traffic carefully. Information about the official events can be obtained from the Union Agricultural Society, Tunbridge, VT 05077 (802-889-5555 or 802-889-3311).

Within 0.1 mile after you start south on VT 110, you can see the Mill covered bridge on your right. Built across the First Branch of the White River in 1883, its structure is multiple kingpost, with a span of 60 feet. Just beyond the bridge on your left, you can buy groceries at the Tunbridge Village Store. A mile farther south, if you turn right off VT 110 onto the unpaved road, you can find the Lower, or Cilley, covered bridge. This bridge, also built in 1883, measures 65 feet. And finally, 1.25 miles farther, on your left, is the 60-foot Howe covered bridge, built in 1879.

27.6 *At the stop sign at the intersection of VT 110 and VT 14, go straight across VT 14 onto the road to South Royalton.*

27.9 *You enter South Royalton along the west side of the green, where the tour began.*

For general information on lodging, restaurants, attractions, and special events, contact the White River Junction Chamber of Commerce, PO Box 697, White River Junction, VT 05001 (802-295-6200).

Where to Stay

Fox Stand Inn, VT 14, Royalton, VT 05058 (802-763-8437), is a homey bed & breakfast with a full restaurant. Innkeepers Jean and Gary Curley offer inexpensive accommodations above their tavern and restaurant. Try to get room #1; it's the largest and quietest. Behind the inn there's a good swimming hole in the White River. Dinner is served indoors and out, Tuesday through Saturday. A hot breakfast is served to all B&B guests.

Shire Inn, Main Street, PO Box 37, Chelsea, VT 05038 (802-685-3031), stands behind a low white fence in one of Vermont's loveliest and most unspoiled villages. The inn is a classic and elegant place. Its six beautifully furnished guest rooms all have private baths; four have working fireplaces. Innkeepers Jay and Karen Keller make fine food a high priority at both dinner and breakfast.

Thetford Hill State Park, Box 132, Thetford, VT 05074 (802-785-2266), is set on 262 acres overlooking the hills of New Hampshire. There are 3 miles of walking trails and 16 mostly wooded sites: 14 for tents or trailers without hookups and 2 lean-tos. There are picnic tables, wood fireplaces, a picnic shelter, and a playground.

Bicycle Repair Services

The Cyclery Plus, US 4, West Woodstock, VT (802-457-3377)

Morris Brothers Mountain Bikes, 20 Bridge Street, White River Junction, VT (802-296-2331)

Woodstock Sports, 30 Central Street, Woodstock, VT (802-457-1568)

11

Fairlee–Haverhill, N.H.

Easy-to-moderate terrain; 24.1 or 16.2 miles

This tour explores a cycling paradise where Vermont and New Hampshire meet along the Connecticut River. Since the cycling is neither difficult nor long, by making a day of it you will have ample time to enjoy what you find along the way, including prosperous horse and dairy farms, glorious river views, extraordinary 18th- and 19th-century architecture, lovely lakes, and a superb antiques shop. For a real treat, make arrangements for a sunset hot-air-balloon ride with veteran pilot Brian Boland. He operates seven days a week out of nearby Post Mills Airport (802-333-9254). Also consider visiting Hanover to explore the campus of Dartmouth College (1769) and visit the shop of the League of New Hampshire Craftsmen at 13 Lebanon Street, which represents some 250 craftspersons. Take your time along this tour; it will reward you well.

0.0 **From the green in Fairlee, ride south on US 5 so you pass the green on your right.**

Aficionados of road food as well as hungry bicyclists find themselves at home and well fed at the Fairlee Diner, less than 0.25 north of the green on the east side of US 5. It is a living artifact of the time when travelers drove on roads, rather than on superhighways. The diner is open daily 5:30 AM–2 PM.

Before leaving Fairlee, consider making a visit to Chapman's, at the northwest corner of the green. No ordinary general store, Chapman's displays thousands of hand-tied fishing flies, lots of stuffed fishing trophies, an enormous selection of wines, antique linens, and rows and rows of used books.

0.4 **Turn right toward I-91.**

Silver Maple Lodge and Cottages is less than a quarter mile south of here on the west side of US 5.

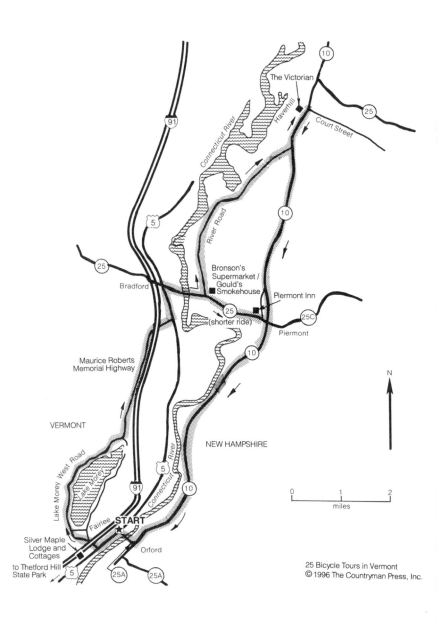

The Victorian

Connecticut River

River Road

Haverhill

Court Street

Bronson's
Supermarket /
Gould's
Smokehouse

Piermont Inn

Bradford

25 (shorter ride)

25C

Piermont

Maurice Roberts
Memorial Highway

VERMONT

NEW HAMPSHIRE

Lake Morey West Road

Lake Morey

Connecticut River

Fairlee

START

Silver Maple
Lodge and
Cottages

Orford

to Thetford Hill
State Park

25A

25A

N

0   1   2
miles

25 Bicycle Tours in Vermont
© 1996 The Countryman Press, Inc.

102

0.6 *Go straight onto Lake Morey West Road, which follows the lake's western shore; the water will be on your right.*

The lake is named after Samuel Morey, who lived in Fairlee, Vermont, and Orford, New Hampshire, in the late 18th century. In 1826 he patented an internal combustion engine, and it seems possible that Morey designed and operated the world's first steamboat. In 1797, 10 years before Robert Fulton launched his *Clermont,* Morey was plying the Connecticut River in a comical little craft, barely large enough to carry himself, a steam boiler, and an armful of wood. Morey showed his boat to Fulton, and some local patriots feel that Fulton, whom history honors as the steamboat's creator, received credit for Morey's invention. Morey went on to hitch an internal combustion engine to a little boat dubbed *Aunt Sally.* Nevertheless, he became discouraged and embittered by his repeated failures to convince the world of the usefulness of his inventions and sank his beloved *Aunt Sally* in Lake Morey. Attempts to locate the venerable boat have proved unsuccessful. Fishing for bass and perch is more promising.

3.7 *Turn left onto Maurice Roberts Memorial Highway.*

This little country road at the northern tip of Lake Morey bears no resemblance to a modern highway. The first mile goes uphill, quite steeply at the end. Then, after about 0.6 mile of easy riding, it goes uphill again for a half mile. From the top, the road shoots swiftly downhill for a mile through three tight curves; ride cautiously.

7.0 *At the stop sign, turn left onto US 5 North, which is unsigned here.*

7.3 *At the traffic light just south of Bradford, turn right onto VT 25 South toward Piermont, New Hampshire, and ride across the Connecticut River.*

Just beyond the river, there's a short climb.

Bradford hosts a traditional country fair and an unusual wild game supper. The Connecticut Valley Fair is held at fairgrounds on US 5, just north of the village, on the third weekend in July. Activities begin on Thursday evening and feature agricultural and homemaking competitions; horse, ox, and tractor pulls; carnival rides; and country-and-western music.

The Bradford Wild Game Supper is held at the United Church of Christ on Main Street and takes place the Saturday before Thanks-

The National Historic District in Haverhill, New Hampshire

giving. Parishioners prepare a gargantuan feast that includes rabbit pâté, fresh and smoked wild boar, venison steak, bear roast, wild-game sausage, buffalo roast, moose burgers, pheasant, and beaver as well as salad, vegetables, and gingerbread. There are six seatings, beginning at 2:30, at which diners consume some 2800 field-dressed pounds of game.

Admission is charged to both the fair and the supper. For further information or reservations, which are a must for the supper, contact the Town Clerk, Bradford, VT 05033 (802-222-4727).

8.2 *In 0.3 mile after you cross the river, turn left onto River Road.*
You can buy food at Bronson's Supermarket and Gould's Smokehouse at this intersection.

Heading northward on River Road, the cycling is easy until the last mile, which climbs a moderate hill.

FOR THE 16.2-MILE RIDE: Do not turn onto River Road. Instead continue straight on NH 25 East for 1.9 miles more, about half of which goes uphill. Then, at the blinking light (in Piermont), turn right onto NH 10 and ride 6.1 miles to Orford.

From there, continue from Mile 23.7 below.

12.1 *At the stop sign, turn left onto NH 10 North, which is un-signed here.*

13.1 *The Haverhill commons are on your right, and you have reached the northernmost point of the tour. To complete the ride, turn around and head south on NH 10.*

The rest of the tour is easy and often downhill.

Before you go, take at least a few minutes to bicycle around the commons and to explore the side streets, where there are many very handsome brick and clapboard Federal houses. Haverhill (1763), a National Historic District, is one of the Granite State's most handsome villages. In the middle of the 19th century it chose not to have the railroad from Boston come into town, so the tracks were curved northward toward Woodsville, which became a commercial center and allowed Haverhill to remain pristine. Exquisite 18th- and 19th-century homes and public buildings, reflecting Haverhill's historic importance as Grafton County seat (1793–1891) face the two commons.

Just 100 yards south of the commons, The Victorian on Main Street is on your right. Here, proprietor Ann Hayden has created one of New England's most enticing—and extensive—collections of soft antiques and vintage jewelry: men's, women's, and children's clothing from beaded flapper dresses to wedding gowns to top hats; table linens, lace curtains, and wonderful white bedspreads; flatware, glassware, and china. To Ann, antique clothing is "a part of history, an art form," and it shows.

At the blinking light in 4.5 miles, you cross NH 25. If you were to turn west there and go 0.2 mile into Piermont, the Piermont Inn would be on your right across from the post office.

23.7 *In Orford, turn right onto NH 25A West toward Fairlee, Vermont.*

In the early 19th century, after visiting Orford, Washington Irving wrote: "In all my travels in this country and Europe, I have seen no village more beautiful." Orford is no longer the thriving village it was prior to the westward exodus of the 1840s and the industrial revolution that silenced local water-powered mills. But it remains a striking village of outstanding architecture on a grand scale. The buildings that line Orford Street compose a district in the National

Register of Historic Places. Most prominent are the seven so-called Ridge Houses. These large mansions stand on enormous lawns, set well back from the east side of the road. They date from 1773 to 1839 and were designed by a Boston architect, probably Asher Benjamin, who was a colleague of Charles Bulfinch.

24.0 At the stop sign in Fairlee, turn left onto US 5 South.

24.1 You are back at the green, on your right, in Fairlee.

For general information on lodging, restaurants, attractions, and special events, contact the White River Junction Chamber of Commerce, PO Box 697, White River Junction, VT 05001 (802-295-6200), and the Hanover Chamber of Commerce, PO Box A105, Hanover, NH 03755 (603-643-3115).

Where to Stay

The Piermont Inn, Piermont, NH 03779 (603-272-4820), was a 1790s stagecoach stop and tavern. Innkeepers Karen and Charles Brown have made it over into a cheery, antiques-furnished inn. The guest rooms are uniformly spacious and charming, but my favorite is the Terrace Ballroom, a high-ceilinged, sunny room with fireplace, double bed, dressing room, and private bath. Breakfast is served indoors, or outside on the flagstone terrace. On Friday and Saturday, dinner is served too.

Silver Maple Lodge and Cottages, RD 1, Box 8, Fairlee, VT 05045 (802-333-4326 or 800-666-1946), centers on a late 18th-century farmhouse that was expanded in Victorian style in the mid-1800s. The farmhouse has cheerful sitting rooms and a huge wrap-around screened porch. If you are sensitive to road noise, talk to innkeepers Scott and Sharon Wright about it, for the lodge sits between US 5 and I-91.

Thetford Hill State Park, Box 132, Thetford, VT 05074 (802-785-2266), covers 262 acres and has just 16 sites; 2 are lean-tos. There are no hookups, but there is a picnic table and wood fireplace at each site, a playground, and a picnic shelter.

Bicycle Repair Services

Brick Store Bicycles, The Green, Strafford, VT (802-765-4441)

Der RadLaden Bicycles, 13 Dartmouth College Highway, Lyme, NH (603-795-4430)

Morris Brothers Mountain Bikes, 20 Bridge Street, White River Junction, VT (802-296-2331)

Omer's & Bob's, Allen Street, Hanover, NH (603-643-3525)

Tom Mowatt Cycles, Olde Nugget Alley, Hanover, NH (603-643-5522)

12
Randolph–Brookfield

Moderate terrain; 42 miles (2.7 unpaved)
Moderate-to-difficult terrain; 26 miles (2.7 unpaved)

A remote valley along the Third Branch of the White River, a floating bridge in an exquisite hillside village, and a rolling ridge overlooking the Green Mountains define this tour. The landscape is quiet and pastoral: a mixture of farmland, small lakes, woods, and streams. On the fringe of the tour stand two small colleges, one a military academy and the other a technical school. Along the route are two charming inns—one on a Morgan horse farm and the other overlooking Vermont's only floating bridge—and a 150-acre campground with a sparkling swimming lake. The longer ride is rated as easier than the shorter, because there is less climbing per total mile, but both rides climb the identical amount of elevation. In the shorter ride most of the climbing is concentrated in 10 rather than 25 miles. I find the shorter ride prettier and more interesting. It takes you to lovely small farms and open fields at the beginning and then a shaded, winding climb through Brookfield Gulf at the end.

In 1975 Randolph witnessed the birth of Vermont Castings, one of the world's leading manufacturers of cast-iron stoves for wood, coal, natural gas, and propane. Though the company still has its foundry in Randolph, the showroom and assembly area have been moved 9 miles down the road to Bethel. Now employing 400 persons and annually producing 50,000 cast-iron stoves, Vermont Castings is publicly "committed to a conservation ethic that mandates the wise use of wood and coal as a viable alternative to exhausting the earth's energy reserves. A natural extension of this belief tells us that a well-made, durable product, as opposed to one of short life which must be replaced and remanufactured, is another sensible way to save our natural resources." The stoves are beautiful as well as efficient. The showroom, on VT 107, 2.5 miles east of Bethel, is open to the public weekdays 9–5.

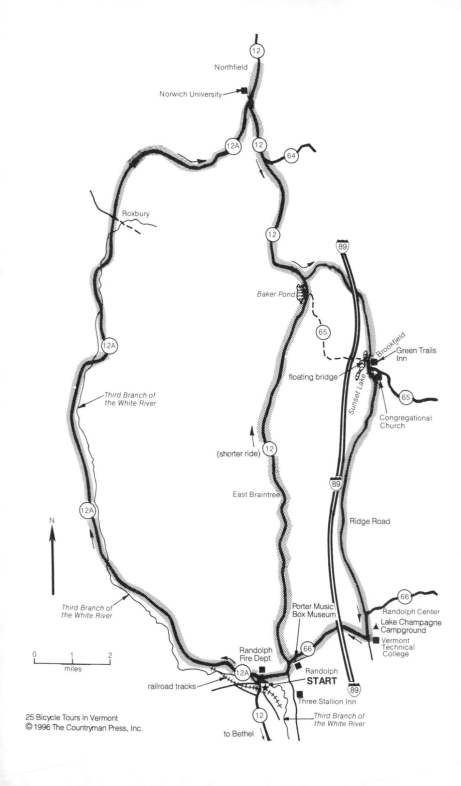

Northfield

12

Norwich University

12A 12 64

Roxbury

12

89

Baker Pond

65

Brookfield

Green Trails Inn

floating bridge

Sunset Lake

65

Congregational Church

12A

Third Branch of the White River

12

(shorter ride)

89

East Braintree

Ridge Road

12A

N

Third Branch of the White River

12A

Porter Music Box Museum

66

Randolph Center

Lake Champagne Campground

Vermont Technical College

Randolph Fire Dept.

66

0 1 2
miles

Randolph
START

89

railroad tracks

Three Stallion Inn

Third Branch of the White River

12

to Bethel

25 Bicycle Tours in Vermont
© 1996 The Countryman Press, Inc.

0.0 *From the center of Randolph, follow Route 12 North, which is also called North Main Street.*

On your way down North Main Street, you pass the Chandler Music Hall and Gallery on your right. Built in 1907 and well known for its fine acoustics and beautifully restored Victorian interior, Chandler hosts an eclectic variety of music: from Richie Havens to Italian opera. The gallery's exhibits change regularly and may feature paintings, sculpture, photographs, or a special collection such as fine Vermont furniture or quilts. The gallery is open Friday through Sunday 11–4. For information about events in the music hall or gallery, call 802-728-9878.

Randolph sits along the Third Branch of the White River at an altitude of 694 feet, the lowest point of the tour.

0.3 *At the T facing the Randolph Fire Department, turn left onto VT 12A North (Park Street) toward Roxbury.*

Just as you make this turn, you pass Slab City Bike & Sports on your left. It's a shop worth visiting. Consider taking one of their guided off-road mountain bike tours. VT 12A has little traffic and makes easy cycling as it follows the Third Branch of the White River. Be very careful crossing the railroad tracks about 5 miles up the road. About 5.5 miles beyond the railroad-track crossing, you reach the Roxbury Fish Hatchery on your left. You can visit—and feed—the young trout being raised here to stock Vermont's streams.

0.3 *FOR THE 26-MILE RIDE: At the T, do not turn left; instead turn right onto Route 12 North (Forest Street). Ride 0.1 mile to the stop sign and there bear left to continue on VT 12 North, which you follow for 10.8 miles.*

The first 7 miles are relatively easy and take you through a quiet, lovely valley of small farms. The next 3.5 miles are exceptionally beautiful, but challenging. You ride uphill through Brookfield Gulf, which resembles a winding crease in the side of a hill. Large, lush trees arch above the shaded road and a little brook spills over its rocky bed. The gulf makes a wonderful contrast with the open meadows and panoramic views along other parts of the tour. At 0.3 mile *beyond* VT 65 (on your right), turn right onto the unpaved road toward Brookfield and the Brookfield floating bridge. The unpaved road surface is hard and smooth.

111

It makes good cycling, but most of the way to Brookfield is still uphill! (Do not use VT 65 to go to Brookfield; it is an unpleasant road for bicycling.) In 1.75 miles, the road becomes paved. Follow the paved road for a mile, ride beneath I-89, and then at the yield sign resume from Mile 29.5 below.

21.4 At the stop sign, turn sharply right onto VT 12 South toward Randolph.

If you need food or drink, ride just 100 yards north on VT 12, toward Northfield, to Lemery's Store on your left. The proprietor, former State Representative Jay Pedley, will take good care of you. He has a full selection of cold drinks and makes subs to order. You might take your food a mile farther north to the handsome Northfield common. The common is oval and surrounded by a striking white rail fence. You can sit on the grass or in the small gazebo. Northfield is the home of Norwich University (1819), a private, coeducational college of 850 cadets. It is the oldest private military academy in the United States; 523 Norwich graduates fought in the Civil War. In 1867 the college moved from Norwich, Vermont, to its present location.

For one weekend, every July, many of the nation's most skilled quilters gather and exhibit their work at the Vermont Quilt Festival in Northfield. For information, call 802-485-7092.

Northfield sits at an altitude of 760 feet, well below Brookfield at 1481 feet, so a considerable challenge lies ahead. VT 12 goes gradually uphill for 5 miles before your next turn.

26.7 Turn left onto the unpaved road toward Brookfield and the Brookfield floating bridge.

The unpaved road surface is hard and smooth. It makes good cycling, but most of the way to Brookfield is still uphill. In 1.75 miles, the road becomes paved.

If you miss the turn to Brookfield, you will reach Baker Pond on your right in a quarter mile and then VT 65 on your left. Though VT 65 does go to Brookfield, do not take it. In this area it is an unpleasant road for bicycling.

29.5 Bear left to ride beneath I-89 and then, at the yield sign, bear right onto the unsigned road.

In 0.2 mile this road becomes unpaved. A quarter mile later, it turns steeply downhill for 0.3 mile. Ride cautiously and beware of sand or gravel on the road.

30.5 *At the stop sign in Brookfield, go straight onto VT 65 East, which may be unsigned here.*

For 0.1 mile VT 65 is not paved.

The current floating bridge—50 feet to your right when you reach this stop sign—is actually the seventh such structure to span the 320 feet across Sunset Lake (also called Clinton Pond and Mirror Pond). The first was built in approximately 1820. That bridge and its successors were essentially rafts buoyed up by empty wooden maple syrup, or later kerosene, barrels. When heavy traffic crosses the bridge, it sinks slightly beneath the surface of the pond. The present bridge, constructed in 1978, floats on polyethylene barrels that are filled with polystyrene. Some people claim that a floating bridge is used here—and it is the only one in Vermont—because the pond is too deep to support a pillared span. Others claim that a tradition is a tradition, and Brookfield simply wouldn't be Brookfield if the bridge didn't float! In any case, the swimming and fishing off the bridge are excellent.

The charming Green Trails Inn is immediately on your left when you reach the stop sign in Brookfield.

30.8 *At the white Brookfield Congregational Church, just after VT 65 becomes paved again, turn right off VT 65 onto Ridge Road toward Brookfield Center. There may not be a street sign here.*

For the next 3 miles, the road rolls up and down short, moderately steep hills.

37.5 *At the stop sign in Randolph Center, go straight onto Route 66 West.*

Most activity in Randolph Center revolves around Floyd's General Store and Vermont Technical College. (Just before the store, on your left, is the entrance to Lake Champagne Campground.) The college enrolls 750 men and women who are studying for degrees in agriculture, business, and engineering. Daily 3 PM–4 PM you can watch an automated milking parlor at work on the campus. If you ride 250 yards beyond the turn at Mile 38.1, the entrance to the milking barn will be on your right.

Floyd's General Store, at the heart of Randolph Center

Randolph Center is also the original home of that especially American horse, the Morgan. It was here that Justin Morgan and his small, rough-coated colt, Figure, settled in 1795. Now Vermont's state animal, the Morgan horse is extolled for the diversity of its abilities. It can be a cowhorse, pleasure horse, equitation horse, or harness horse. The Vermont Morgan Horse Farm in Weybridge is on the Middlebury–Vergennes tour.

38.1 At the stop sign, turn right to continue on VT 66 West toward Randolph.

The next 3 miles descend rapidly back into Randolph.

40.7 At the blinking light, continue straight on VT 66 West.

In 0.1 mile, you reach the Porter Music Box Museum and Shop. It's on your left, at the second driveway beyond the biking light. Here you can learn about the manufacturing and history of music boxes. Several exquisite boxes, musical automata, a 1926 Steinway Duo-Art Aeolian reproducing piano, and some of the unique Porter boxes made on the premises are on display. The museum is open Monday through Saturday, 9:30–5. Admission is charged.

Just beyond the museum is Lower Stock Farm Road, on your

left. If you turn there, you will reach the Three Stallion Inn in 0.6 mile. It's a magnificent spot, whether you are stopping for cocktails and dinner or a relaxing overnight.

41.5 *At the stop sign in Randolph, bear left onto VT 12 South.*
Beware of the traffic at this intersection.

41.7 *At the intersection beside the Randolph Fire Department on your right, turn left to continue on VT 12 South, which is also North Main Street, toward Bethel and Rutland.*

42.0 *You are back in the center of Randolph where you began.*

For general information on lodging, restaurants, attractions, and special events, contact the Randolph Chamber of Commerce, 66 Central Street, Randolph, VT 05060 (802-728-9027).

Where to Stay

Lake Champagne Campground, PO Box C, Randolph, VT 05061 (802-728-5298), is a 150-acre retreat of spacious fields, sweeping mountain views, a delightful 3-acre swimming lake, hot showers, and facilities for everything from tents to full-sized RVs. Open Memorial Day weekend through mid-October.

Green Trails Inn, Brookfield, VT 05036 (800-243-3412 or 802-276-3412), sits on 17 acres overlooking the floating bridge and Sunset Lake. Innkeepers Sue and Mark Erwin provide charming accommodations in the 1840s Marcus Peck House and an 18th-century guest house. You can select a room or suite with antique beds, private or shared bath, fireplace, or Jacuzzi tub. My favorites are the Stenciled Room, with its hand-decorated plaster walls that date from the 1830s, and Miss Butters Suite, with its fireplace and two rooms. The inn serves a full gourmet breakfast and prepares dinners for small groups by reservation.

Three Stallion Inn at the Green Mountain Stock Farm, Randolph, VT 05060 (800-424-5575 or 802-728-5575), has the facilities of a small resort with the personality and scale of a country inn. The inn is a gracious, 100-year-old farmhouse with an inviting wraparound porch. Under the loving care of innkeepers Betty and Al Geibel, the Three

Stallion offers its guests swimming and fishing in the Third Branch of the White River, 50 kilometers of hiking and mountain-biking trails, a full restaurant, two all-weather tennis courts, a fitness center, swimming pool, sauna, and hot tub.

Bicycle Repair Services

Bicycle Express, Depot Square, Northfield, VT (800-247-7430 or 802-485-7430)

Slab City Bike & Sports, Junction of VT 12 and VT 12A, Randolph, VT (802-728-5747)

Waitsfield–Warren

Easy-to-moderate terrain; 14.7 miles
Moderate terrain; 18 miles (0.3 unpaved)

The Waitsfield–Warren area, known as the Sugarbush Valley or Mad River Valley, offers extraordinarily pretty cycling amid the attractions of one of the East's major ski resorts. ("Sugarbush" is the generic term for any woods of sugar maple trees. The word derives from the time when sap was collected and boiled to make sugar, rather than syrup. The process, which takes place in the early spring, is still called sugaring whether its product is sugar or syrup. The Valley and two of its three ski areas take their names from the stands of sugar maples on Lincoln Peak and the neighboring hills.) The Valley, as locals know it, offers a wide variety of activities. You can go soaring in a glider out of the Warren airport, horseback riding at any of several stables, hiking on challenging or easy trails, golfing at the Robert Trent Jones golf course, and trout fishing or canoeing on the Mad River. There's also tennis at many inns and hotels, polo to watch or try to learn, organized off-road mountain biking, summer concerts, theater, nightlife, and lots of arts, crafts, and antiques galleries. The restaurants, bakeries, and special food shops can satisfy the appetites of the most hungry gourmet. Despite all these goings-on, the Valley does not seem crowded or overdone.

The longer version of this tour is definitely the more pleasant and beautiful, but it is more difficult than the shorter one. The longer route bypasses most of VT 100, where motorized traffic can be heavy. Both rides visit two villages, each with its own covered bridge, and explore panoramic countryside at the base of the Lincoln range of the Green Mountains. The views are stupendous, the terrain has two challenging climbs on the longer ride—one on the shorter—and lots of descent.

0.0 Turn left out of the Mad River Green Shopping Center, a half mile north of the intersection of VT 100 and VT 17, onto VT 100 North.

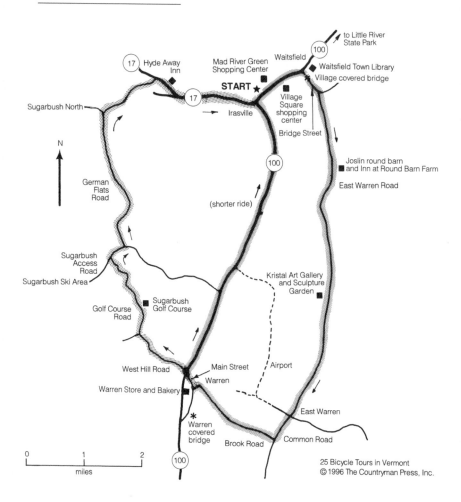

Before leaving the shopping center, you might stop at Green Mountain Coffee Roasters or the Breadbasket Bakery for some fine coffee, freshly made bread, pastry, cheese, delicatessen cold cuts, or other treats. If you want information about local events, pick up a copy of the latest *Sugarbush Area Guide*. You can make free local phone calls thanks to the hospitality of the Waitsfield Telecom Company. There are public telephones for this purpose in the Waitsfield and Irasville shopping centers and the villages of Waitsfield and Warren.

Just as you start up VT 100, the Cheese Shop is on your right in Village Square. It sells a wide selection of local and imported cheeses as well as crackers, wines, and sweets—all of which will taste especially good when you reach the top of the hill outside Waitsfield.

0.8   *Just before you pass the Waitsfield Town Library (in a beige brick building) on your right, turn right onto Bridge Street so you pass the library on your left.*

You come immediately to the Bridge Street Bakery on your right. It's a good place for pastries, fresh bread, soups, and coffee.

Twenty yards farther on, you cross the Village or Big Eddy covered bridge. Built in 1833 and recently restored by Milton Graton and Sons, the bridge reaches 113 feet over the Mad River. There's good swimming beneath the bridge. Just beyond it, East Warren Road begins an ascent that is nearly 3 miles long. The grade is steady but seldom very steep. It's the first of the two trying climbs on the longer ride; it's the only trying climb on the shorter ride. Both are followed by terrific descents.

1.2   *At the fork, continue straight uphill on East Warren Road.*

In about a mile and a quarter, the rare, handsome Joslin round barn rises on your left. Constructed in 1910, it is the last round barn left in the Mad River Valley and one of only a few still standing in Vermont. The barn is now the centerpiece of the Inn at Round Barn Farm.

About 4 miles beyond the inn is the Kristal Art Gallery and Sculpture Garden on your right. It's a delightful spot with a first-rate selection of American and European paintings and sculptures. The charming owner, Hanni Saltzman, welcomes cyclists and encourages them to relax or picnic in her sculpture garden—an ideal place to enjoy the snacks you carried up the hill.

A quarter mile beyond the gallery, East Warren Road tips down into an increasingly fast, exhilarating descent into Warren.

6.8   *At the crossroad, go straight onto Common Road toward Warren Village.*

Off to the west (on your right), the trails of the Sugarbush Ski Area stand out clearly on the wooded slopes of Lincoln Peak (elevation 3975 feet).

The Joslin round barn (1910) in Waitsfield

7.4 *Follow the main road as it curves 90 degrees to the right. On some maps the road changes its name here to Brook Road, but in any case there is no street sign.*

The descent gets progressively steeper as you approach Warren. Heed the road signs and ride the last half mile slowly.

9.3 *At the stop sign in Warren, turn right onto Main Street.*

Before you make your turn, consider visiting the Warren Store and Bakery, which you reach by turning left onto Main Street and riding 50 yards. Located in a former stagecoach inn and library, the store stocks a delectable variety of food, including dried fruits, nuts, penny candy, fresh produce, and excellent breads and sandwiches. The upstairs boutique sells clothing, fabrics, and decorative accessories. Next door are two arts and crafts galleries.

While you are at the store, get directions to The Arch, a natural bridge of stone carved by the Mad River as it cuts through a rocky, jagged gorge. If you feel like stretching your legs with a short hike, ask the shopkeepers to point the way to the mile-long trail leading up Lincoln Brook. And before you leave Warren, stop to look at the Warren covered bridge that Walter Bagley built in 1880. The Mad River makes for calm and clear swimming just above the waterfalls that flow below the bridge. It's less than a third of a mile from the store to the bridge and swimming spot.

9.5   At the stop sign, go straight across VT 100 onto West Hill Road, which goes uphill.

> ONLY FOR THE 14.7-MILE RIDE: Do *not* go across VT 100. Instead turn right onto VT 100 North and ride 5.2 miles to the Mad River Green Shopping Center on your left, where the tour began. The ride up VT 100 is much easier than the ride via West Hill Road, but be prepared for heavy traffic. As the main artery of the Sugarbush Valley, VT 100 connects Warren to Waitsfield and feeds traffic to the many businesses that have sprung up near the Valley's three ski areas—Mad River Glen, Sugarbush, and Sugarbush North.

9.7   At the fork, bear left to continue on West Hill Road.

The next mile is tough, no doubt about it. But the payoff is great: charming roads, stunning views, and a terrific ride downhill.

10.6   At the T in front of the weathered sugarhouse, turn right onto Golf Course Road.

In 75 yards, the road surface becomes unpaved. The pavement resumes after 0.3 mile. Just as you're reaching that point, you also reach the Sugarbush Golf Course, designed by Robert Trent Jones.

As you ride through the golf course, the road drops into a very steep and winding descent for 0.75 mile. Ride cautiously. From the bottom of the hill, there is one last climb—of just 0.5 mile.

12.1   At the stop sign, turn right onto Sugarbush Access Road, which is unsigned here.

12.4   Turn left toward Sugarbush North Ski Area onto German Flats Road.

In 0.6 mile you start downhill for nearly 3 miles.

15.9   At the stop sign, turn right onto VT 17 East, which is unsigned.

It's gently downhill for the next 1.75 mile. You reach the Hyde Away Inn on your left in 0.25 mile.

17.7 At the stop sign, turn left onto VT 100 North.

Over the next 0.3 mile, both sides of the road offer interesting assortments of eateries, shops, and galleries.

18.0 On your left is the entrance to the Mad River Green Shopping Center, where you began.

For general information on lodging, restaurants, attractions, and special events, contact the Sugarbush Chamber of Commerce, PO Box 173, Waitsfield, VT 05673 (802-496-3409 or 800-82VISIT).

Where to Stay

Hyde Away Inn, VT 17, RD 1, Box 65, Waitsfield, VT 05673 (802-496-2322), is a favorite stopping place for local bicyclists. Run with great care and affection by Bruce Hyde and his wife, Margaret, the Hyde Away is casual, comfortable, and reasonably priced. The inn has grown out of a cluster of 150-year-old farm buildings, including a silo, sawmill, and barn. A sunny deck overlooks a swimming pond, stocked with rainbow trout that you're welcome to fish for. Behind the inn there are several mountain-bike trails, ranging from easy to tough. Children are most welcome, and there is a special menu for them. Breakfast and an interesting selection of dinner choices are served.

Inn at Round Barn Farm, East Warren Road, Waitsfield, VT 05673 (802-496-2276), is a deluxe and much heralded place. It sits beside an exquisite round barn—one of only eight still standing in Vermont. Innkeepers Jack and Doreen Simko accurately describe their inn as "a place that is elegant, luxurious, and charming without the least bit of pretension." There is a lap pool, wicker-filled solarium, stone terrace, and well-stocked library.

Little River State Park, RD 1, Box 1150, Waterbury, VT 05676 (802-244-7103), is an extraordinary park, covering 12,000 acres that include the 900-acre Waterbury Reservoir. The reservoir is available for swimming, boating (rentals are offered at the park), and fishing. Marked hiking trails lead up Mount Mansfield. The 101 sites include 20 lean-tos and some remote sites along the shoreline of the lake. Self-contained motorized campers are welcome, but there are no hookups.

Bicycle Repair Services

Clearwater Sports, VT 100, Waitsfield, VT (802-496-2708)

Mad River Bike Shop, VT 100, Waitsfield, VT (802-496-9500)

Onion River Sports, 20 Langdon Street, Montpelier, VT (802-229-9409)

14
Brandon–Fort Ticonderoga

Easy-to-moderate terrain; 18.5 miles
Moderate-to-difficult terrain; 44 miles

Revolutionary history, apple orchards, prosperous dairy farms, and panoramic mountain vistas characterize this tour through the southern Champlain Valley, "Land of Milk and Honey." To maximize the superlative long views of the Adirondack and Green Mountains, ride the route on a clear day. Leaving Brandon and then twice crossing the Otter Creek, an important Native American travel route 200 years ago, you cycle parts of the old Crown Point Military Road, which Lord Jeffery Amherst cut through the wilderness from Charlestown, New Hampshire, to Lake Champlain in 1759. It was this road that Colonel Henry Knox and his army of farmers used during the winter of 1775 to haul 59 cannons overland from Fort Ticonderoga to Boston, where they played a critical role in expelling the British. The 44-mile ride merits a moderate-to-difficult rating, because the ride back to Brandon from Fort Ticonderoga gains considerable elevation.

0.0   From the Brandon green, ride north on US 7.

US 7 is narrow; beware of traffic.

Brandon was chartered in 1761, and fine post-Revolutionary and Victorian homes line its wide streets. Stephen A. Douglas, "The Little Giant" who in 1860 ran for president as a Democrat against Abraham Lincoln, was born here in 1813. The story-and-a-half cottage that was his birthplace sits at the northern end of the village, on your left as you leave town on US 7. The cottage now serves the local Daughters of the American Revolution as their headquarters and is irregularly open to the public.

Douglas and Lincoln differed not about the abolition of slavery—in 1860 neither favored abolition—but about the question of slavery in US territories. Douglas and the Democrats favored allow-

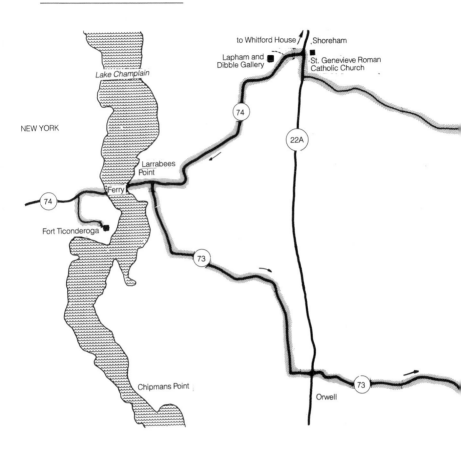

ing the voters in each territory to decide by ballot whether or not to permit slavery. Lincoln and the Republicans advocated Congressional legislation to prohibit slavery in the territories. Neither position suited the eight cotton states, which, following the lead of Jefferson Davis, withdrew from the Democratic Party and nominated their own presidential candidate, John C. Breckinridge, then the vice president. With the Democrats split, Lincoln won a sound electoral victory (59 percent), though he received only 40 percent of the popular vote.

Vermont was the first state in the United States to prohibit slavery; Vermont took that step in 1791. In 1860 Vermont voted four to one for Lincoln over its native son Douglas.

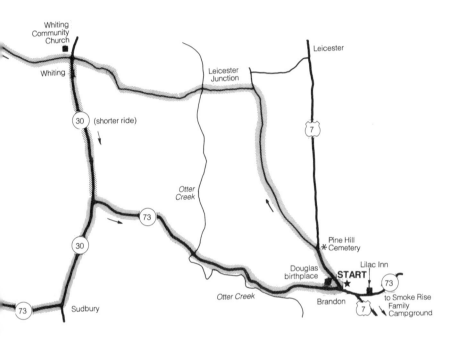

25 Bicycle Tours in Vermont
© 1996 The Countryman Press, Inc.

N

0   1   2

miles

Whiting
Community
Church

Whiting

Leicester

Leicester
Junction

30   (shorter ride)

*Otter
Creek*

73

30

Pine Hill
* Cemetery

Douglas
birthplace

Lilac Inn

START

73

73   Sudbury

Otter Creek

Brandon

7

to Smoke Rise
Family
Campground

1.5   *At the Pine Hill Cemetery (on the right), turn left onto the unsigned road that runs northwest off US 7.*

You climb gently uphill the last 1.5 miles and overlook a spectacular panorama of the high peaks of the Adirondacks.

4.8   *Beside two houses (on your left)—the first has two dormers and the other is a single-story ranch house—turn left onto the unsigned road between the two houses so that you pass the ranch house on your right.*

9.0   *At the stop sign in Whiting, go straight across VT 30 onto the unsigned road toward Shoreham.*

FOR THE 18.5-MILE RIDE: Do *not* go straight; instead turn

127

left onto VT 30 South and ride 3 miles to the crossroad. There turn left onto VT 73 East and follow it 6 miles back to Brandon. Then proceed from Mile 43.6 below.

In May 1775, when Ethan Allen wanted to gather the Green Mountain Boys for their attack on Fort Ticonderoga, he dispatched Whiting blacksmith Samuel Beach as his messenger. The hardy Vermonter ran 64 miles in 24 hours to summon the backwoods clan for its sally across Lake Champlain.

Just as you leave Whiting you pass the Whiting Community Church, built in 1811, on your right.

In 4 miles you reach the Vermont Department of Fish and Wildlife Access Area to Richville Pond, a weedy bass and water-fowl pond.

15.7 **At the stop sign, turn right onto VT 22A North, which has high-speed traffic.**

16.2 **At St. Genevieve Roman Catholic Church (on the right) in Shoreham, turn left onto VT 74 West toward Larrabees Point and Ticonderoga.**

You can get food or a snack at the Shoreham Country Store on your right in 100 yards. About 10 houses past the store is the outstanding Lapham and Dibble Gallery, which restores and sells fine American paintings and prints. The gallery is definitely worth a visit; it's open Tuesday through Saturday 9–5.

Shoreham sits at the heart of Addison County's prosperous apple-growing district and features a cooperative apple-storage plant. Although more McIntosh are harvested than any other variety of apples, scores of kinds are grown in Addison County. From Shoreham, VT 74 descends 300 feet to Larrabees Point on Lake Champlain, which is 95 feet above sea level, the lowest elevation in Vermont.

22.6 **At Larrabees Point, stop to take the tiny Shorewell Ferry across Lake Champlain. After disembarking on the New York side, go straight onto NY 74 West.**

The Shorewell Ferry (802-897-7999), which has been running for more than 200 years, operates 8 AM–6 PM. The crossing takes only 6 minutes; consequently you should not have to wait more than 15.

Cyclists are welcome, and are charged about $2 round trip.

After the five Great Lakes, Champlain, covering 435 square miles, is the largest body of fresh water in the United States. Long and narrow, it begins 35 miles south of Larrabees Point and stretches northward 136 miles, the last 18 falling in Canada.

At its widest point, north of Burlington, the lake measures 15 miles across, but most of it is much narrower. In winter it freezes to an average depth of 22 inches—enough to support cars and light trucks as well as ice fishers. Champlain is one of the few lakes in North America that flow northward; it empties into the St. Lawrence River. A series of 12 locks near Whitehall, New York, connects the lake at its southern end to the Hudson River. The swimming at Larrabees Point is not attractive.

The section of NY 74 that leads to Fort Ticonderoga is nearly all uphill.

23.2 *At the sign for Fort Ticonderoga, turn left and follow the mile-long driveway to the fort. After your visit, retrace your way back to the ferry and return to Vermont.*

Between mid-May and mid-October, visitors are welcome at Fort Ticonderoga 8–5. Admission to the fort and its fine military museum is well worth the charge. A restaurant, gift shop, and large pleasant picnic area are located outside the stockade and are accessible without charge. The descendants of William Ferris Pell, who purchased the fort in ruins in 1820, have restored it magnificently. Now a National Historic Landmark, Fort Ticonderoga is still owned and managed by the Pell family. A fife-and-drum corps often performs outside the fort.

Militarily, the fort was key to Lake Champlain and served first the French, who built it, then the British, the Revolutionary colonists, and the United States. Symbolically it has long been a monument to the audacity of Ethan Allen and his 83 Green Mountain Boys, who captured it from the sleeping British commander La Place in the morning darkness of May 10, 1775. Although their triumph was due to surprise rather than military force, it nevertheless greatly buoyed the spirits of the Revolutionary troops.

23.0 *From the ferry landing at Larrabees Point, go straight onto VT 74 East.*

129

23.6 *Turn right onto VT 73 East and follow its twists and turns through Orwell and Sudbury all the way back to Brandon.*

This portion of the route—the 16 miles from Larrabees Point to Otter Creek, 3 miles west of Brandon—makes the tour more demanding than moderate cycling. VT 73 mounts several hills, some steep and some long. These climbs are relieved by stretches of level riding and an occasional downhill run, but the ride is difficult because it climbs the 450-foot difference between Brandon and Lake Champlain.

Orwell is the last place to buy food and drink until you reach Brandon, 14 miles away. During the middle of the 19th century, Orwell became prosperous as a center of Vermont's vigorous wool industry. In the 1830s Merino sheep were the state's principal livestock, and most of the state was cleared for their pasture. Though sheep raising faded in Vermont after the Civil War, it is now enjoying a revival.

The Otter Creek makes poor swimming. At 75 miles the state's longest river, it flows lazily northward from the town of Mount Tabor to Lake Champlain near Vergennes. Along the way it gathers the runoff of thousands of acres of pastureland as well as some industrial and residential waste.

43.6 *At the yield sign, turn right onto US 7 South.*

44.0 *You are back in Brandon where the tour began.*

For general information on lodging, restaurants, attractions, and special events, contact the Addison County Chamber of Commerce, 2 Court Street, Middlebury, VT 05753 (802-388-7951), and the Brandon Area Chamber of Commerce, PO Box 267, Brandon, VT 05733 (802-247-6401).

Where to Stay

Lilac Inn, 53 Park Street, Brandon, VT 05733 (802-247-5463), sits on one of Vermont's hidden treasures, a wide avenue of broad lawns and tall trees lined with historic homes. The inn has been lovingly created from a 1909 Georgian mansion by Melanie and Michael Shane—she an architect and interior designer, he a builder with a dash of culinary experience. The inn regularly hosts concerts and dances; call ahead for

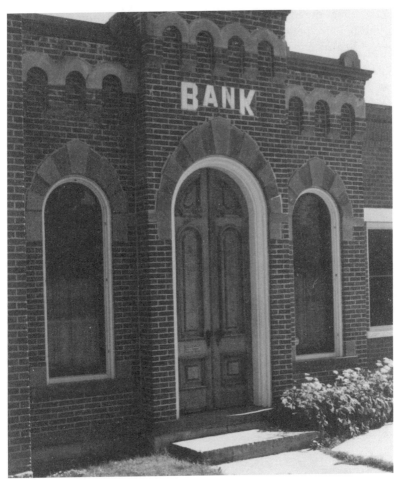

The First National Bank of Orwell, built in 1887

a schedule. Breakfast is served daily—try the French toast or omelets; dinner Wednesday through Saturday.

Whitford House, RD 1, Box 1490, Vergennes, VT 05491 (802-758-2704), is actually located in the town of Addison, about 10 miles off this route. A shaded veranda welcomes you for morning coffee or a cool afternoon drink, and the well-stocked library and fireplaces invite you to relax after dinner. Innkeepers Bruce and Barbara Carson are wonderful hosts. They prepare a fine dinner and will also put up a lunch that you can carry along on your ride.

Smoke Rise Family Campground, US 7, Brandon, VT 05733 (802-247-6472), has 50 open and wooded sites, unlimited tenting, a swimming pool, picnic tables, and fireplaces.

Bicycle Repair Services

Bike & Ski Touring Center, 74 Main Street, Middlebury, VT (802-388-6666)

Great Outdoors Trading Company, 41 Center Street, Rutland, VT (802-775-6531)

Green Mountain Schwinn Cyclery, 133 Strongs Avenue, Rutland, VT (802-775-0869)

Marble City Bicycles, 1 Scale Avenue, Rutland, VT (802-747-1471)

Mountain Tread-n-Shred, 150½ Woodstock Avenue, Rutland, VT (802-747-7080)

Skihaus of Vermont, Merchants Row, Middlebury, VT (802-388-6762)

Sports Peddler, 158 North Main Street (US 7), Rutland, VT (802-775-0101)

15
Middlebury–Vergennes:
A One- or Two-day Ride

Easy terrain; 7.1 (1.4 unpaved); 16.6 (1.4 unpaved); 29.7 (6.1 unpaved); or 42.5 miles (8.1 unpaved)

This tour offers a perfect blend of country cycling and Vermont village attractions. Because the terrain and distances suit cyclists of all abilities, this tour is really four tours that range in length from 7.1 to 42.5 miles. Families or groups of friends can bicycle together for a while and then divide into smaller groups according to the distances they prefer. If they're patient they can even regroup toward the end of the rides. Best of all, the route also makes a great two-day ride. Spend one night in Middlebury and another in Vergennes. That way, you can ride all 42.5 miles, but do 28 the first day, have time for a riverboat cruise down the Otter Creek, and do 14 miles the second day.

Nestled in the heart of the Champlain Valley, "Land of Milk and Honey," these rides explore fertile dairy farmland overlooking New York's Adirondack Mountains and Vermont's Otter Creek. The creek produces dramatic waterfalls in Middlebury and Vergennes and accounts for much of their historic architecture. Each town boasts a wonderful variety of homes, churches, and commercial buildings that once served a vigorous 19th-century economy driven by waterfalls.

Middlebury is renowned as a college town and folk-art center and is far more cosmopolitan than its population of 8000 suggests. It offers a pleasing variety of attractions that include the Vermont State Craft Center, the Vermont Folklife Center, the Sheldon Museum, several antiques dealers, restaurants and inns recommended in national guides, and often concerts, either outdoors or inside at the Center for the Arts at Middlebury College.

0.0   With your back to the Middlebury Post Office, turn right on Main Street (VT 23 North and VT 125 West) and ride cau-

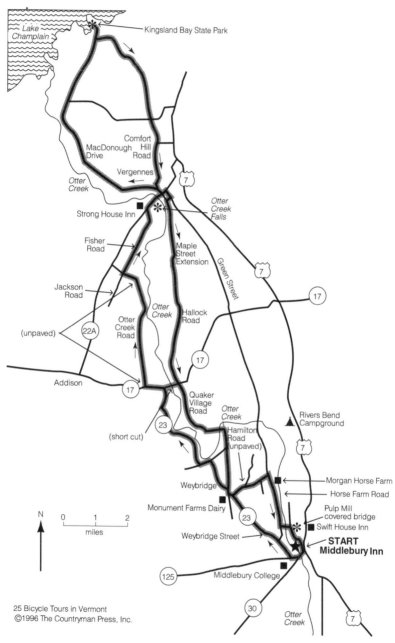

Lake
Champlain

Kingsland Bay State Park

Comfort
MacDonough Hill
Drive Road

Vergennes

Otter
Creek

7

Strong House Inn

Otter Creek
Falls

Fisher
Road

Maple
Street
Extension

Green Street

7

Jackson
Road

17

Otter
Creek

Otter
Creek
Road

Hallock
Road

(unpaved)

22A

17

Addison

17

Quaker
Village
Road

Otter
Creek

Rivers Bend
Campground

(short cut)

23

Hamilton
Road
(unpaved)

7

Weybridge

Morgan Horse Farm

Horse Farm Road

Monument Farms Dairy

23

Pulp Mill
covered bridge

Swift House Inn

Weybridge Street

**START
Middlebury Inn**

N

0   1   2
miles

125

Middlebury College

30

Otter
Creek

7

134

tiously through the village of Middlebury. You cross the bridge above the falls of Otter Creek in 0.1 mile.

Middlebury has been a town of significance for two centuries. To gain a sense of this history and really see what it has left behind, go to the Vermont Book Shop behind the orange awning at 38 Main Street and buy *A Walking History of Middlebury* by Glenn M. Andres. Then take a morning or afternoon to let this 80-page history guide you through the village. As Andres writes in his introduction: "Middlebury has remained to a remarkable degree the village that the 18th and 19th centuries built . . . Not merely of local historic interest . . . [Middlebury's buildings] are of such range and quality that they can be taken as representative of almost every major style of American building from the colonial period onward." For up-to-date information on activities in Middlebury and nearby, contact the Addison County Chamber of Commerce, Court Square, Middlebury, VT 05753 (802-388-7951).

You can get an excellent sandwich—to carry along or eat at a picnic table overlooking the falls—at Noonie's Deli in the Historic Marbleworks or the Storm Café in Frog Hollow.

0.2 *At the traffic island, bear right onto VT 125 North (College Street). Just as you make this turn, you pass the Otter Creek Bakery on your right.*

At Otter Creek Bakery, you can eat outside, even as early as 7 AM, and enjoy any number of delectable freshly baked treats as well as creative sandwiches.

At some time during your visit to Middlebury, take a walk or at least a ride through the campus of Middlebury College, which begins on College Street, 0.25 mile beyond your approaching turn.

From rectangular Painter Hall, built of locally quarried gray stone in 1815 and now the oldest college building in Vermont, to the recently completed asymmetrical Center for the Arts, built of pink Tadaussac granite from Quebec and designed by New York architects Hardy, Holzman, and Pfeiffer, the college architecture stimulates the eye. The campus itself is a New England hillside classic with broad views of the mountains and sweeping lawns, shaded by majestic trees of many species.

To learn what special events are happening, either stop by the box office at the arts center or call 802-388-3711 (ext. SHOW). In July and August, you may hear little English spoken on campus. During those months, this liberal arts college of 2000 women and men transforms itself into an academy of foreign languages, where all students swear to speak only their language of study.

0.3   Turn right to continue on VT 23 North (Weybridge Street).

You might enjoy stopping in about a mile to look back at Middlebury. The steeples of the Congregational Church (1806–09) and the college's Mead Chapel (1916) rise in front of the Green Mountains.

3.0   At the intersection just beyond the brick Congregational Church of Weybridge (on your right in Weybridge), go straight to continue on VT 23 North. Immediately beyond the intersection, you pass a cemetery on your right and the grade drops into a steep descent. Control your speed.

Before leaving Weybridge, indulge yourself with a half pint of the best chocolate milk anywhere. Just walk left across the intersection to Monument Farms; you can see it from the church. Monument Farms, which has been owned and run by the James and Rooney families since 1930, tends its own herd of 350 Holsteins and packages their milk weekdays here at the plant.

> FOR THE 7.1-MILE RIDE: Do not go beyond the brick Congregational Church of Weybridge (on your right in Weybridge Hill); instead, just *before* the Congregational Church, turn right onto Hamilton Road, which is unpaved. Ride 1.4 miles to the T and then proceed from Mile 39.8 below. Beware of loose gravel along Hamilton Road.

7.6   At the stop sign, turn left onto Route 17 West toward Addison. Beware of the traffic on Route 17.

> FOR THE 16.6-MILE RIDE: Do *not* turn left onto VT 17 West. Instead, turn right onto VT 17 East and ride 0.5 mile across the bridge over Otter Creek to the crossroads. There, turn right onto Quaker Village Road, the first right you can make, and ride 4.3 miles to the stop sign. The final 2 miles rise steadily up a moderate hill. When you reach the stop sign, proceed from Mile 38.3 below.

8.4 *Turn right onto Otter Creek Road, which is the first right you can make. Otter Creek Road is not paved for the first 3 miles.*

Few roads connect a cyclist with the agricultural landscape of New England as lovingly as this one. Take it slowly so you can enjoy it longer.

12.2 *At the crossroads (with Jackson Road to your left), turn right onto Fisher Road, which is unpaved for the first 1.8 miles.*

Vermont's Green Mountains run along the eastern horizon to your right.

14.3 *At the stop sign, turn right onto VT 22A North. Beware of high-speed traffic.*

As you're standing at this stop sign, the Strong House Inn is directly across from you, on the opposite side of VT 22A.

14.9 *At the blinking light, just after you cross the bridge above the falls of Otter Creek (in Vergennes), turn left onto MacDonough Drive, which is unsigned here. In 0.1 mile you pass N. Maple Street on your right. MacDonough Drive becomes unpaved in 5 miles and remains unpaved for 2 miles.*

The next 12.8 miles, which I call the Kingsland Bay Loop, cover easy terrain, have very little traffic, and take you to a secluded state park on Lake Champlain where you can picnic and swim.

In the winter of 1813–14, Thomas MacDonough, after whom MacDonough Drive is named, used the basin below the waterfalls to build three ships of Vermont lumber in 40 days! One was the 734-ton, 26-gun *Saratoga*. Using these and nine refurbished gunboats, MacDonough saved Vermont from British occupation by defeating the British on September 11, 1814, in the decisive battle of Plattsburgh. One of these gunboats, the 54-foot *Philadelphia*, used by Benedict Arnold, was later raised from the bottom of Lake Champlain and is now on display at the Smithsonian Institution. The cold, fresh water of the lake makes a nearly perfect medium for the preservation of wood. You can see a replica of the *Philadelphia*, and other objects reflective of the lake's 10,000-year history, at the Lake Champlain Maritime Musuem (802-475-2317) at the entrance to the Basin Harbor Club 4.5 miles from here in Panton.

FOR THE 29.7-MILE RIDE: Do *not* turn left onto MacDonough Drive. Instead, continue straight up the steep hill on VT 22A for 0.2 mile more to the traffic light in the center of Vergennes. Then proceed from Mile 27.9 below.

21.9 *At the sign for Kingsland Bay State Park (on your left), bear right to continue on the main unpaved road, which becomes paved in 0.4 mile.*

Allow yourself time to visit Kingsland Bay State Park. It surrounds a small Lake Champlain harbor where cruising sailboats find shelter from the lake's sudden blows. The swimming is fine, and you can picnic or just stretch out on a well-kept, shaded lawn that overlooks the water. Admission is charged between Memorial Day and Labor Day.

25.3 *At the stop sign at the crossroad, continue straight on the unsigned road.*

26.1 *At the fork, bear slightly right onto Comfort Hill Road, which may be unsigned. In 1.25 miles the road drops steeply downward and then ends at a stop sign. Keep your speed under control and be ready to stop.*

27.5 *At the stop sign, turn left back onto MacDonough Drive.*

27.7 *At the blinking light and stop sign, turn left onto VT 22A North (Main Street) and climb up the steep hill into the center of Vergennes.*

If you are spending the night at the Strong House Inn, turn right here and ride 0.6 mile. The inn will be on your right. While you are in Vergennes, consider taking a narrated scenic cruise aboard a riverboat on the Otter Creek. Call Otter Creek Cruises at 802-475-2465 for information and schedule.

27.9 *At the traffic light (in Vergennes), turn right onto Green Street.*

Before leaving Vergennes, indulge yourself with a sweet treat, sandwich, or beverage at Beth's Bakery, which faces Main Street on your right just before you reach the traffic light. When you're in Vergennes, it's always fun to visit the Kennedy Brothers Factory Marketplace 0.6 mile straight ahead on Main Street (VT 22A East), especially if you like antiques. It's filled with the discoveries of scores of local dealers, and you can also get a sandwich and a Ben & Jerry's ice cream cone there at the Owl's Basket Deli.

28.1 *Turn right onto School Street.*

28.2 *At the stop sign, turn left onto South Maple Street, which in a half mile becomes Maple Street Extension and then in another 3 miles Hallock Road.*

The terrain rolls gently up and down for the next 5 miles as you ride through some of Vermont's finest dairy country. More milk is produced in the Champlain Valley than anywhere else in Vermont. Though some Vermonters used to claim that the state had more cows than people, it now has just under one for each three Vermonters. Nevertheless, that represents an enormous investment, since the average value of a milker is $1250. Between 1983 and 1993, the number of cows being milked in Vermont dropped from 190,000 to 162,000, but the amount of milk produced rose slightly because the output per cow jumped from 12,695 pounds per year to 15,414—an increase of 21 percent! During the same period, the price of milk fell from $14.20 per 100 pounds to $13.44, and the number of dairy farms dropped from 3216 to 2265. The 1990s continue to be very difficult times for most Vermont dairy farmers, who account for 70 percent of the agricultural income of the state. The balance derives mostly from other livestock and maple syrup.

34.0 *At the stop sign at the crossroads, continue straight onto Quaker Village Road.*

In just over 2 miles, you will start up a moderate hill that persists for 2 miles.

As you ride along Quaker Village Road, you can occasionally see Otter Creek. It is Vermont's longest river—75 miles. It runs northward from North Dorset to Lake Champlain just 8 miles west of Vergennes. Though pretty to look at and good for fishing and canoeing, Otter Creek is not an inviting place to swim. The clay along its shores and some agricultural runoff give the water a brown hue.

38.3 *At the stop sign (in Weybridge), turn left onto VT 23 South and ride just 0.1 mile past the Congregational Church of Weybridge (on your left).*

38.4 *Just beyond the Congregational Church of Weybridge, turn left* onto Hamilton Road, which is unpaved. Beware of loose gravel on this road.

39.8 At the T, turn right onto Horse Farm Road, which is paved but unsigned.

In 0.5 mile you reach the University of Vermont Morgan Horse Farm on your left. Make sure to stop; it's a great place to visit, rest, or picnic. Admission is charged. The farm, a National Historic Site, is gathered about a great mansard-roofed barn, built in 1878 in the French Second Empire style. Information and guided tours are available there. About 70 registered Morgans are stabled at the farm, and some are usually out in the pastures or training ring. Several are national champions.

In 1795 a singing master by the name of Justin Morgan brought a strikingly small colt named Figure from Massachusetts to Randolph, Vermont, to pay a debt. Morgan rented the 14-hand colt to a farmer who discovered that Figure had unusual stamina and quickness, a plucky disposition, and lots of style. Figure, who soon became known as "Justin Morgan," passed these fine qualities along to many sons and daughters and thereby began the development of North America's first breed of light horse. Morgan himself died in 1798, unaware of what his little Figure had begun.

Today Morgans are revered for their versatility and handsome appearance. They are trained for plowing, cutting cattle, dressage, jumping, pleasure riding, show, police work, driving carts, and trotting. During the Civil War, Morgans distinguished themselves in the First Vermont Cavalry. In fact, a Confederate soldier captured by the First Vermont was heard to protest that "it was your hawses that licked us." The Morgan is also Vermont's state animal.

The Morgan Horse Farm, which is now operated by the University of Vermont, was left to the United States in 1906 by a wealthy Middlebury resident, Joseph Battell, who loved Morgans deeply. Battell was a thoughtful person—some might say prescient—and he hated motor vehicles. In a slim book on the subject, he wrote: "With what more lethal weapon can man be assaulted than the terrible and destructive motor car trespassing on the highway? Sooner or later it will come to this—the automobiles will be driven from the highways or the horses will be driven from the highways."

The main barn (1878) of the University of Vermont's
Morgan Horse Farm in Weybridge

41.6 At the yield sign, bear left and ride through the Pulp Mill covered bridge over Otter Creek. In the bridge the light is dim, and there are gaps between the floorboards. Consider walking your bicycle through.

The Pulp Mill Bridge is one of only two 2-laned covered bridges in Vermont. The other is at the Shelburne Museum. There are only six of these bridges left in the entire country! This one spans 179 feet and was built in approximately 1820.

42.2 At the stop sign, turn left onto Seymour Street, ride through the underpass, and immediately turn right to continue on Seymour Street, which may be unsigned. Ride carefully, for you're now back in the village of Middlebury.

42.5 At the stop sign, turn right onto Main Street and coast 10
yards to the Middlebury Post Office on your right, where the
tour began.

For general information on lodging, restaurants, attractions, and special
events, contact the Addison County Chamber of Commerce, 2 Court
Street, Middlebury, VT 05753 (802-388-7951).

Where to Stay

Middlebury Inn, US 7, Middlebury, VT 05753 (802-388-4961 or 800-
842-4666), is a well-kept, rambling, 165-year-old, brick village inn.
The ceilings are high, the hallways wide; cozy libraries and little sitting
areas are hidden among the guest rooms. The staff is attentive and
friendly. The inn serves breakfast, lunch, and dinner in its large dining
room and on its fine, broad porch that overlooks the village green and
the most outstanding Federal-style church in Vermont.

Strong House Inn, Route 22A, Vergennes, VT 05491 (802-877-3337),
offers comfortably elegant lodging amid a potpourri of antiques and floral wallpapers. The inn was built as a home in 1834 in the Federal style
and is currently listed on the National Register of Historic Places. The
cheery accommodations range from Samuel's Suite, which includes a
library with fireplace and a private sunporch, to the English Garden
Room and French Country Room, which share a bath. Breakfast and
afternoon refreshments are included in the room charge; dinner can be
arranged for groups of 12 or more.

Swift House Inn, Stewart Lane, Middlebury, VT 05753 (802-388-9925),
is an outstanding, Four Diamond AAA country inn. Each room has a
distinctive personality, lots of space, and often an oversized whirlpool
bath. Guests also have use of the inn's sauna and steam room: a luxurious way to complete a fall day of cycling! Innkeepers Andrea and John
Nelson have created this fine inn over the past 10 years, and know lots
of local history to enhance the pleasure of your stay. Continental breakfast and gourmet dinners are served. The inn's wine list has earned it
the Award of Excellence from *The Wine Spectator*.

Rivers Bend Campground, PO Box 9, New Haven, VT 05472 (802-388-9092), is set on a remote site where the New Haven River enters Otter Creek. There are wooded, open, and river sites plus all the amenities you'd expect from a modern campground.

Bicycle Repair Services

Bike & Ski Touring Center, 74 Main Street, Middlebury, VT (802-388-6666)

Skihaus of Vermont, Main Street, Middlebury, VT (802-388-6762)

16
North Ferrisburgh–Essex, N.Y.

Easy-to-moderate terrain; 31.0 miles (4.2 unpaved) with optional 5-mile side trip to the Shelburne Museum or 26.5 miles (4.2 unpaved)

This is a splendid figure-eight tour, featuring the sparkling waters of Lake Champlain, panoramic views of the Green Mountains and the Adirondacks, and handsome farms. A delightful half-hour ferry trip connects two circular rides: one in Vermont, the other in New York. Although about a quarter of Vermont's 548,000 residents live within 25 miles of here, this tour uses roads with extremely little traffic. And Essex, New York, is an ideal destination: quiet, charming, and interesting—a perfect place for lunch, browsing, swimming, sailboat watching, or overnight. The entire hamlet is a National Historic Site. And finally, the tour offers mostly easy cycling and good access to the Shelburne Museum, which houses one of the nation's greatest collections of American folk art.

0.0 *From North Ferrisburgh, at the intersection of US 7 and Stage Road, ride west on Stage Road between Jimmo's Store and the North Ferrisburgh Post Office.*

1.0 *At the stop sign, turn right onto Greenbush Road.*

3.3 *At the stop sign, turn left onto Thompson's Point Road.*

In 0.1 mile, you pass a plaque on your right that commemorates the discovery of the Vermont state fossil. In 1849, an 11,000-year-old fossil of a small beluga whale was found about 9 feet below the surface a little north of here in what had been the Champlain Sea. The 10-foot skeleton is now on display in the Perkins Museum of Geology off Colchester Avenue at the University of Vermont in Burlington. The museum is open 8 AM–8 PM Monday through Friday, and 9–5 Saturday and Sunday.

3.8 *At the crossroads, turn right onto Lake Road, which becomes unpaved in 75 yards.*

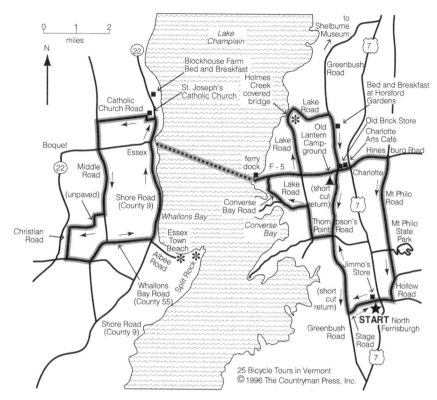

4.6 *Just beyond the point where Lake Road becomes paved and just beyond a "Dangerous Intersection" sign, turn left onto Converse Bay Road, which is unsigned and becomes unpaved in 50 yards.*

Converse Bay Road runs gently downhill to Lake Champlain and affords lovely views of sailboats anchored in Converse Bay.

5.5 *At the intersection with an unpaved road on your left, go straight to continue on Converse Bay Road, which is still unsigned.*

6.1 *At the T, just beyond the Charlotte Sailing Center on your left, turn left onto VT F-5, which is unsigned there. VT F-5 is paved.*

6.3 *You are at the ferry dock, where you catch the Lake Champlain Ferry to Essex, New York.*

During most of the cycling season, the ferry runs every half hour on the half hour. It takes 30 minutes to make the crossing. The charge for a bicyclist and bicycle is $3 one way or $3.75 round trip. You can verify the schedule and charge by calling 802-425-2504. There is usually a Ben & Jerry's ice cream stand at the ferry landing.

6.3 *After disembarking from the ferry in Essex, walk to the stop sign and turn right toward Willsboro, New York, onto NY 22 North.*

Allow yourself an hour or two to explore Essex. The entire village was placed on the National Register of Historic Places in 1975. It is one of the best-preserved pre–Civil War villages in America.

Essex was one of the first European settlements on the west shore of Lake Champlain. It was chartered in 1765 and then devastated during the American Revolution. But during the first half of the 19th century, when Lake Champlain was the primary route for commerce between Canada and the American republic, Essex became a magnet for energy and ambition. Young Americans built a fine harbor here that attracted commerce and wealth. And their work was further rewarded in 1823 when the Champlain Canal connected the southern end of the lake to the Hudson River and hence New York City. By 1850, Essex had become one of the largest towns on the lake.

This prosperity enabled the people of Essex to construct fine buildings of stone, brick, and timbers that still stand today. Stop at the Essex town offices to pick up a copy of the free pamphlet, "Essex: An Architectural Guide." It lists 28 buildings of interest in the village of Essex and 18 more on the outskirts.

Just as transportation gave rise to Essex's prosperity, so it took it away. Shortly after the Civil War, the railroad reached northeastern New York, and Lake Champlain lost its monopoly on shipping. Cargo began to follow the tracks of the railroad instead of the waters of the lake. Essex then became a late-19th-century summer resort for Bostonians and New Yorkers, until travelers abandoned railroad trains for private passenger cars. It has just recently begun to recapture its appeal to travelers.

6.9 *Turn left onto Catholic Church Road (which is unpaved) so that you pass St. Joseph's Catholic Church on your right after you turn.*

Blockhouse Farm Bed & Breakfast is located on NY 22 just 0.2 mile beyond—that is, north of—Catholic Church Road.

Catholic Church Road is extremely hard-packed with little loose material on its surface. It goes uphill ever so gradually and becomes paved in 1.3 miles.

8.6 *At the stop sign, turn left onto Middle Road, which is also Essex County 66 North.*

Middle Road goes gently uphill for 0.7 mile.

9.4 *At the stop sign, go straight to continue on Middle Road and Essex County 66 South.*

11.2 *Turn right onto Christian Road.*

Christian Road goes uphill for 0.75 mile. Stop to take a look at the views behind you. Just as you reach the top of the hill and start down, Christian Road becomes unpaved and yields stunning views north and southward along the valley. The road becomes paved again after 0.6 mile. Keep your speed under control, because Christian Road makes a sudden 90-degree left turn just as the descent is ending.

13.3 *At the yield sign at the T, turn left onto Whallons Bay Road, which is unsigned here and is also Essex County 55.*

Whallons Bay Road goes gently uphill.

14.0 *At the intersection, follow Whallons Bay Road as it curves leftward.*

Almost immediately, Whallons Bay Road starts downward toward Lake Champlain, affording superb views of Camels Hump and Mount Mansfield in Vermont.

Just before your next turn, you also get a great view of Split Rock on the far shore of Whallons Bay. Split Rock, which Native Americans called Roche Regio, marked the boundary between the nations of the Iroquois and the Algonquins. Later, the Treaty of Utrecht (1713–14) established the rock as the dividing point between the English and French dominions.

14.6 *At the intersection with Middle Road on your left, continue straight on Whallons Bay Road.*

The descent really gets rollicking from here to the lake.

16.0 *At the yield sign, turn left onto Shore Road, which is also Essex County 9 North.*

If you'd like to go swimming at the best spot on the tour, turn right onto Shore Road, ride 50 yards, and then turn left onto Albee Road and ride 25 yards more to the Essex Town Beach. It is partly sandy, beautiful, and nearly deserted.

18.7 *At the blinking light in Essex, go straight onto Main Street, which is also NY 22 North.*

Essex has several art galleries, antiques shops, restaurants, and an ice cream shop. You can pick up more information about them at the Essex Inn or the Essex Town Office, both just behind you on the other side of Main Street.

18.8 *Turn right onto the ferry landing for your return trip to Vermont. It takes a half hour.*

18.8 *After disembarking from the ferry, follow the signs for VT F-5.*

The first half mile is uphill.

20.3 *Turn left onto Lake Road.*

In 1.75 miles you cross the Holmes Creek through the little Leonard Sherman–Holmes Creek covered bridge. It's just one lane wide, built in the tied arch style, and 39 feet long. Just beyond the bridge is the Charlotte Town Beach, where you can take a swim in Lake Champlain.

> *FOR THE 26.5-MILE RIDE (Though only 4.5 miles shorter than the full tour, this shortcut avoids about 2 miles of climbing and as much descent):*
>
> *Do not turn left. Instead, continue straight on VT F-5 and ride 1.1 mile to the blinking light—the last half mile is uphill. At the blinking light, turn right onto Greenbush Road, which is unsigned here.*

If you want a snack, you can get one at the Old Brick Store, which is on your left at this intersection. If you want a first-class sandwich, a good cup of coffee, or ice cream, continue on VT F-5 for 0.1 mile more to the Charlotte Arts Café, on your left.

Follow Greenbush Road 1.9 miles. In 0.4 mile you pass the entrance to the Old Lantern Campground on your right;

and 0.75 mile beyond that you pass Manchester's Raspberries and then Pelkey's Blueberries, both also on your right.

The middle of July through late August is raspberry season; August is blueberry season. The berries at both places are excellent and well worth the stop.

As you're going downhill and reach an intersection with a road on your left, carefully turn left and then immediately bear right to continue on Greenbush Road, which is still unsigned. (If you miss this turn, you'll reach a set of railroad tracks in a quarter mile.) Follow Greenbush Road 2.2 miles more, which you rode in the opposite direction at the beginning of the tour. Then, turn left onto Stage Road and follow it 1.0 mile back to North Ferrisburgh, where you began.

22.3 *Follow Lake Road as it swings 90 degrees to the right and passes the town baseball field on your right.*

23.5 *At the stop sign, turn right onto Greenbush Road, which is unsigned here.*

In 0.2 mile, you ride beneath a railroad trestle and go uphill for a half mile. A half mile beyond the railroad trestle, the entrance to the Bed & Breakfast at Horsford Gardens is on your left.

If you can spare at least a couple of hours, you can cycle north on Greenbush Road to the Shelburne Museum. It's just 2.5 good cycling miles away. Instead of turning right onto Greenbush Road, turn left and ride 2.4 miles to the traffic light at US 7 in Shelburne. From there, you can walk your bicycle 0.1 mile down the shoulder of the highway to the entrance to the museum.

Nowhere in Vermont and few places in the United States display a finer or more varied collection of Americana. Founded in 1947 by Electra Havemeyer Webb, the Shelburne Museum consists of 37 buildings and the SS *Ticonderoga*, the last vertical-beam passenger and freight sidewheeler remaining intact in this country. Spread over 45 beautifully groomed acres, the museum is open daily 10–5 from late May to late October. Admission is charged.

The museum reflects the eclectic taste of its founder, who began collecting American craft and folk art before its artistic merit

The Adirondack Mountains as seen from
Mt. Philo Road in North Ferrisburgh

was widely recognized. Among many other items, the museum
contains railroad memorabilia, sculptured folk art such as cigar-
store figures and waterfowl decoys, Audubon prints, a 525-foot-
long scale model of a circus parade, and two galleries of paintings.

25.1 *At the stop sign and blinking light, turn left onto VT F-5, though
there is no route marker there.*

If you're looking for a cold drink or snack, you can get one at the
Old Brick Store, which is on your left at this intersection. If you
want a first-class sandwich, a good cup of coffee, or some ice
cream, continue on VT F-5 for 0.2 mile more to Charlotte Arts
Café, also on your left.

151

25.4 *At the traffic light, go straight and very carefully across US 7 onto Hinesburg Road, which is unsigned.*

There is a bicycle lane on Hinesburg Road, which goes uphill for the first half mile.

26.1 *Immediately beyond the "Dangerous Intersection" sign, turn right to continue on Hinesburg Road.*

26.7 *At the stop sign and blinking light, turn right onto Mt. Philo Road, which is unsigned here.*

Mt. Philo Road climbs two hills, each 0.75 mile long, and then goes mostly downhill with one half-mile climb near the end.

In 2.5 miles, you reach the entrance to Mt. Philo State Park (on your left). It's a steep 1.25-mile ride or walk to the summit, and well worth the effort, for the views of Lake Champlain, the coast where you've ridden, and the Adirondacks are spectacular. Try it.

30.7 *At the stop sign at the T (in North Ferrisburgh), turn right onto Hollow Road.*

31.0 *At the stop sign, go carefully straight across US 7, and you are back in North Ferrisburgh where the tour began.*

For general information on lodging, restaurants, attractions, and special events, contact the Vergennes Area Chamber of Commerce, PO Box 335, Vergennes, VT 05491 (802-877-3111), the Lake Champlain Regional Chamber of Commerce, 60 Main Street, Suite 100, Burlington, VT 05401-8418 (802-863-3489), and the Essex Town Office, Main Street, PO Box 355, Essex, NY 12936 (518-963-4287).

Where to Stay

Bed & Breakfast at Horsford Gardens, 2058 North Greenbush Road, Charlotte, VT 05445 (802-425-2811), is a charming spot to enjoy a special piece of Vermont from a different perspective. The B&B stands at the center of the state's oldest nursery (1893). There are fields of lilacs and flowering crabapples, perennials growing in French intensive–style beds, 40 acres of grounds, two ponds, and several walking trails.

Blockhouse Farm Bed & Breakfast, NY 22, PO Box 353, Essex, NY 12936 (518-963-8648), is exquisite. Its 1836 Greek Revival exterior has been painstakingly restored and is now a beauty in pale yellow with white trim and four graceful columns. Inside it is crisply contemporary: An open living room with tall windows and an arched ceiling provides a magnificent view of Lake Champlain and the Green Mountains. The guest rooms are equally interesting and striking. Susan Callahan and Ron Allbee are cordial hosts and provide a full breakfast using natural foods and fruit.

Old Lantern Campground, Greenbush Road, PO Box 221, Charlotte, VT 05445 (802-425-2120), is a spacious, friendly campground with large grassy and wooded sites, enormous trees, a swimming pool, and lots of recreational facilities. Be sure to spend a little time with owner Earl Burns while you're there.

Bicycle Repair Services

Bob's Bike Repair Shop, 214 Main Street, Winooski, VT (802-655-4965)

Champion Cycles, 2105 Shelburne Road, Shelburne, VT (802-985-5354)

Climb High, 1861 Shelburne Road, Shelburne, VT (802-985-5055)

Earl's Cyclery and Fitness, 135 Main Street, Burlington, VT (802-862-4203)

Essex Junction Bicycles, 50 Pearl Street, Essex Junction, VT (802-878-1275)

North Star Cyclery, 100 Main Street, Burlington, VT (802-863-3832)

Planetary Cycles, 422 Pine Street, Burlington, VT (802-862-3154)

Ski Rack, 81 Main Street, Burlington, VT (802-658-3313)

Winooski Bicycle Shop, 26 Main Street, Winooski, VT (802-655-3233)

17
Bristol–Starksboro

Easy-to-moderate terrain; 24.2 miles (1.3 miles unpaved)

This tour nestles in the Champlain Valley, some of the most beautiful farmland in the Northeast. Though there are a few short, steep climbs, the terrain is relatively flat. The farms are pleasingly small, and the foot-hills of the Green Mountains scallop the horizon. Dairy farming is still dominant here, but apples, honey, maple syrup, wool, lamb, and beef are also produced. From late July through mid-September roadside stands overflow with delicious ripe vegetables.

The Champlain Valley was created during the Pleistocene glacial age. A huge sheet of ice crept southward from Labrador, rearranging rocks and soil, sculpting the mountains, and widening the valley. Waters from the melting ice and invading sea then flooded the valley to a depth of a hundred feet. Marine fossils are still being discovered here, well above sea level.

Bristol is a quiet, unpretentious, pretty village. Consider starting your day with breakfast at the Main Street Diner at 24 Main Street. The home-made bread is excellent, either as French toast with maple syrup or with eggs. For a good cup of coffee and a baked treat, don't miss the Bristol Bakery at 8 Main Street. The tour starts in the center of Bristol.

0.0 *At the traffic light at the intersection of Main, West, and North Streets—with the village green on your left—turn left onto North Street.*

In 1.75 miles you pass the headquarters of Vermont Bicycle Touring (VBT) in a pale yellow barn and farmhouse (1848) on the right. VBT, which I founded in 1972, is the oldest American firm offering country-inn bicycling vacations. VBT is now owned and operated by Travel Ventures, Ltd. If you need bicycle repair service, you can get it there.

2.1 *Follow the main road—from here northward known as Monkton*

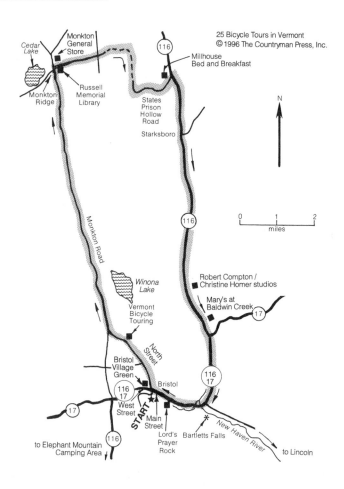

Road, though it is unsigned—as it curves to the right. Thereafter, follow the main road straight; do not turn onto the side roads.

In 1.75 miles, by the Vermont Department of Fish and Wildlife Access Area sign on the right, is an unpaved road that leads to Winona Lake, good for northern pike and largemouth bass. A large variety of Native American relics has been uncovered along the shores.

Three miles beyond the turnoff to the pond, Monkton Road tips slightly upward. The slope increases gradually for a mile and then suddenly turns steep into what may feel like a wall. Fortunately, it lasts just 0.4 mile.

9.3   *At the intersection in Monkton Ridge, go straight but ride only 100 yards to the first road on your right. There, bear right onto the unsigned road that goes downhill past the Russell Memorial Library, housed in a small white clapboard building, on your right.*

If you miss this turn, you reach the Monkton General Store on your right in 100 yards. You can buy a cold drink or creemee there.

Before heading eastward out of town, consider riding through this one-street village to enjoy a view of the Adirondacks sweeping across the western horizon and the top of Camels Hump (elevation 4083 feet), peeking over the Green Mountains in the east.

From Monkton Ridge, the road runs downhill for 1.5 miles.

10.7   *At the crossroad, go straight onto the unsigned road, which becomes unpaved in 0.1 mile. The name of this road is States Prison Hollow, but it is unsigned here, and there is no prison nearby.*

The road rolls steeply uphill for a half mile and then downhill for a half mile. It stays unpaved for 1.3 miles. Then, about a mile farther on, you encounter another steep half-mile climb.

Just after you cross a small bridge and just before your turn onto VT 116, you reach the driveway on your left of the Millhouse Bed & Breakfast. This striking homestead of finely restored buildings sits on a knoll above the Great Falls of Lewis Creek. The principal structures, both listed on the National Register of Historic Places, are the Hoag Mill (1799) and the Knight House (1831). The mill, which operated as a gristmill and then as a sawmill until the 1930s, is now a private home. Its walls are 3 feet thick.

14.0   *At the stop sign, turn right onto VT 116 South, which is unsigned here, and follow it all the way back to Bristol.*

For the first 0.75 mile you ride gradually uphill. Then an easy half mile carries you into Starksboro, where a solitary general store stands on your right. From the store you climb a difficult half mile to the height of the land, and thereafter the cycling is easy all the way to Bristol. Starksboro was named for the American Revolutionary General John Stark, hero at the battles of Bunker Hill and Bennington.

In 5.75 miles, you reach the studios of Robert Compton and Christine Homer. Robert has made his living as a potter since 1972. His extensive experience has blossomed into an eclectic variety of work that includes *raku,* sawdust firing, pit-fired pottery, and stoneware. His most remarkable works are hanging aquariums (5 and 10 gallons) and waterfall aquasculptures. The waterfalls range from 3 to nearly 7 feet high. They bring the reflected light and playful tones of falling water into a home or outdoor garden. Christine Homer weaves scarves, blankets, and shawls. Her work integrates traditional techniques with modern fibers and contemporary designs.

It's definitely worth stopping; you can have your purchases shipped to you. The studios are open daily 10–6, May through October. If you stop on a Saturday between June and October, you can often attend a *raku* firing. *Raku* is a Japanese word meaning "happiness" or "joy."

In 0.75 mile you reach Mary's at Baldwin Creek (on your left), a fine restaurant and bed & breakfast. In 1993 *Fodor's* ranked Mary's as one of the top 10 restaurants in New England. Chef Doug Mack creates an ingenious cuisine that's unusual and delicious and an Epicurean Sunday brunch. Reservations (802-453-2432) are recommended, though not necessary.

Two and quarter miles beyond Mary's, just before VT 116 curves right across a small bridge, you reach on your left a paved road that runs uphill to Lincoln and Warren. If you ride up that road just a third of a mile, you can take a dip in an old-fashioned swimming hole. The New Haven River tumbles alongside the road through a series of playful cascades. The most popular place to swim is at the base of Bartletts Falls, at the top of the first rise. If you ride farther, you can often find a pool all to yourself.

Continuing along VT 116, you reach the stolid Lord's Prayer Rock (1891) in 1 mile on your left. Here, thanks to the generosity and righteousness of a Buffalo, New York, physician, Joseph Greene, who spent his boyhood in Bristol, the Lord's Prayer is inscribed on the face of an enormous boulder. Apparently Greene thought the profane language of teamsters, urging their horses along Bristol's muddy roads a century ago, might be improved by this immense invocation. There's no evidence that the good doctor's efforts went unheeded, but, although the roads are now paved, the hillsides of Bristol still occasionally ring with the blasphemous exclamations of travelers.

24.2 At the traffic light, you are again beside the green on Main Street in Bristol.

The Flying Fish at 11 Main Street is a good place to extend your vacation into the evening. Owner Doug Mack (also of Mary's at Baldwin Creek) features Caribbean food, complimentary jukebox music (Jimmy Buffet and reggae), beers on tap, and a pool table.

If you're in Bristol on a Wednesday evening around 8 between late May and early September, you can hear a free concert, performed by a citizens' band in the cupola on the green.

For general information on lodging, restaurants, attractions, and special events, contact the Addison County Chamber of Commerce, 2 Court Street, Middlebury, VT 05753 (802-388-7951).

Where to Stay

Mary's at Baldwin Creek, Route 116, PO Box 312, Bristol, VT 05443 (802-453-2432), is a small bed & breakfast in a historic farmhouse with large flower gardens and walking paths that lead to the creek and into the woods. For dining, Mary's is hard to beat. Innkeepers/restaurateurs Linda Harmon and Doug Mack are talented and delightful.

The Millhouse Bed & Breakfast, PO Box 22, Starksboro, VT 05487 (802-453-2008), was built in 1831. Innkeepers Pat, Ron, and Suzy Messer meticulously maintain their charming inn and the antiques that furnish it. You can take a dip in the Great Falls of Lewis Creek and enjoy your breakfast on the breezeway overlooking them. The Millhouse is open May through October; reservations are required.

Elephant Mountain Camping Area, Route 116, RD 3, Box 850, Bristol, VT 05443 (802-453-3123), has 50 tent and trailer sites, a swimming pool, and a children's play area. It's well off the road and a fine place for families.

Bicycle Repair Services

Bike and Ski Touring Center, 74 Main Street, Middlebury, VT (802-388-6666)

Skihaus of Vermont, Main Street, Middlebury, VT (802-388-6762)

Vermont Bicycle Touring, Monkton Road, Bristol, VT (802-453-4811)

NORTHWESTERN VERMONT

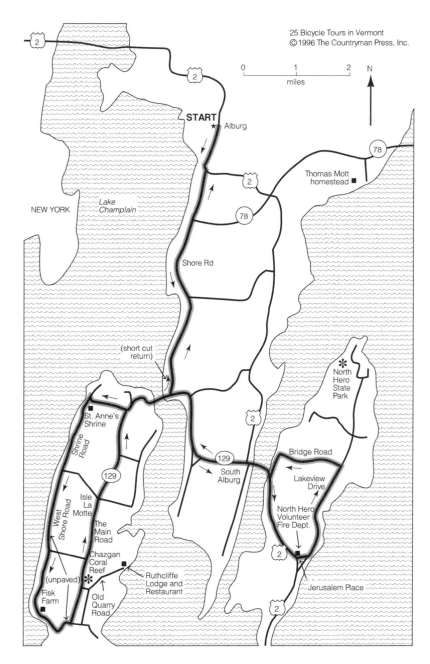

25 Bicycle Tours in Vermont
© 1996 The Countryman Press, Inc.

0   1   2   N
        miles

START ★ Alburg

NEW YORK

Lake Champlain

Shore Rd

(short cut return)

St. Anne's Shrine

Shrine Road

West Shore Road

Isle La Motte

The Main Road

Chazgan Coral Reef

(unpaved)

Fisk Farm

Old Quarry Road

Ruthcliffe Lodge and Restaurant

South Alburg

North Hero State Park

Bridge Road

Lakeview Drive

North Hero Volunteer Fire Dept.

Jerusalem Place

Thomas Mott homestead

18
Alburg–Isle La Motte

Easy terrain; 22.9 (2.5 unpaved) or 34.9(2.5 unpaved) miles

The northwestern corner of Vermont is its most panoramic and perhaps its most blissful, for here you are at the center of the Lake Champlain Basin. Lush, flat farmland spreads across the landscape; the Green Mountains stand as a sentinel at the eastern horizon, as do the Adirondacks in the west; Lake Champlain itself runs up the center; and the towns are very small and quiet. Cycling along America's sixth largest lake, you can see for a hundred miles. The terrain is especially easy and the traffic light, so these roads are particularly well suited for riders of all levels of experience and strength.

The tour follows level terrain right along the bucolic shorelines of two islands: Isle La Motte and North Hero. You are nearly always in sight of the water, and when you're not, you can often see mountains instead. Along with panoramic views and excellent swimming, the tour leads to some charming black marble and stone architecture, the oldest coral reef in the world, and the site of the first Catholic Mass in North America (1666). If you ride during July or August, you can also see the Royal Lipizzan stallions perform. Call 802-372-5683 for information.

0.0   With your back to the Town of Alburg Municipal Building, turn right onto US 2 East. Beware of the traffic on US 2.

Like many other Vermont towns along the Canadian border, but especially those on Lake Champlain, Alburg has seen its share of smuggling. During the winter, contraband was readily sledded over the ice. One story tells of an Alburg smuggler whose load crashed into the freezing water when the ice below him broke. The quick Vermonter saved himself, but his clothes were so drenched they immediately froze stiff. Unable to mount his horse or even walk, the savvy outlaw threw himself on the ice, clutched the trailing harness, and made his horses drag him to salvation.

Three miles from here, the healing waters at Alburg Springs were an important destination for mid-19th-century travelers from New York and southern New England. The health faddists of that day traveled by train to "take the waters" here, as they did to more than a dozen other mineral springs around Vermont.

0.7 *Turn right onto Shore Road, which is unsigned here.*

You are now riding along the west coast of New England. Lake Champlain flows northward—unlike most North American lakes—118 miles from Whitehall, New York, to Canada. With 435 square miles of surface and depths to 400 feet, Champlain was once the principal transportation route between New York City and Montreal. Now mostly pleasure boats travel up the Hudson, through the New York State Barge Canal and locks into Champlain, and then north into the Richelieu River to Montreal. Scores of species of fish live in the lake. Bass, walleye, yellow perch, northern pike, lake trout, and landlocked salmon are the most popular with fishermen. And nearly everyone is still seeking positive identification of "Champ," the lake's elusive long-necked monster. In the winter, when the lake freezes deep enough to drive across, hardy Vermonters put out their fishing shanties and catch the sweetest smelt and perch a frying pan ever cooked.

5.1 *At the stop sign, turn right onto the unsigned road toward St. Anne's Shrine and Isle La Motte. In 0.1 mile, you ride across a concrete bridge.*

Great historical dramas have played out upon this lakeshore. Samuel de Champlain wrote that he camped and hunted here on July 2 and 3, 1609. In 1665, swashbuckling French gallants, under the direction of a Captain de La Motte, built a fort here. And just a year later, adventuresome Jesuits celebrated the first Catholic Mass in the North American wilderness, where St. Anne's Shrine now stands. More than a century later, in 1776, Benedict Arnold set sail off the western shore of the island for Valcour Island to battle the British. Only a year before, Arnold had accompanied Ethan Allen and the Green Mountain Boys in their successful attack on Fort Ticonderoga.

6.2 *Turn right toward St. Anne's Shrine onto Shrine Road, which is unsigned here.*

Statue of French explorer Samuel de Champlain and
Native American, St. Anne's Shrine, Isle La Motte

In a mile you reach St. Anne's Shrine. It is built on the site once occupied by Fort St. Anne, Vermont's oldest European settlement (1666). Nestled among lofty pines at the edge of the lake, the shrine is an inviting place to pause for reflection or rest. Eucharist celebrations are offered daily in a simple open-air structure. The Edmundite fathers and brothers who oversee the shrine also maintain a sandy, public beach, picnic tables, and a cafeteria. The shrine is open May 15 to October 15. Also on this site is a grand, granite statue of Samuel de Champlain and an unidentified Native American. It is here to commemorate Champlain's 1609 landing on Isle La Motte.

8.5 *Turn right onto West Shore Road, which is unsigned here, and keep the shoreline of Lake Champlain on your right. West Shore Road becomes unpaved in 2.4 miles and remains unpaved for 2.5 miles. The surface is well-packed.*

In just under 3 miles, you reach the strikingly beautiful Fisk Farm on your left. This small group of stone, black marble, and clapboard buildings is no longer a working farm, but has become a place for people to enjoy the setting and one another. The reborn Fisk Farm has been created by a remarkable woman, Linda Vaughn Fitch, who began to fulfill her dream by restoring the horse and carriage barn. "It's a metaphor," she writes, "this barn. A challenge to rise up and create something out of rotting timbers, old dreams, and moments of cathedral-like inspiration."

On Sunday afternoons, 2–5, Linda and her friends host tea and art exhibitions in the garden. Try to arrange your riding to fit their schedule. If you're lucky, you can also arrange to stay here.

12.5 *At the intersection just after the road becomes paved, go straight onto the Main Road, which is unsigned here.*

At the next intersection—in 0.6 mile—you reach a small stone building on your right that houses the Isle La Motte Historical Society. If you were to turn right here onto what is known as Old Quarry Road, but is not signed, you'd reach Ruthcliffe Lodge at the end of the road in precisely 1 mile.

Immediately north of this intersection is an overgrown pasture, where you can see many pale gray outcroppings of the Chazgan Coral Reef, the oldest coral reef in the world. It is dramatic evidence of the Champlain Valley's earlier life as the floor of an ocean. To get a good look at the reef and the fossils in it, you must walk into the pasture; get permission from Tom LaBombard. To find him, turn right at the historical society building and ride about a half mile to a barn on your left, which is the office of Tom LaBombard's RV campground. If you do walk into the pasture, beware of poison ivy.

14.9 *At the crossroads in Isle La Motte village, continue straight onto VT 129 East.*

You can get a sandwich made to order at the Isle La Motte Country Store, 100 yards down the side street to your left at this intersection.

17.7 *At the T, just beyond the concrete bridge that you crossed at Mile 5.1, turn right to continue on VT 129 East toward US 2. You'll pass a small cemetery on your left in 0.1 mile.*

In about a mile and a half, you ride up a gentle grade for a half mile.

North and South Hero are named after the heroic Vermonters who fought in the Revolutionary War. In 1779, the independent nation of Vermont granted the two largest islands in Lake Champlain to Ethan Allen, Samuel Herrick, and 363 other Revolutionary War veterans.

FOR THE 22.9 MILE RIDE: Do *not* turn right. Instead turn left onto Shore Road, which is unsigned, and retrace your way back to Alburg. Follow Shore Road 4.5 miles to the stop sign. There, turn left onto US 2 West and ride 0.7 mile to the Town of Alburg Municipal Building, which will be on your left.

20.4 *At the stop sign, turn right onto US 2 East toward Burlington. Beware of traffic on US 2.*

22.6 *Just 0.1 mile beyond the North Hero Volunteer Fire Department (on your left), turn left onto Jerusalem Place.*

22.8 *At the stop sign, turn left onto Lakeview Drive.*

The lake will now be on your right.

24.8 *Turn left onto Bridge Road.*

The entrance to North Hero State Park is 1 mile farther north of this intersection on Lakeview Drive.

26.5 *At the stop sign, turn right onto US 2 West, which is unsigned here.*

27.0 Turn left onto VT 129 West toward Isle La Motte and St. Anne's Shrine.

29.7 At the intersection with the road on your left that goes south onto Isle La Motte, follow the main road, now called Shore Road but unsigned, as it curves to your right. The lake will now be on your left.

34.2 At the stop sign, turn left onto US 2 West.

34.9 You are back at the Town of Alburg Municipal Building, which is on your left.

For general information on lodging, restaurants, attractions, and special events, contact the Lake Champlain Islands Chamber of Commerce, PO Box 213, North Hero, VT 05474 (802-372-5683).

Where to Stay

Ruthcliffe Lodge and Restaurant, Old Quarry Road, Box 32, Isle La Motte, VT 05463 (802-928-3200), sits at the end of the road on a great, shaded lawn facing east over Lake Champlain to the Green Mountains. The swimming and boating are superb; the setting exquisite. Although architecturally a motel, this lodge has a homey and friendly air. Each guest room is individually decorated, and faces the panoramic water view. Innkeepers Mark and Katherine Infante are warm hosts. Mark is the chef, and his Italo-American dinners are well known locally. Breakfast and lunch are also served.

Thomas Mott Homestead, Blue Rock Road, RFD 2, Box 149B, Alburg, VT 05440 (802-796-3736), sits directly on the shore of Lake Champlain in a white 1838 farmhouse. Friendly innkeeper Pat Schallart greets you with good cheer and a freezer full of complimentary Ben & Jerry's ice cream. If it's available, try Ransom's Rest; it has its own fireplace and balcony. There are also two canoes. Outstanding breakfasts are prepared for each guest from a large selection of hearty treats.

North Hero State Park, RD 1, Box 259, North Hero, VT 05474 (802-372-8727), sits on 399 acres on the shore of Lake Champlain. There is a beach, boat rentals, launching ramp, fishing, and playground as well as 117 sites, which include lean-tos, picnic tables, and fireplaces. The park is open mid-May through early October.

Bicycle Repair Services

Foot of the Notch Bicycles, Church Street (VT 108), Jeffersonville, VT (802-644-8182)

Northstar Cyclery, South Main Street, St. Albans, VT (802-524-2049)

Porter's Bike Shop, 116 Grand Avenue, Swanton, VT (802-868-7417)

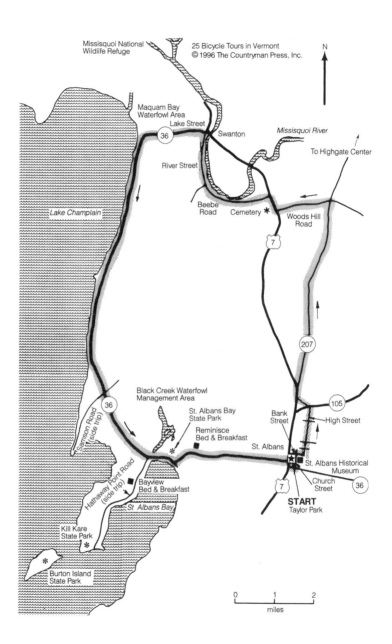

Missisquoi National Wildlife Refuge

25 Bicycle Tours in Vermont
© 1996 The Countryman Press, Inc.

N

Maquam Bay
Waterfowl Area
Lake Street

36

Swanton

Missisquoi River

To Highgate Center

River Street

Lake Champlain

Beebe
Road

Cemetery *

Woods Hill
Road

7

207

105

Black Creek Waterfowl
Management Area

Samson Road
(side trip)

36

St. Albans Bay
State Park

Reminisce
Bed & Breakfast

Bank
Street

High Street

St. Albans

Hathaway Point Road
(side trip)

Bayview
Bed & Breakfast

St. Albans Bay

St. Albans Historical
Museum

Church
Street

36

7

START
Taylor Park

Kill Kare
State Park
*

*
Burton Island
State Park

0   1   2
miles

19

St. Albans–Swanton

Easy terrain; 25 miles plus two side trips of 2.2 and 6 miles

From St. Albans, this tour follows quiet roads without hills or much traffic through the farmlands of the Champlain valley, along the Missisquoi River, and for more than 7 miles down the northern shore of Lake Champlain. Henry Ward Beecher thought St. Albans sat "in the midst of a greater variety of scenic beauty than any other [place] I can remember in America." But this niche of Vermont has witnessed many changes in the 100 years since Beecher was writing. Old roadside trees have died or been removed, and in places houses crowd the banks of the lake and river. Prepare yourself to feel occasionally frustrated by what humankind has done to nature's raw material.

The tour is ideal for a family with young children. The riding is easy and there's lots to do. Besides dozens of stirring views, there is a fine place to swim and barbecue and exceptional opportunities to see waterfowl. The tour also lends itself especially well to the early and late parts of the cycling season. There is less traffic at those times, and Lake Champlain tempers the climate, hastening spring and stalling the cold. With no leaves on the trees the views are better, and with fewer vacationers about, the roads are nearly yours alone. Moreover, if you do the tour in April, you can combine it with a visit to the Vermont Maple Sugar Festival in St. Albans. That is a joyous occasion, with sugar on snow, lumberjack contests, square dances, pancake breakfasts, a fiddling contest, and much more. Before leaving St. Albans you might want to pick up some food, since the selection is better here than elsewhere along the route.

0.0 *From the traffic light on US 7 at the southwestern corner of Taylor Park, the large green in the center of St. Albans, ride uphill on Fairfield Street (also VT 36 East).*

By leaving St. Albans on residential roads, rather than on US 7, the tour avoids a great deal of traffic and allows you to enjoy some interesting architecture.

St. Albans has witnessed some curious events because of its proximity to Canada. Before the railroad reached St. Albans, potash was the city's only salable product, and Montreal its only market. But in 1807 the passage of Thomas Jefferson's Embargo Act outlawed trade with all foreign nations, and the good folk of St. Albans became deeply involved in smuggling. One St. Albans merchant hired a craft, named *Black Snake,* to run potash into Canada. His business thrived for several months until the border patrol discovered *Black Snake* and chased it down Lake Champlain. At Burlington a bloody battle ensued, with the smugglers killing three federal officers and wounding several others before losing their craft. Opposition to the Embargo Act ran so deep in Vermont, as it did throughout New England, that only one of the smugglers was executed. The others were imprisoned and subsequently pardoned.

With the completion of the railroad in 1850, prosperity came to St. Albans. Ironically, that prosperity indirectly caused the most memorable day in St. Albans's history. At 3 o'clock in the afternoon on October 19, 1864, 22 rebel soldiers seeking funds for the Confederacy converged on St. Albans. They entered all the banks simultaneously, unburdened them of more than $200,000, killed one man, and wounded several others. The rebels then hustled their booty across the border to Canada, burning the Sheldon covered bridge behind them. Thus did St. Albans become the site of the Civil War's northernmost engagement.

Mementos of the raid, including photographs, some of the stolen currency, and a broadside entitled "Orleans County Awake, Rebels in Vermont!" are exhibited at the St. Albans Historical Museum, which faces the eastern edge of Taylor Park. The museum's large and diverse collection also contains two interesting medical exhibits. One consists of the memorabilia of William Beaumont, a surgeon who studied in St. Albans from 1810 to 1812 and contributed greatly to medical research by reporting on the digestive system of a patient who had a permanent hole in his stomach from a gunshot wound. The other exhibit contains the furnishings from Dr. George Russell's Arlington, Vermont, office, made famous by Norman Rockwell in his painting *The Family Doctor,* which appeared on a 1947 cover of the *Saturday Evening Post*. The museum also contains period costumes and railroad memorabilia. It is open Tuesday through Saturday 1–4 during July and August and by appointment; call 527-7933. Admission is charged.

0.1 *Turn left onto Church Street and ride north along Taylor Park.*

On your right will be the St. Albans Historical Museum, St. Paul's United Methodist Church, the Franklin County Courthouse, and the Romanesque First Congregational Church.

0.2 *Turn right onto Bank Street, which is unsigned here.*

0.4 *Turn left onto High Street.*

1.5 *At the stop sign at the T, turn left onto VT 105 South, which is unsigned here. Ride downhill just 100 yards and then go straight off VT 105 onto the unsigned road.*

1.7 *At the stop sign, turn right onto US 7 North.*

Bicycling on US 7 requires your complete attention. There is no shoulder, and traffic may be heavy. Vehicles may stop suddenly or turn quickly onto or off the road.

2.6 *Just beyond the traffic light, turn right off US 7 onto VT 207 North toward Highgate Center and I-89.*

Just before reaching the next turn, if the weather is clear, you can see Jay Peak (elevation 3861 feet) off to your right. In less than a half mile, you will be out of St. Albans and in beautiful Vermont dairy country, where tall blue Harvestore silos and solid barns punctuate the skyline.

6.9 *At the crossroad, turn left onto Woods Hill Road, which is unsigned here.*

8.2 *At the stop sign, turn right onto US 7 North.*

8.6 *Just 0.2 mile beyond the cemetery (on your left), turn left off US 7 onto Town Highway 2 (Beebe Road). At its western end, in Swanton, this road is called River Street.*

Over the next 2 miles you follow the Missisquoi River toward Lake Champlain. Missisquoi means "much grass" and "many waterfowl." The Missisquoi National Wildlife Refuge covers 4792 acres of marshland less than 5 miles away, so you might see some interesting birds. More than 180 species—including osprey, great horned owl, bald eagle, and great blue heron—have been sighted in the refuge.

10.3 *At the stop sign, bear right to stay on River Street, which is unsigned here. Be sure you follow the Missisquoi River; do not ride across the railroad tracks.*

11.0 *On the outskirts of Swanton, turn left onto Lake Street, which is VT 36 South. You will cross a set of railroad tracks in 0.1 mile. You can easily miss this turn; if you do, you will reach a stop sign in 75 yards.*

You can pick up food for a picnic in Swanton by riding to the stop sign and then turning right onto Route 78 East.

Like St. Albans, Swanton is no stranger to smuggling. Bootleggers of the Roaring Twenties who hauled Canadian whiskey into Swanton were the spiritual descendants of the Vermont farmers who drove cattle into Canada to sell to the starving British soldiers during the War of 1812.

Each year near the end of July, Swanton produces a festival that includes arts and crafts exhibits, band concerts, barbershop-quartet singing, a lumberjack roundup, a chicken barbecue, a parade, and a fairway with rides and concessions. For details and a schedule, contact the Swanton Chamber of Commerce, Box 182, Swanton, VT 05488 (802-868-7200).

A mile and a half after turning onto VT 36, just as Lake Champlain comes into view, you reach a grassy picnic area on your right. A good place for lunch! Lake Champlain is the sixth largest body of fresh water in the United States. It covers 435 square miles and, beginning in Quebec, Canada, stretches 118 miles down Vermont's western border. In the winter the lake usually freezes to a depth of 2 feet and supports a multitude of fishing shanties. Although private homes, cottages, and trees occasionally obstruct your view, you can often see across the lake to the Adirondack Mountains. A mile and a quarter after the road pulls away from the lakeshore, Camels Hump (elevation 4083 feet), Vermont's fourth highest peak, comes into view far in the southeast. Once you know its name, you can always identify it.

19.1 *OPTIONAL 2.2-MILE SIDE TRIP: At the crossroad, turn right onto Samson Road. Samson Road heads west through a*

meadow to the lake and then follows the shoreline for 0.75 mile.

Since no buildings stand between the road and the lake, the views are especially wonderful. This section of Lake Champlain is called the Inland Sea, since it is nearly entirely separated from the remainder of the lake by islands and sandbars. Retrace your way back to VT 36 and continue southward.

23.2   *OPTIONAL 6-MILE SIDE TRIP: Turn right onto Hathaway Point Road to get to Kill Kare State Park and Bayview Bed & Breakfast.*

Bayview Bed & Breakfast is on your right in 0.9 mile. As you continue toward the state park, Hathaway Point Road offers a delightful ride along the edge of St. Albans Bay. Kill Kare State Park (admission charged) is 2 miles beyond the B&B. Kill Kare is a perfect destination, whether for a meal or just some relaxation. The park sits on a spit of land at the southern end of Hathaway Point. Rolling lawns are bounded by the lake on the east, south, and west. The park provides barbecuing grills, a beach, swings for young children, and toilet facilities. If you can arrange it, try to arrive in late afternoon and stay to cook a barbecue. From Kill Kare you catch the boat to Burton Island State Park, which offers even better swimming as well as good fishing and camping. For the boat schedule, call 802-524-6353.

30.6   *Reminisce Bed & Breakfast is on your left.*

As you continue toward St. Albans, VT 36 is also called Lake Street.

33.2   *At the traffic light, you are facing Tyler Park in St. Albans, where the tour began.*

For general information on lodging, restaurants, attractions, and special events, contact the St. Albans Area Chamber of Commerce, 2 North Main Street, St. Albans, VT 05478 (802-524-2444).

Where to Stay

Reminisce Bed & Breakfast, Lake Road, Box 183, St. Albans, VT 05478 (802-524-3907), is an exquisite 1830s Federal farmhouse. It sits behind a deep lawn on a 550-acre working dairy farm. Run by the mother-daughter team of Mary and Michele Boissoneault, this immaculately maintained house has fireplaces, large public rooms, a broad front porch, and a back deck that overlooks the swimming pool. Breakfast includes maple syrup made on the farm.

Bayview Bed & Breakfast, Hathaway Point Road, RD 3, Box 246, St. Albans, VT 05478 (802-524-5609), is an unassuming farmhouse that faces St. Albans Bay. It's an easy 2-mile ride to Kill Kare State Park for swimming and picnicking. Hosts Sandy Sweenie and Ruthie Baraby are congenial. Their three guest rooms are clean and simple and share two baths.

Burton Island State Park, Box 123, St. Albans Bay, VT 05481 (802-524-6353), is reached by a tiny ferry from Kill Kare State Park. This lovely 250-acre island remains undeveloped except for sites set aside for camping, swimming, and picnicking. All the modern camping amenities are provided, plus boat rentals and slips for 100 boats. Fishing off this charming island is usually good.

Bicycle Repair Services

Foot of the Notch Bicycles, Church Street (VT 108), Jeffersonville, VT (802-644-8182)

Northstar Cyclery, South Main Street, St. Albans, VT (802-524-2049)

Porter's Bike Shop, 116 Grand Avenue, Swanton, VT (802-868-7417)

20
Montgomery–Richford

Moderate-to-difficult terrain; 22.6 or 33.7 miles

Beginning just 8 miles from the Canadian border, this tour has everything a hardy cyclist could want: extraordinary beauty, roads free of traffic, a perfect balance of challenge and exhilaration, and a superb inn to come home to. The tour winds through rolling farmlands fringed by thousands of sugar maples and bounded by the mountains. The longer ride curves into Canada for 5 miles and climbs over a major hill in the midst of miles of well-tended apple orchards, an aromatic treat in mid- to late May. Falling at the northern end of the Green Mountain chain, the route is relatively hilly, though it never crosses a mountain pass, and so warrants a moderate-to-difficult rating. But the undulations of the terrain provide several outstanding downhill runs and countless sweeping views of the mountains. Both routes begin with an easy ride past two covered bridges on the Trout River and culminate in a crescendo of hard work and exquisite reward that ends as you sweep through a third covered bridge.

0.0 *From the Black Lantern Inn in Montgomery, follow VT 118 North.*

Off the southwestern side of VT 118—to the left as you ride out of Montgomery—are two old covered bridges, built by Sheldon and Savannah Jewett. Both stretch 80 feet across the Trout River and shade good swimming and fishing holes. You reach the first, known as Longley or Harnois bridge, 1.5 miles from Montgomery; it went into use in 1863. The second, the Comstock bridge, was erected 20 years later and is visible 2 miles after the first.

4.8 *At the stop sign at the T in East Berkshire, turn left to continue on VT 118 North, ride just 75 yards, and turn right to continue farther on VT 118 North.*

You're now just 6 miles east of Enosburg Falls, one of a few towns

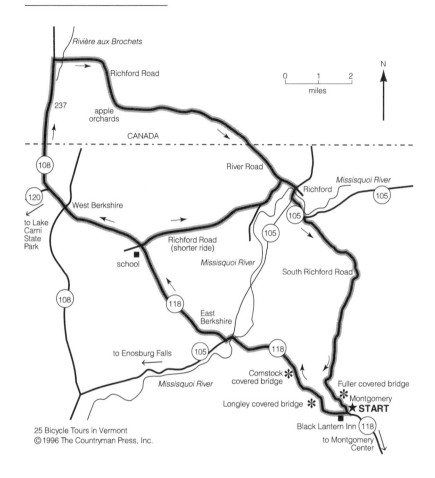

25 Bicycle Tours in Vermont
© 1996 The Countryman Press, Inc.

that the Republic of Vermont chartered during its 14 years as an independent nation (1777–1791). Enosburg Falls is now best known for maple syrup and the Vermont Dairy Festival. The festival takes place on the village green on the first Friday, Saturday, and Sunday of June. It features a parade, livestock shows, horse-pulling contests, barbecues, and lots of country fiddling and square dancing. Since the festival draws considerable traffic to the area and VT 105 has no shoulder, it's best not to ride there. It would be fun to combine an early springtime ride with a visit to the Dairy Festival.

In the early 19th century an Enosburg settler named Isaac Farrar developed wooden spouts for tapping sugar-maple trees. Though the effectiveness of the spouts quickly led to their widespread use, Farrar's neighbors nevertheless accused him of "scientific farming," which then was not the vogue that it has become. Later in the 19th century Enosburg Falls acquired a substantial reputation as the home of panaceas and patent medicines, "guaranteed" to cure nearly every ill of man and beast. At least four local entrepreneurs amassed fortunes with their cures, and some people say that descendants of the original manufacturers still pursue the business.

About 1.5 miles of the next 2.5 go uphill. Along the way, stop to take a look at the view behind you. To the east stands Jay Peak (elevation 3861 feet), readily identifiable by its cone-shaped top on which a ski lift is perched.

9.0 **FOR THE 22.6-MILE RIDE: At the crossroad by the Berkshire Elementary School on your left, turn right onto Richford Road, which is unsigned.**

For about a mile you climb a moderate grade, but then the road turns downward into a wonderful 4-mile descent facing one of the most panoramic views in Vermont. Before you stands the Jay Peak range; to your left in Canada is the hump of Pinnacle Mountain; and on the clearest of days Mount Mansfield, at 4393 feet Vermont's tallest summit, is visible far to the south, over your right shoulder.

Ride 4.7 miles to the T and there turn right onto River Road, which is unsigned. You immediately cross a bridge and pass a hardware store on your right. Just 0.2 mile farther on the right is a grassy picnic area overlooking the Missisquoi River. Follow River Road just 0.5 mile to the blinker in Richford. From there, continue as below from Mile 25.5.

9.5 **At the next crossroad, go straight to continue on VT 118 North.**
Much of the next 2 miles rolls downhill.

11.7 **At the end of VT 118 in West Berkshire, go straight onto VT 108 North toward Frelighsburg, Quebec.**

12.3 **At the junction of VT 120, continue straight onto VT 108 North.**

Across to Missisquoi River to Jay Peak

About 11 miles northwest of here, at Eccles Hill in Quebec, the Fenians, a secret Irish brotherhood organized in the 1850s to gain independence for Ireland, marshaled an attack on Canada in 1870. Nearly 1000 Fenians came to Vermont by train from Boston. They fought one small battle—the only violent encounter of their unsuccessful attempt to acquire land for a New Ireland—and then fled back across the border, where the US marshal promptly arrested their leaders.

13.8 *Report to Canadian Customs at the international border.*

US citizens should carry a driver's license or documentation of citizenship, such as a passport or birth certificate. Others should have a green card, passport, or other documentation acceptable to US Customs. If you have any doubt about your documentation, stop at US Customs, on your left before you cross the border.

After you leave customs, the road is known as Quebec 237 Nord.

16.2 *Turn right onto Richford Road toward Richford. You immediately cross the Rivière aux Brochets.*

In 0.25 mile you can see Pinnacle Mountain on your left and the heart-pounding hill you will soon be climbing. Though it's only 1 mile long, it is a major climb. Apple orchards and a few cornfields stretch for miles along both sides of the road, making this a ride especially wonderful in May and September. Once you reach the top and begin your 2-mile descent into Richford, mountains of nearby Quebec and Vermont fill the horizon in a panorama that wraps around you.

23.7 *Report to US Customs at the international border.*

Keep your speed under control, for you will reach a stop sign in 1.3 miles while you are still descending.

25.0 *At the stop sign, go straight onto River Road, which is unsigned.*

You immediately cross a bridge and pass a rural hardware store on your right. Just 0.2 mile farther on the right is a grassy picnic area overlooking the Missisquoi River.

25.5 *At the blinking light in Richford, turn right, cross the bridge over the Missisquoi River, and follow the signs onto VT 105 East.*

Richford stands amid enormous natural beauty, but the village bears the scars of misfortune and adversity. More than once ravaged by fire and flooding, Richford has also suffered recent economic hardship as the hardwood-furniture businesses that once supported much of the town have fallen on bad times. But in March and April the area comes alive with sugar-making, for Richford stands near the center of Franklin County, the largest syrup-producing area in Vermont.

There are several small supermarkets and a luncheonette in Richford.

25.8 *At the next blinking light, turn left onto VT 105 East.*

26.5 *Just 0.2 mile beyond Richford Villa mobile home park on your right, turn right onto South Richford Road, which is unsigned.*

You immediately start up a tough hill. The hill rises steeply for about 0.75 mile and then continues gradually but relentlessly for 2.5 miles more to the top. The road then goes wonderfully downhill all the way to Montgomery! At the outskirts of Montgomery it passes through the Fuller or Blackfalls covered bridge, built over

Black Falls Creek in 1890 by Sheldon and Savannah Jewett.

33.7 *At the stop sign in Montgomery, turn right onto VT 118 North
and ride 25 yards to the Black Lantern Inn, where you began.*

For general information on lodging, restaurants, attractions, and special
events, contact the Smugglers Notch Area Chamber of Commerce, PO
Box 364, Jeffersonville, VT 05464 (802-644-2239), or the St. Albans
Area Chamber of Commerce, 2 North Main Street, St. Albans, VT 05478
(802-524-2444).

Where to Stay

Black Lantern Inn, Route 118, Montgomery Village, VT 05470 (802-
326-4507), is one of my favorites. This inn opened as a stagecoach
stop in 1803. Its cozy guest rooms and suites offer a choice of whirlpool tubs (perfect for a weary cyclist), fireplaces, and antique furnishings. An old swimming hole is nearby too, as are golf and tennis.
Innkeepers Rita and Allan Kalsmith are the best. Rita oversees the outstanding dining room, which offers superb continental food, and Allan,
who tends the bar and is also a lawyer, will charm the weariest cyclist
with his stories of the northland.

Lake Carmi State Park, RD 1, Box 1710, Enosburg Falls, VT 05450
(802-933-8383), sits on 482 acres of rolling farmland. There are 178
wooded campsites, 35 lean-tos, and 2 cabins. You can swim from the
beach, rent a boat, or launch your own. It's a pretty spot. No hookups
are available.

Bicycle Repair Services

Foot of the Notch Bicycles, VT 108, Jeffersonville, VT (802-644-8182)

Northstar Cyclery, South Main Street, St. Albans, VT (802-524-2049)

Porter's Bike Shop, 116 Grand Avenue, Swanton, VT (802-868-7417)

21
Stowe–Morrisville

Easy-to-moderate terrain; 20.6 miles

Following delightfully untrafficked roads in the magnificent countryside just north of Stowe, this tour affords panoramic views of Mount Mansfield and the peaks that surround it. The tour is short and makes an excellent focus for a weekend of recreation and relaxation for families. By heading directly into the countryside, which includes 35,000 acres of state forest, you completely avoid Stowe's tourist accommodations and cycle through an arcadia of small farms and fishing ponds. There's plenty of time to visit Vermont's most venerable four-season resort and its award-winning, 5.3-mile Recreation Path, which makes a superb addition to the tour's 20 miles.

Though a town of only 3500 people, Stowe is a center of both Alpine and Nordic skiing and nearly every warm-weather sport you can imagine: tennis, bicycle racing, horseback riding, polo, rock climbing, hiking, swimming, fishing, in-line skating, soaring, and golfing on the highest course in the state. There is a competitive edge to the place; year-round most residents of Stowe seem to be working out, sharpening a technique, or mastering some new sport. But despite all this activity and attractions such as summer theater, a balloon festival, and classic auto shows, Stowe, more than any other skiing center in the state, retains its integrity as a Vermont village: unhurried, independent, and friendly. For cyclists who enjoy quiet activities, Stowe offers concerts, art exhibits, and three ways to get to the top of Mount Mansfield, Vermont's tallest summit. You can drive there, take the skiers' gondola, or walk up. And you can descend the same way, or sled down on the Alpine Slide. Stowe is also less than 10 miles from Ben & Jerry's ice cream factory and Cold Hollow Cider Mill. The tour begins at the Stowe Community Church (1863), whose slim spire soars high above the adjacent buildings at the center of Stowe village.

0.0   *From the Stowe Community Church, follow VT 100 (Main Street) North.*

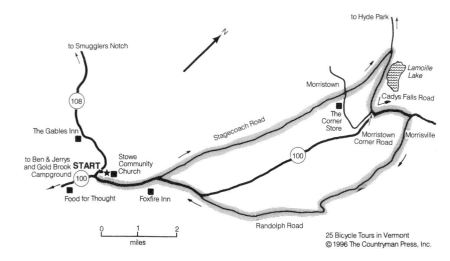

25 Bicycle Tours in Vermont
© 1996 The Countryman Press, Inc.

Stowe was founded in 1794 and its history as a resort began about 50 years later. Thanks to the hard work and dedication of its townspeople, Stowe village has preserved its historic appearance and in 1978 was listed on the National Register of Historic Places.

Since there is little opportunity to buy food along the route, you may want to get something before leaving town. If you haven't yet eaten breakfast, treat yourself by going to the Gables Inn, 1.5 miles out of town on VT 108. From 8 AM till noon, the Gables serves a marvelous menu of homemade specialties—from eggs Benedict to kippers and Belgian waffles. You sit on the inn's porch or at white tables with yellow umbrellas on the lawn facing Mount Mansfield. On weekends call ahead to make a reservation (802-253-7730). Food for Thought is another of my favorites; it sits just off the east side of VT 100 about a mile south of the village. They make delicious, mostly vegetarian, sandwiches on their own wholegrain breads and offer an extensive selection of tasty, natural foods. Delicatessen fare is available in town at Mother's Deli and Bakery, diagonally across Main Street from the church.

1.6   By the Foxfire Inn (on the right), bear left off VT 100 onto Stagecoach Road.

After 1.5 miles of relatively level terrain, Stagecoach Road curves

Mount Mansfield seen from the North

uphill for 1.2 miles, then levels off for about 0.75 mile, and turns uphill again for a half mile. Once you reach the top, all the difficult climbing of the tour is behind you, and you immediately begin to reap dividends. From the crest the road runs downhill for more than a mile to Morristown.

Along Stagecoach Road you get your first long views of Mount Mansfield, at 4393 feet Vermont's highest peak, and its surrounding mountains—Dewey (elevation 3360 feet), Spruce Peak (3320 feet), Madonna (3640 feet), and White Face (3715 feet).

7.4   At the stop sign at the crossroad in Morristown, with the Corner Store on your right, go straight to continue north on Stagecoach Road.

The road shoots downhill again for more than a mile. The last half of the hill is steep, occasionally sandy, and ends abruptly at an intersection, so take it slowly and carefully.

8.7   At the stop sign, turn right onto Cadys Falls Road, which may be unsigned here.

Within 0.5 mile you are cycling along Lamoille Lake on your left.

10.0   At the stop sign, turn left onto Morristown Corner Road, which may be unsigned here.

10.1   At the stop sign, turn left onto VT 100 North.

10.8   At the traffic island on the edge of Morrisville, turn right onto Randolph Road.

Soon a sweeping view of the Mount Mansfield range comes into sight on your right. If you use your imagination, you may be able to see a resemblance between Mansfield and the profile of a human face with forehead, nose, lips, chin, and Adam's apple. After completing your bicycle tour, consider going to the top of Mansfield. You can get there by hiking, driving the toll road, or taking the Mount Mansfield Gondola. Call ahead to verify its time of operation (802-253-3000). The views from the summit are among the most spectacular in Vermont.

17.6   At the stop sign, turn left onto VT 100 South.

20.6   You are back in Stowe by the Community Church.

A visit to Stowe is incomplete without at least a brief trip on the Stowe Recreation Path. It takes you off the roads onto a 5.3-mile, paved surface that meanders from behind the Community Church toward the base of Mount Mansfield. Reserved for nonmotorized transportation, the path is the perfect place to take your child tricycling, to teach yourself in-line skating, or just to relish the absence of motor vehicles in your favorite way. President George Bush honored the path, which was designed and built with a combination of private donations, state funds, town taxes, and federal grants, as his 119th Point of Light. It offers wonderful views of Mount Mansfield and the West Branch River.

Another very special place is Smugglers Notch, on VT 108, 3.5 miles north of its intersection with VT 100 at the center of Stowe. The Notch, a pass between Mount Mansfield and Sterling Mountain, reaches an elevation of 2162 feet. It earned its name during the War of 1812, when smugglers took cattle and other commodities through it to Canada in violation of Thomas Jefferson's Embargo Acts. The temperature in the Notch is markedly lower than elsewhere in the vicinity and sustains rare ice-age flora not found even at higher elevations. Thousand-foot cliffs rise on either side of the road, and you are likely to see rock climbers clinging to the outcroppings. In the annual June Stowe Bicycle Race, cyclists climb through the Notch on the 50-mile course, over which they average nearly 28 miles an hour!

For general information on lodging, restaurants, attractions, and special events, contact the Stowe Area Association, Main Street, Stowe, VT 05672 (800-247-8693 or 802-253-7321).

Where to Stay

The Gables Inn, 1457 Mountain Road, Stowe, VT 05672 (802-253-7730), has long been a favorite of mine and many other cyclists. It's a classic Vermont country inn decorated with floral wallpaper, stenciling, and simple antiques. The inn is entirely smoke-free, centrally air-conditioned, and outfitted with both a swimming pool and an outdoor hot tub. The most luxurious suites have double Jacuzzi tubs, king-sized beds, and working fireplaces. Best of all, every guest gets to enjoy the charming hospitality of innkeepers Sol and Lynn Baumrind and "the best breakfast in Stowe."

Gold Brook Campground, VT 100, Stowe, VT 05672 (800-483-7683 or 802-253-7683), offers 100 sites for tents and campers. The tent sites are nicely wooded, and everyone can swim in Gold Brook, the Waterbury River, or a pool. Gold Brook also has free hot showers and a large playground.

Bicycle Repair Services

AJ's Mountain Bike, Mountain Road, Stowe VT (802-253-4593)

Action Outfitters, Mountain Road, Stowe VT (802-253-7975)

Chuck's Bikes, Main Street, Morrisville, VT (802-888-7642)

The Mountain Bike Shop, Mountain Road, Stowe, VT (802-253-7919)

Stowe Hardware, Main Street, Stowe, VT (802-253-7205)

Stowe Mountain Sports, Mountain Road, Stowe VT (802-253-4896)

22
Montpelier–Maple Corner

Moderate-to-difficult terrain; 24.8 miles (2.5 unpaved), plus optional 3-mile side trip to Kents Corner

This tour enables you to visit the political capital of Vermont, and to enjoy quiet bicycling along country ponds and splashing streams. It takes you to lovely 19th-century town architecture, and offers swimming, fishing, tennis, and a good museum. Be sure to allow yourself time to tour the state capitol, visit the Vermont Historical Society, and eat at one of the three restaurants run by the New England Culinary Institute, at Sarducci's, or at the Inn at Montpelier.

Once you are outside the small city of Montpelier (population 8300), you encounter little traffic. The tour's most difficult hills occur about halfway through the ride, when you climb a moderate grade for 3 miles, the second half of which is unpaved and nicely shaded. The tour continues with a 7-mile series of short rolling hills, like the teeth of a rip saw, each about a half mile up and an equal distance down. The tour concludes with a rollicking 2-mile descent into Montpelier.

0.0 **With your back to the Vermont State House, turn left onto State Street (US 2 East).**

You can find a better selection of food in Montpelier than along the route, although you can get a sandwich at the Maple Corner Store at Mile 14.0.

Montpelier is the smallest state capital in the United States. It is also the seat of Washington County, which Jeffersonian Republicans, who controlled the Vermont House of Representatives in 1810, originally named Jefferson County. Four years later, when the Federalists took power, they renamed the county Washington.

Recently the state's two major parties have shared power about equally. Democrats have held the governor's office for 21 years since 1962; Republicans for 13. The state's three-person congressional

25 Bicycle Tours in Vermont
©1996 The Countryman Press, Inc.

0   1   2
miles

N

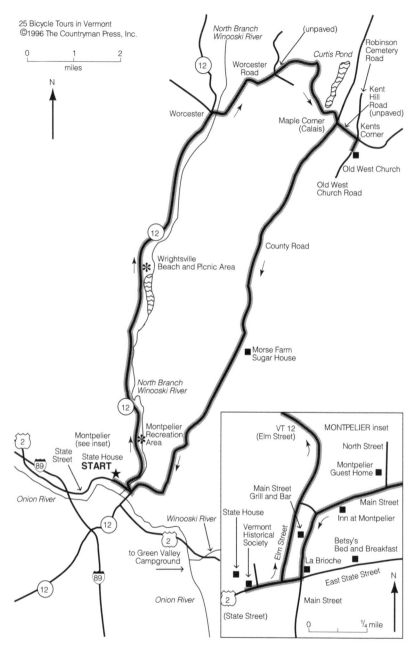

North Branch
Winooski River

(unpaved)

Curtis Pond

Robinson
Cemetery
Road

Worcester
Road

12

Worcester

Kent
Hill
Road
(unpaved)

Maple Corner
(Calais)

Kents
Corner

Old West Church

Old West
Church Road

County Road

12

Wrightsville
Beach and Picnic Area

Morse Farm
Sugar House

North Branch
Winooski River

12

Montpelier
Recreation
Area

Montpelier
(see inset)

2

State
Street

89

State House
START

Onion River

12

Winooski River

2

to Green Valley
Campground

12

89

Onion River

MONTPELIER inset

VT 12
(Elm Street)

North Street

Montpelier
Guest Home

Main Street
Grill and Bar

Main Street

Inn at Montpelier

State House

Vermont
Historical
Society

Elm Street

Betsy's
Bed and Breakfast

La Brioche

East State Street

N

2
(State Street)

Main Street

0   1/4 mile

delegation has usually contained a senator from each party and a Republican congressman. Since 1991, however, the state's sole Representative has been an independent, Bernie Sanders, who describes himself as a socialist. In 1992, for only the second time in history, the Green Mountain State cast its three electoral votes for a Democratic presidential candidate, Bill Clinton.

Politics runs broad and deep in the Green Mountain State. The Vermont General Assembly is a part-time, citizen legislature. Its members must run for election every two years, and seldom serve more than four terms. They are teachers, farmers, businesspeople, retirees, lawyers, and doctors. And, relatively speaking, a large proportion are women. In 1993–94, when 34 percent of Vermont's state legislators were women, the state ranked fourth highest in the United States for its ratio of female to male legislators. The legislature meets from January through April or May, and despite its nonprofessional character it has passed nationally significant legislation on family leave, human rights, smoking, environmental protection, and health care. Most Vermonters know their legislators, which is not surprising since each of the 150 state representatives has a constituency of about 3800 people. The 30 senators represent an average of 18,000.

The present Vermont statehouse, the third since 1805, was completed in 1859. Many of the original furnishings are still in use, and most rooms have been restored to their mid-19th-century elegance.

With its Italianate style, Greek Revival portico, six enormous granite columns, and gold dome, the statehouse looks like a capitol. The 57-foot-high dome is covered with 24-carat gold; atop the dome stands a hand-carved, 14-foot-high statue representing the spirit of agriculture.

The statehouse deserves a close look: you can explore on your own or join a tour—on the half hour, 10–3:30, Monday through Friday, July through mid-October, and Saturday, 11–2:30. The building is open year-round Monday through Friday 8–4 or until much later when the legislature is in session.

0.1   *On your left is the Vermont Historical Society. It is housed in a replica of the Pavilion Hotel, here from 1870 to 1966.*

As you climb the broad wooden steps, you cross a wide veranda that looks the same as it would have if you were a visitor 100 years ago. The lobby is Victorian, the settees covered in horsehair, the furniture dark and elaborately carved. The museum invites you to a colorful trip into Vermont's past: costumes, furnishings, tools, paintings, photographs, maps, and a library where you can trace family roots.

0.2 *At the redbrick Washington County Court House (1832), turn left onto Elm Street.*

0.4 *At the blinking light, continue straight on Elm Street.*

In 1.3 miles, you reach the Montpelier Recreation Area on your right. There are tables for picnicking and courts for tennis.

You can also picnic—and swim—at the Wrightsville Reservoir Beach and Picnic Area on your right in another 3 miles. The Wrightsville Dam, which creates the reservoir, was constructed between 1933 and 1935 by the Civilian Conservation Corps of the New Deal. The principal purpose of the dam is to prevent water from the Winooski River's North Branch, which you are riding alongside, from flooding Montpelier.

9.6 *At the 1912 Worcester Town Hall on your right, turn right toward Maple Corner. A sign for Maple Corner (Calais) is painted on an old wooden board but it faces away from you and may be difficult to see.*

For slightly more than 3 miles you climb a moderate grade beside a small stream. Hemlocks, maples, and beeches offer some shade and make this little road a special treat in the fall.

11.5 *At the crooked intersection, where all the roads become unpaved, continue straight toward Calais so you follow the middle of the three roads. The road you take is called Worcester Road, though you won't see its road sign for another mile and a half.*

In just under 2 miles you reach the fishing access to Curtis Pond. It's a nice spot for resting—and fishing, if you've brought your gear.

14.0 *At the stop sign in Maple Corner, turn right onto County Road, which may be unsigned. For about 100 yards County Road is unpaved. It turns to pavement just beyond the Maple Corner Store.*

At the Maple Corner Store on your right, you can get a cold drink, a sandwich, and some friendly chat about Calais, which prides itself on being the only town in Vermont with not an inch of road that has felt the heat of asphalt.

FOR THE 3.0-MILE SIDE TRIP TO KENTS CORNER—a lovely, unspoiled, tiny hamlet of historic buildings, including the 1837 Kent Tavern and Old West Church: Just 20 yards beyond the Maple Corner Store—right where County Road becomes paved—turn left onto Kent Hill Road, which is unpaved. Follow Kent Hill Road, which is firmly packed and tilts slightly downward, for 0.7 mile to the four-cornered intersection with Old West Church Road and Robinson Cemetery Road. If you'd like to explore further, turn right onto Old West Church Road and ride another 0.7 mile to the Old West Church; it has not been altered since it was built in 1823–25. It epitomizes the stalwart severity and fine proportions of old Vermont meetinghouses. Calais townspeople still use the church for summer services and an extraordinary Christmas Eve service, though the building has neither central heating nor electricity. Retrace your way back to County Road at Maple Corner and turn left to continue to Montpelier.

For the better part of 7 miles, County Road rolls up and down short hills a half to three-quarters of a mile long. It's challenging riding that yields an ideal opportunity to shift rapidly through the full range of your gears.

Just as you're gliding down one of the last hills, keep an eye out for the Morse Farm Sugar House on your left. In the summer you can get fruit, ice cream, and creemees as well as maple syrup and cold drinks. Best of all, you can see how Vermont farmers and Native Americans before them boiled maple sap to make that most delicious of sweeteners, maple syrup!

About 0.75 mile beyond Morse Farm, you reach the top of the final hill. The Worcester range of the Green Mountains stands at the horizon to the east. The final 2 miles go down an increasingly steep and winding hill into Montpelier. You have a grand view of the statehouse, but be sure to keep your speed fully under control.

Near the bottom of the hill, County Road becomes Main Street, which runs past the Inn at Montpelier on your left into the center of town.

The Vermont State House in Montpelier

In 1980, an extraordinary school for chefs, the New England Culinary Institute, was founded in Montpelier. "We felt the best way to learn culinary arts," said Francis Voigt, one of the two founders, "was not by reading a textbook but by cooking in a real restaurant—under the guidance of a talented chef-teacher." NECI students spend 75 percent of their time preparing and serving wonderful food. The institute operates three restaurants in Montpelier: the Main Street Bar and Grill and the Chef's Table on your right at 118 Main Street and La Brioche Bakery on your left at 89 Main Street. Two blocks farther down Main Street at number 3 is Sarducci's, a delightful Italian restaurant, highly favored by state legislators.

24.5 *At the traffic light, turn right onto State Street.*

24.8 *The statehouse is on your right, where you began.*

Special events often occur on the statehouse lawn and elsewhere in Montpelier. For information, contact the Statehouse Sergeant at Arms (802-828-2228) and the Onion River Arts Council (802-229-9408).

Eight miles away, in Graniteville, is the world's largest granite quarry. All but one of the quarries are owned by Rock of Ages, which has made its operations a showcase for visitors. You will see a surrealistic landscape dominated by immense quarrying pits, roaring drills, and seemingly ant-sized workers. The exhibits are open, May through October, Monday through Friday 8:30–3:30. For a special treat, take the open-car train ride to the working quarries; it runs every half hour, 9:30–3:30, June through September.

For general information on lodging, restaurants, attractions, and special events, contact the Central Vermont Chamber of Commerce, PO Box 336, Barre, VT 05641 (802-229-5711 or 802-229-4619).

Where to Stay

Betsy's Bed & Breakfast, 74 East State Street, Montpelier, VT 05602 (802-229-0466), provides relaxed and casual lodging in a restored Queen Anne residence. The style is Victorian with high ceilings, carved woodwork, and sunlight spilling through lace curtains. Innkeepers Betsy and Jon Anderson serve a generous and leisurely breakfast that may feature Vermont specialties or delicacies from Betsy's southern past.

Inn at Montpelier, 147 Main Street, Montpelier, VT 05602,(802-223-2727), is a stately, elegant inn. An imposing porch provides a perfect setting for cocktails or an early morning visit with your favorite newspaper. The ambiance is gracious and luxurious with antique furnishings and every modern amenity. The dining is outstanding: gourmet meals and a fine wine cellar.

Montpelier Guest Home, 22 North Street, Montpelier, VT 05602 (802-229-0878), is an 1890s Victorian home with extensive sun-filled gardens. Innkeeper Karen Kitzmiller is a state legislator and her husband, Warren, owns the outstanding bicycle/cross county ski shop, Onion River Sports, at 20 Langdon Street, Montpelier. Guests who arrive by bicycle or who stay at least two nights receive a discount. No meals are served; treat yourself to breakfast at the Main Street Grill or La Brioche Bakery.

Green Valley Campground, US 2, Box 21, East Montpelier, VT 05651 (802-223-6217), 5 miles northeast of Montpelier, has 35 grassy sites, swimming, a community fireplace, and playground.

Bicycle Repair Services

Centerstate Bicycles, 120 River Street, Montpelier, VT (802-229-4549)

Demers' Repair, Inc., 81 South Main Street, Barre, VT (802-476-7712)

Onion River Sports, 20 Langdon Street, Montpelier, VT (802-229-9409), and 395 North Main Street, Barre, VT (802-476-9750)

Park Pedals, Cabot, VT (802-563-2252

NORTHEASTERN VERMONT

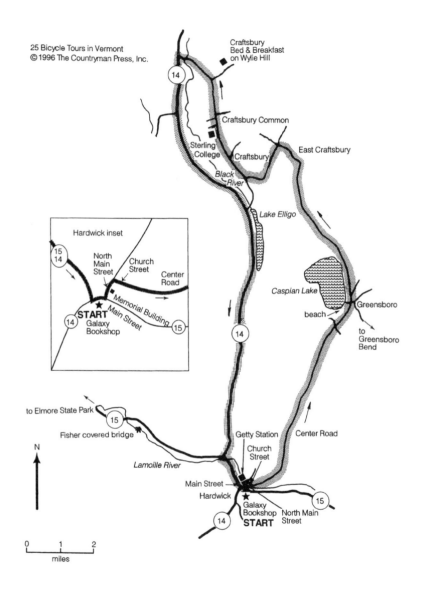

25 Bicycle Tours in Vermont
© 1996 The Countryman Press, Inc.

Craftsbury
Bed & Breakfast
on Wylie Hill

Craftsbury Common

East Craftsbury

Sterling
College

Craftsbury

Black
River

Lake Elligo

Caspian Lake

Greensboro

beach

to
Greensboro
Bend

Center Road

Getty Station

Church
Street

to Elmore State Park

Fisher covered bridge

Lamoille River

Main Street

Hardwick

Galaxy
Bookshop
START

North Main
Street

Hardwick inset

North
Main
Street

Church
Street

Center
Road

Memorial Building

START
Galaxy
Bookshop

Main Street

N

0   1   2
miles

Hardwick–Craftsbury Common

Difficult terrain; 32.8 miles

Starting in Hardwick, this tour explores an extraordinary pocket of Vermont's Northeast Kingdom. Named by former US Senator George Aiken, the Northeast Kingdom is roughly a square, 40 miles on a side, bordering Canada and New Hampshire. Long an economic backwater, this region of glacial lakes and conifer forests possesses a sort of pastoral magic. The path taken by this tour is no exception, although Craftsbury Common and Greensboro are now prosperous summer resorts. In that respect the tour highlights an especially privileged part of the Kingdom. But the magic persists: in Caspian Lake, in the nearly deserted road winding its way through the Craftsburys, and in Hardwick, where lives of hardship in the midst of beauty are still the rule. Spend a full day making the tour, if you can, for few places offer better opportunities to meet such a diversity of people than do Hardwick, Greensboro, and Craftsbury Common. The difficult portion of the tour comes in its first half; the final third is as easy as it is beautiful.

0.0 *Starting at the Galaxy Bookshop—a lovely little bookstore—on Main Street (also VT 15 East) in Hardwick, ride or walk just 0.1 mile to your first left.*

If you approached Hardwick from the west, you may have noticed an unusual covered bridge on the south side of VT 15, about 4 miles west of Hardwick. The Fisher covered bridge, which extends 103 feet over the Lamoille River, was built in 1908 by the St. Johnsbury and Lamoille Railroad Company. It is the last railroad covered bridge in use in Vermont and one of only a few left in the country. A cupola, which runs its full length to provide a vent for engine smoke, distinguishes this covered bridge from others. Scheduled for replacement in 1968, the bridge was saved by private donations and state funds, which paid for the installation of supportive steel beams beneath its floor.

0.1 *Immediately beyond the Getty station (on your left), turn left onto North Main Street, which immediately crosses a bridge over the Lamoille River.*

Hardwick was a simple agricultural town until 1868, when Henry R. Mack discovered granite nearby. Then the area went through a dramatic transformation, becoming one of the granite centers of the nation. Like a booming mining town, it rode the crest of prosperity into a period of frenetic, haphazard growth that ended in the 1920s.

Hardwick has recently gained statewide attention as the home of the Craftsbury Chamber Players. This group of skilled professionals, who teach and perform in metropolitan areas most of the year, gives concerts each Thursday during July and August at 8 PM. They choose to play in the Hardwick Town House because of its exceptional acoustics.

On the last Saturday in July, Hardwick is also home to a fiddling contest. Drawing performers from throughout New England, this competition also attracts more than 1000 spectators. Fiddling contests are great fun, especially if you have the taste and energy for a day of music, revelry, and dancing. The Hardwick event runs from approximately 10 AM to 7 PM; admission is charged. In July 1995, for the first time, Hardwick also hosted a major reggae festival. It featured eight bands from the United States and abroad and drew an estimated 50,000 fans. To confirm future dates and locations, contact the Hardwick town manager's office (802-472-6120).

You can buy food to carry along in Hardwick or later in Greensboro.

0.2 *At the crossroad by the large gray stone Memorial Building on your right, turn right onto Church Street toward Greensboro. Within the next mile or so, Church Street becomes Center Road, though no sign marks the change.*

The Memorial Building, constructed of local granite, contains a room made of marble from Proctor, Vermont, and houses a valuable collection of old coins and paper currency.

This section of the tour is its most strenuous. For the first 1.75 miles, the road rises steadily and steeply. Then after descending for a mile, it rolls upward over smaller hills for 3 miles, gaining height until it reaches Greensboro at an elevation of 1463 feet, 800 feet above Hardwick.

5.9 *At the crossroad, go straight toward Greensboro to continue on Center Road, which is unsigned here.*

In 0.75 mile you can see on your left a small sign for a public beach indicating the 0.25-mile-long road to Caspian Lake. Surrounded by low hills and wooded shores, Caspian ranks as one of Vermont's most beautiful and undisturbed large lakes. Its crystalline waters are fed by springs and offer splendid swimming from a sandy shore at the edge of a parklike lawn maintained by the town of Greensboro.

6.7 *Beside Willey's Store on your right in Greensboro, bear left so that you pass the tiny village green on your right.*

Willey's Store offers a fine selection of food for a picnic. Across from Willey's is the Miller's Thumb, a pleasant place to browse. Owners Rob and Anne Brigham import Italian and Portuguese ceramics and also sell an attractive assortment of paintings, antiques, and furniture. Their shop was a gristmill in the 1850s. Greensboro has become a rather exclusive summer retreat especially favored by writers and professors.

6.9 *At the curve just beyond the United Church of Christ on your left, go left to follow East Craftsbury Road.*

Over the next 3 miles, the road rolls up and down several short hills and then goes downhill nearly 4 miles into East Craftsbury. At the crest of the hill, Highland Lodge, which serves lunch, is on your right. Stop to look at the view of Caspian Lake.

In East Craftsbury, you may enjoy visiting the Old Forge, which will be on your left. The shop is a direct importer of Scottish, Irish, Welsh, and English sweaters and tweeds. In 0.4 mile beyond the Old Forge, the road bends into an exhilarating 1.5 mile descent into the Black River valley. Beware of the last half mile; it's steep and ends at a stop sign.

14.2 *At the stop sign, turn right onto the unsigned road that goes through Craftsbury to Craftsbury Common.*

You reach Craftsbury in 1 mile. If you are not carrying food or have not already eaten, you should stop at one of the two stores there, because they are the last ones on the route. Since Craftsbury Common is much more beautiful and interesting than Craftsbury, it is worth waiting to picnic there.

Though barely a mile long, the ride up to the broad plateau where Craftsbury Common sits is demanding. But at the top you suddenly find yourself in an almost surreal collection of trim houses, uniformly gleaming with white clapboards and green shutters, and commanding views across broad valleys to mountains in the east and west. Entirely free of commercial establishments, this village surrounding a broad green must be one of the most memorable in New England. Its spotless neatness accentuates the simplicity of line and color in its architecture. Giant sugar maples shade lawns set behind white picket fences. And elegantly presiding over the village is the towering spire of the United Church of Craftsbury (1820).

Craftsbury Common is also the home of Sterling College. Founded in 1958 as a traditional boys' preparatory school, Sterling quickly altered direction toward liberal studies that emphasize outdoor challenges and nonacademic experience. Granted higher-education status in 1978, Sterling began granting associate of arts degrees four years later. It now enrolls approximately 90 students.

16.3 *From Craftsbury Common, continue to follow the main road straight through town, keeping the common on your left.*

From the common you glide speedily downhill nearly 3 miles back into the Black River valley.

Less than a mile beyond the common is the unpaved road on your right that leads to Craftsbury Bed & Breakfast on Wylie Hill. It's just a half mile off the route.

18.8 *At the stop sign, turn left onto VT 14 South.*

VT 14 tilts slightly downward virtually the entire way back to Hardwick.

In 6 miles you reach Lake Elligo on your left. It is long, narrow, and a good place to swim. A quarter mile beyond the State Fishing Access on your left is a place reserved for public swimming. The Abenakis called the Black River, which flows into Lake Elligo, Elligo-sigo, which means "a good place to hunt [or return to] in springtime."

31.6 *At the stop sign, turn left onto VT 14 South/VT 15 East toward Hardwick.*

*32.8 At the T in Hardwick, turn left to continue on VT 15 East,
which is now Main Street, and ride 25 yards to the Galaxy
Bookshop on your right where you began.*

For general information about lodging, restaurants, attractions, and special events, contact the Hardwick Area Chamber of Commerce, PO Box 111, Hardwick, VT 05843, (802-472-5906).

Where to Stay

Somerset House Bed & Breakfast, 24 Highland Avenue, Hardwick, VT 05843 (802-472-5484), is a gracious 1899 Victorian house in a quiet residential neighborhood. I like the round and balcony rooms best. Innkeepers Ruth and David Gaillard serve terrific breakfasts, using eggs from free-range hens and organically raised vegetables whenever possible. Their great sweeping porch overlooking the perennial garden is an enticing place to sit, morning or night.

Craftsbury Bed & Breakfast on Wylie Hill, Craftsbury Common, VT 05827 (802-586-2206), is Craftsbury's longest-operating traditional bed & breakfast, 1.5 miles from the common. It is peaceful and panoramic here. Innkeeper Margaret Ramsdell has lived in Craftsbury for more than 30 years, and few people can tell you more about it. Her guest rooms are comfortable and pleasant with shared baths; I like the rooms upstairs best. She serves a full country breakfast.

Elmore State Park, Box 93, Lake Elmore, VT 05657 (802-888-2982), occupies 709 acres and has tent sites, 15 lean-tos, and hot showers, but no hookups. There's fishing, swimming from a beach, boats to rent, and hiking trails as well as a snack bar, picnic tables, and fireplaces.

Bicycle Repair Services

Chuck's Bikes, Main Street, Morrisville, VT (802-888-7642)

Park Pedals, South Walden Road, Cabot, VT (802-563-2252)

24
Barnet–St. Johnsbury

Moderate-to-difficult terrain; 35.5 miles or 53.1 miles (2.6 unpaved)

From the tiny settlement of Barnet on the Connecticut River, this tour explores the exquisite countryside and tiny villages of what former US Senator George Aiken evocatively dubbed the Northeast Kingdom. It is the part of Vermont that has changed the least.

The first 13 miles bring challenge along with dramatic beauty as you leave the river valley and ride westward into the hills of Caledonia County. The terrain is sometimes arduous, but the charm of the Kingdom's tiny towns and undulating hills makes the effort worthwhile. At its midpoint the tour enters St. Johnsbury and necessitates a little cycling on roads that are neither pretty nor quiet. But that city offers surprising attractions as well: an extraordinary public art gallery that features one of the greatest of Albert Bierstadt's paintings, a fine museum of natural history, superb Victorian architecture, and a comprehensive exhibit of the process of making maple syrup. The longer tour crosses into New Hampshire for a final 10 easy miles along the Connecticut River. Here you ride through rich farmlands with long views across the river to Vermont.

0.0   *From Barnet, with the Barnet Village Store on your left and Barnet Post Office on your right, ride west—uphill and away from US 5—just 15 yards to the granite plaques honoring Barnet's war dead. There bear left onto the unsigned road. In 0.1 mile you cross a bridge and pass the 1854 Barnet Congregational Church on your right.*

During the first week of October, Barnet joins Peacham and five other nearby towns in the Northeast Kingdom Annual Fall Foliage Festival. The celebration lasts a week. A different event—usually involving food, but sometimes also dancing, hiking, livestock, or crafts—is scheduled in each town daily. For details, call the Barnet town clerk (802-633-2256).

205

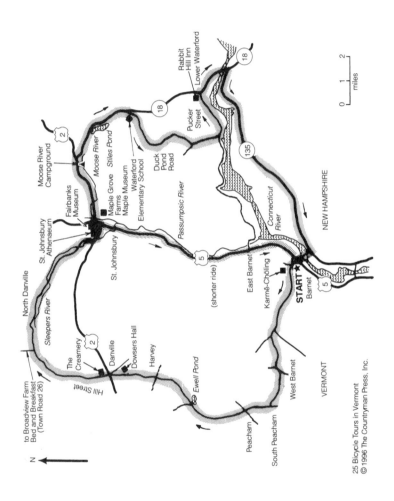

25 Bicycle Tours in Vermont
© 1996 The Countryman Press, Inc.

0.3 *At the stop sign, turn right toward West Barnet, Harvey's Lake, and Peacham onto West Barnet Road, though it is unsigned here. In 0.1 mile you pass beneath I-91. Thereafter, do not turn onto any of the side roads.*

Immediately you start a hearty climb that lasts a mile as you begin to work your way out of the Connecticut River valley.

In 0.5 mile you reach the driveway to Karmê-Chöling, a Buddhist meditation center, which sits 0.25 mile off the road on your right. Karmê-Chöling was founded in 1970 by a Tibetan Buddhist master and author, Vidyadhara Chögyam Trungpa Rinpoche. The center focuses on Buddhist and Shambhala teachings.

Architecturally, Karmê-Chöling is a vibrant juxtaposition of Vermont, Tibetan, and Japanese design. It sits on 540 acres of woodland, meadows, and ponds. The central building is a blend of farmhouse and shrine that features the first Kagyü shrine room in North America and a meditation hall for 200 people. Guests are most welcome. But it's wise to call ahead (802-633-2384) just to make sure no special event that might interfere with a visit is going on.

5.0 *In West Barnet, follow the main road—actually called Main Street—so that you pass the Presbyterian Church of West Barnet on your left and then the West Barnet General Store on your right. Do not turn onto Old West Road.*

5.2 *Just beyond the West Barnet Garage on your left, turn right onto the unsigned road.*

For the next 1.5 miles you head steadily up a modest grade. South Peacham sits at 1000 feet; Barnet was at 452 feet.

6.7 *At the T, in front of the South Peacham Store, turn right toward Peacham and Danville.*

You now encounter the most difficult climb of the tour. In barely a mile you climb more than 900 vertical feet to reach Peacham at 1908 feet. Don't feel weak if you have to stop; the grade averages 17 percent!

7.7 *In Peacham continue straight.*

The Peacham Store and the Peacham Corner Art Guild are both on your left. The store makes soup, chili, salads, unusual sandwiches, and coffee, including espresso and cappuccino. The art guild, a cooperative, features the work of 20 local crafters who take turns staffing the shop. Their wares include photography, children's clothing, quilting, and homemade foods.

Peacham is a sparkling village of white clapboard houses that seem virtually unchanged since they were built 150 or more years ago. Some date to the 18th century. The village has something of an aristocratic air. Perhaps it derives from the fine architecture, perhaps from the former professors, ambassadors, literati, and artistic luminati who have moved there.

From Peacham to Danville the cycling is much easier. You descend nearly 600 feet in elevation over the next 6 miles. The terrain continues its dramatic rolls, but goes down more than up. In the late fall the hillsides turn yellow-orange thanks to the predominance of larch trees, also called tamaracks. This unusual genus of pine is deciduous; its green needles change color and fall off in autumn.

14.6 *At the blinking light in Danville, go straight across US 2 onto Hill Street toward North Danville. Thereafter, follow the main road; do not turn onto the side roads.*

Danville sits on a plateau, commanding long views of New Hampshire's White Mountains. The next 10 miles offer many pleasant places to picnic. Hill Street Park, which has picnic tables and shelter, is on your right in 0.2 mile. Later on, you can just pick a spot along your way.

The Danville General Store will make a grinder to your order. Or you can eat at the Creamery Restaurant, on the right side of Hill Street, 50 yards after you cross US 2. The Creamery is open Tuesday through Saturday and features homemade soups, sandwiches, and salads.

After climbing for 1.5 miles, Hill Street turns downhill as you descend to St. Johnsbury. The first 1.75 miles of descent are moderate. The next mile is steep and fast. And the final 4 go downhill gently.

About three-quarters of the way down the steepest part of the hill, you reach Town Road 26 on your left. It goes to Old North Church and the Broadview Farm Bed & Breakfast.

Danville is the birthplace (in 1792) of Thaddeus Stevens. A vigorous and outspoken opponent of slavery, he also fought Lincoln's plan for reconstructing the South after the Civil War because he considered it too lenient. Stevens was a representative from Pennsylvania to the US House of Representatives from 1849 to 1853 as a Whig, and from 1859 until his death in 1868 as a Republican. Leader of the Congressional Radical Republicans, Stevens broke with Andrew Johnson when Johnson vetoed a bill to protect the newly freed blacks from vengeful codes being legislated against them by many southern states. Stevens went on to lead the successful battle for the 14th Amendment and to conduct the House impeachment proceedings against Johnson.

Danville may be best known as the dowsing headquarters of the nation. The 5000-member American Society of Dowsers is located here in Dowsers Hall, just 0.25 mile down Brainerd Street.

Dowsing is a quest for information, usually done by holding a forked stick or angle rod over the ground until the stick or rod moves to indicate a find. According to the society, anyone can do it, and children younger than 16 are almost all sensitive. In these days of exotic technology, dowsing seems almost supernatural. According to the society, "Information comes to the dowser through a means other than the five senses." Dowsers most often seek underground sources of water, but they may also search for buried objects and even missing persons. The most skilled dowser can stand at the edge of a field—or even over a map—and determine where water or some other object is located, how deep it is, and, in the case of water, how rapidly it is flowing. A good dowser can certainly unsettle the crustiest skeptic.

If you visit the society's headquarters—open 9–5 weekdays—you can obtain some basic instruction and free literature. The annual dowsers convention, which met in Danville for 25 years, is now so large that it gathers instead at Lyndon State College in Lyndonville, Vermont.

23.0 *At the stop sign, turn left onto US 2 East, which is a divided highway at this point. Ride carefully on the shoulder.*

23.6 *Continue straight on US 2 East, which is still a divided highway. Do not turn right toward I-91 or I-93. Continue to ride on the shoulder.*

24.5 *Continue straight on US 2 East toward US 5. From this point on, the highway is no longer divided.*

25.1 *At the triangle in front of St. Johnsbury Academy, bear left onto US 2 East. Do not follow the signs for US 2 East for trucks.*

Situated at the confluence of the Passumpsic, Moose, and Sleepers Rivers, St. Johnsbury, with a population of about 7600, is the largest town in the Northeast Kingdom. Much of its history, marvelous architecture, and cultural life derives from the imagination and generosity of the family of Thaddeus Fairbanks (1796–1886), inventor of the platform scale and founder of the Fairbanks-Morse Scale Works. Many of the grand homes and public buildings along Main Street (US 2) were built between 1830 and 1870, when the company's prosperity led to a tripling of the town's population. In the 1960s, when an out-of-state conglomerate acquired Fairbanks-Morse and the St. Johnsbury scale works was threatened by closure, townspeople raised money among themselves to subsidize the cost of a new manufacturing plant.

St. Johnsbury Academy, founded by the Fairbanks family in 1842, is an independent, private, coeducational secondary school for about 880 students. Approximately 140 students board. A great many of the others come from nearby Vermont and New Hampshire towns that have no public high schools. These towns provide their students with vouchers they can use to pay tuition to the schools of their choice.

Three other things are especially noteworthy about St. Johnsbury: the St. Johnsbury Athenaeum, the Fairbanks Museum of Natural Science, and the Maple Grove Farms Maple Museum. They are described below.

FOR 35.5 MILE RIDE: Turn right onto US 5 South and follow it 10.4 miles to Barnet. When you get there, the Barnet Village Store and Post Office will be on your right. US 5 follows the Passumpsic River. Much of the traffic that formerly used US 5 now takes I-91.

25.3 *Turn right to follow US 2 East, here called Eastern Avenue, toward VT 18.*

The St. Johnsbury Athenaeum is now on your left. It should not be missed, for it contains the extraordinary Albert Bierstadt painting *Domes of the Yosemite*. The Athenaeum, which was built and given to the town by Horace Fairbanks, Thaddeus's nephew, is at 30 Main

Street. Designed by John Davis Hatch of New York City, the building is a superlative example of Victorian architecture. It contains a 45,000-volume library and an art gallery lit by an enormous skylight in a domed ceiling. The gallery is the oldest American art gallery still preserved as it was when it was built—in 1873. It houses a permanent collection of nearly 100 canvases, many from the Hudson River School. Included are works by Jasper Cropsey, Asher B. Durand, James and William Hart, and Worthington Whittredge. But the pièce de résistance remains the 10-by-15-foot *Domes of the Yosemite*. When it was acquired, *The New York Times* lamented that "it is now doomed to the obscurity of a Vermont town where it will astonish the natives." To that, Fairbanks replied, "The people who live in this obscurity are nevertheless quite capable of appreciating the dignity it lends to this small village." Bierstadt was apparently not offended by the painting's location, for he returned often to view it and retouch it. The Athenaeum is open without charge six days a week.

The Fairbanks Museum of Natural Science is down the street from the Athenaeum. It is probably the town's most elegant architectural work. Lambert Packard designed it in the Richardsonian style, with towers, arches, and carvings of limestone and red sandstone. The interior, finely made of golden oak and cherry, is highlighted by a 30-foot-high barrel-vaulted ceiling. The collection includes some 3000 animals, most preserved in glass cases. The displays are truly eclectic: big cats, birds of paradise, Civil War artifacts, snakes, Zulu war shields, and one of the world's largest collections of hummingbirds. Patron Franklin Fairbanks said at the museum's 1890 dedication: "I wish it to be the people's school . . . to teach the village the meaning of nature and religion." The museum also contains Vermont's only public planetarium—it seats 50— and the Northern New England Weather Center, which provides the region with daily forecasts and much education. In the basement, physical phenomena are cleverly presented by push-button displays that almost beg to be manipulated. The museum is open Monday through Saturday 10–4 (and until 6 PM in July and August) and 1–5 on Sunday. Admission is charged.

25.5 *At the stop sign, turn left to continue on US 2 East, which is now called Railroad Street.*

25.7 At the stop sign, turn right to continue on US 2 East across the Passumpsic River.

Most of the next 3 miles is a compromise. The eastern outskirts of St. Johnsbury along US 2 are congested and not pretty, but they form a necessary link in the route. Most of the way is also uphill.

In 1 mile you reach Maple Grove Farms Maple Museum on your right. Here you can tour the world's largest maple sugar candy factory, see a movie showing how maple syrup is made— it takes about 40 gallons of sap to make 1 gallon of syrup—and visit an exhibit of sugar-making equipment. If you decide to purchase some candy, examine the label closely to see whether you are getting pure maple sugar or a blend of maple and cane sugars. From May to late October, the museum is open 8–5 seven days a week.

Two miles beyond Maple Grove Farms Maple Museum, the entrance to Moose River Camp Ground is on your right.

28.7 At the blinking light, turn right onto VT 18 South toward I-91 and I-93.

The road goes uphill for 1 mile and then levels off beside Stiles Pond. Traffic on VT 18 can get heavy, but not as heavy as on US 2.

31.6 Turn right toward Waterford Crushed Stone and Pike Industries Asphalt Plant onto Duck Pond Road, which is unsigned here. In 0.3 mile you pass the entrance to the Waterford Elementary School on your right. Though there is no sign for the school, if you look up the driveway you can see it.

Just 1.75 miles beyond the school, Duck Pond Road tilts downhill for 1.25 miles. Just as the downhill ends, by the sign for Waterford Sand and Gravel, the road becomes unpaved. You now follow unpaved roads for 2.6 miles.

36.2 Follow Duck Pond Road, which is still unpaved and not signed, around to the left. Do not turn onto the unpaved road entering from your right.

37.4 At the yield sign, 0.2 mile after the road surface becomes paved, turn left onto Pucker Street, which is unsigned.

Just before your next turn, you ride through the tiny hamlet of Lower Waterford. Several buildings, including Rabbit Hill Inn, date from the late 18th century.

Looking across the Connecticut River at Lower Waterford

40.0 *At the stop sign, turn right onto VT 18 South and ride across the Connecticut River into New Hampshire.*

41.5 *At the stop sign, turn right onto NH 135 South toward Monroe.*

As you ride south along a rolling ridge overlooking the river, you can see Lower Waterford and Barnet rising out of the trees in Vermont. It is a fine way to complete your ride.

51.5 *Turn right onto Barnet Road, which is unsigned, and ride back across the Connecticut River into Vermont.*

52.3 *At the stop sign, turn right onto US 5 North, which is not signed here.*

52.5 *Do not turn toward I-91 and West Barnet, Harvey's Lake, and Peacham.*

53.1 *Just after crossing a bridge, turn left and you are back at the Barnet Village Store and the post office in Barnet.*

For general information on lodging, restaurants, attractions, and special events, contact the Northeast Kingdom Chamber of Commerce, 30 Western Avenue, St. Johnsbury, VT 05819 (802-748-3678).

Where to Stay

Broadview Farm Bed & Breakfast, RD 2, Box 153, St. Johnsbury, VT 05819 (802-748-9902), is a charming place, actually in North Danville. (St. Johnsbury is merely its mailing address.) Gracious innkeepers Joe and Molly Newell have created four comfortable, casual guest rooms—my favorite is the Whittier room—in their homey, slate-roofed country mansion. It's decorated with the mementos of an active family's 30 years of travels with the US Army and countless equestrian competitions. The Newells make their own maple syrup, have a wonderful old square Steinway, and are raising two Holstein oxen that they hope will one day help them do the sugaring.

Rabbit Hill Inn, Lower Waterford, VT 05848 (802-748-5168), is a much-heralded, luxurious country inn. Innkeepers John and Maureen McGee have created seductive guest rooms with lace, Jacuzzi whirlpools for two, and canopy beds. The charming bar doubles as a backgammon and checkers room. The dining room is spacious and candlelit; afternoon tea and breakfast are served. The inn also has a wonderful, spring-fed swimming pond.

Moose River Campground, RD 1, St. Johnsbury, VT 05819 (802-748-4334), sits on an elbow of the scenic Moose River. The swimming is good and so especially are the wooded tent sites along the river's edge. There are also hookups and sites for RVs. Owners Clem and Julie Potvin are great hosts. Ask Clem about his service as a member of the state police.

Bicycle Repair Services

East Burke Sports, East Burke, VT (802-626-3215)

Park Pedals, South Walden Road, Cabot, VT (802-563-2252)

Village Sport Shop, US 5, Lyndonville, VT (802-626-8448)

Western Auto Associate Store, 34 Depot Street, Lyndonville, VT (802-626-5035)

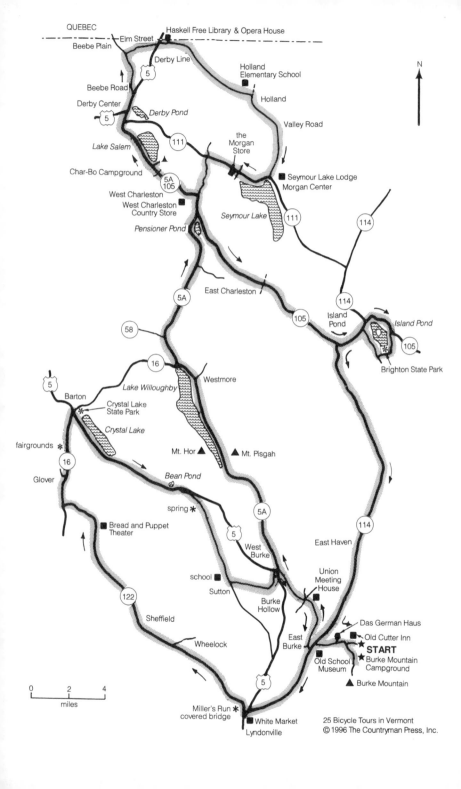

QUEBEC

Haskell Free Library & Opera House

Elm Street

Beebe Plain

Derby Line

(5)

Beebe Road

Derby Center

(5)

Derby Pond

Lake Salem

Char-Bo Campground

(111)

(5A) (105)

West Charleston

West Charleston Country Store

Pensioner Pond

Holland Elementary School

Holland

Valley Road

the Morgan Store

Seymour Lake Lodge
Morgan Center

Seymour Lake

(111)

East Charleston

(5A)

(58)

(16)

(105)

(114)

(114)

Island Pond

Island Pond

(105)

Brighton State Park

Lake Willoughby

Westmore

Barton

Crystal Lake State Park

Crystal Lake

fairgrounds ✳

(16)

Glover

Mt. Hor ▲

▲ Mt. Pisgah

Bean Pond

spring ✳

(5A)

(5)

Bread and Puppet Theater

school ▪

Sutton

West Burke

Union Meeting House

East Haven

(114)

(122)

Sheffield

Wheelock

Burke Hollow

East Burke

Das German Haus

Old Cutter Inn

START ★

★ Burke Mountain Campground

Old School Museum

▲ Burke Mountain

(5)

Miller's Run ✳
covered bridge

▪ White Market

Lyndonville

0   2   4
miles

N

25 Bicycle Tours in Vermont
© 1996 The Countryman Press, Inc.

25
Lakes of the Northeast Kingdom: A Three-day Tour

Using inns: 136.6 miles. Using campgrounds: 124.2 or 152.3 miles.
Each day's distance and terrain are stated at the beginning of that day's
   directions.

Vermont's northern piedmont and glaciated Connecticut River highlands have been known as the Northeast Kingdom since former US Senator George Aiken so dubbed them in 1949. This region, the most sparsely settled of the state, retains an ethereal quality, difficult to define, yet evident to those who take the time to explore it.

Totaling as much as 152 miles over three days, this tour uncovers the deep glacial lakes, conifer forests, tiny villages, and hillside farms that evoke the magnificent serenity—and the mystery—for which the Kingdom is renowned. Each day brings you to a sparkling lake—Island Pond, Lake Willoughby, Crystal Lake, and Seymour Lake—where swimming is a joy. On clear days from the hill towns of Sutton, Sheffield, and Holland you can view the White Mountains of New Hampshire as well as the Greens of Vermont. Indeed, before leaving East Burke, drive the 2.5-mile toll road up Burke Mountain (elevation 3627 feet) to survey the topography that awaits you. The climb is so steep that even if you make it up by bicycle, you must still negotiate a much-too-hazardous descent. From the peak of Burke Mountain nothing obstructs your view, and with the aid of a compass and map you can identify the major geological formations you will soon be seeing by bicycle. For me the Northeast Kingdom—in temperament and appearance—is really the Vermonter's Vermont.

The tour is deliberately constructed to provide several choices. The shortest ride is a one-day, 51.5-mile circle connecting East Burke and Barton, described as Day One; the mid-length ride is a one- or two-day, 72- to 108-mile tour between East Burke and Morgan Center, consisting

217

just of Days Two and Three; the longest ride is a three-day, 124- to 152-mile combination of Days One, Two, and Three.

Fall starts early in the Kingdom; if you're looking for autumn colors in mid-September, this is the tour to do. It is designed so you may use either country inns or campgrounds, and so you encounter the most difficult rides when you can be free of your panniers.

Day 1

East Burke–Barton Loop: *Moderate-to-difficult terrain; 51.5 miles*

0.0 *From either the Old Cutter Inn or Burke Mountain Campground, follow the Burke Mountain Resort road downhill to East Burke.*

2.2 *At the stop sign in East Burke, turn left onto VT 114 South, which is unsigned here, and follow it to Lyndonville.*

In 50 yards you reach Bailey's Country Store on your left. Here you can get groceries, cold drinks, a grinder made to order, dried fruit by the ounce, penny candy, and frozen yogurt. This attractive store sells lots of other things as well: sweaters, Christmas decorations, clothes, pottery, and wine. Get your snacks for the morning either in East Burke or 5 miles later in Lyndonville. Little is available afterwards until you reach Barton.

East Burke's Old School Museum stands 200 yards south of Bailey's on the same side of the road. This 18-by-23-foot retired schoolhouse contains a potpourri of items from its past: primers, pupils' desks, musical instruments, and a globe made by a local resident in about 1800. If the door is locked, you can get a key at the Burke Mountain Clubhouse next door.

7.0 *At the blinking light on the outskirts of Lyndonville, turn left onto US 5 South. Beware of traffic on US 5.*

7.8 *At the next blinking light, which is in Lyndonville, go straight off US 5 onto Main Street, which is unsigned here.*

The best selection of food for the next 20 miles is here at White Market, on your left at this light.

On Wednesday evenings during the summer, the Lyndonville band performs at the bandstand on the village green across from

White Market. The Caledonia County Fair, which in true Vermont style combines livestock and agricultural exhibitions with the attractions of a traveling carnival, also happens in Lyndonville during August. For further information, contact the Lyndonville Town Clerk, 20 Park Avenue, Lyndonville, VT 05851 (802-626-5785).

7.9 *At the stop sign, turn right onto Center Street and follow the signs for VT 122 North.*

Within 0.75 mile, you will pass Lyndon Institute, on your left, go through Miller's Run covered bridge—56 feet long, built in 1878—and then bear left onto VT 122. Lyndon Institute, an independent coeducational day and residential secondary school, was founded in 1867. It takes great pride in its small classes—10 to 20 students—which, in its own words, "provide the personalized attention essential to the growth of each individual."

A mile and a half beyond Wheelock, VT 122 begins working its way uphill through Sheffield for 3.5 miles. The grade begins gently but turns steep in the final mile. The top of the hill marks the Connecticut River–Lake Champlain watershed; most rivers to the east flow into the former, while those to the west flow into the latter. Pause to look behind you at the view; on clear days you can see all the way to New Hampshire's Mount Washington. Then enjoy the 3-mile downhill run that lies ahead and look out for moose.

At Wheelock, there is a lovely little green shaded by 80-foot white pines, with a picnic table and hexagonal bandstand.

In 1785, during Vermont's brief tenure as an independent nation (1777–91), the General Assembly took the unusual action of granting land to a college in another country. Having no college of its own and wishing to ensure its sons opportunities for learning, Vermont granted half the township of Wheelock to New Hampshire's Dartmouth College. As late as 1815 the rent paid by Wheelock townspeople to Dartmouth accounted for a major portion of the college's revenue. Though Dartmouth no longer levies rents on citizens of Wheelock, the college still does adhere to the policy it initiated in 1828 of charging no tuition to those sons and, more recently, daughters of Wheelock who are offered admission.

The home of the Bread and Puppet Theater is 2 miles down the hill on VT 122. It is on your right in a three-story red farmhouse across the road from a long, low, one-story shed with a rusty roof.

There may well be a hand-painted old school bus parked there as well. The hill is quite steep when you reach Bread and Puppet; try not to go too fast.

The Bread and Puppet Theater was founded by Peter Schumann in 1962 on New York City's Lower East Side. It moved to Vermont in 1970. This powerful, innovative company has, in its own words, presented "massive spectacles with 100 participants" in the United States, western and eastern Europe, and Latin America. Their pageants, often performed outdoors, address "well-known social, political, and environmental issues or simply the common urgencies of our . . . age." Using gigantic masks, stilt walkers, mime, and music in forceful and fun-loving dramatizations—often with sharp political messages—Bread and Puppet creates extraordinary theater accessible to adults and children alike.

Bread and Puppet has created a museum here in a 100-year-old hay barn. It houses scores of enormous masks, marvelous puppets, paintings, and other graphics. They make a striking scene in the dark, cavernous barn. The museum is open May to October, 10–5 daily. Admission is free; donations are welcome.

23.9 At the stop sign, turn right onto VT 16 North toward Barton.

In 3 miles you pass the entrance to the Barton Fairgrounds on your left. Some of the major shows exhibited there are the Memorial Day Horse Show; the Fourth of July celebration, which includes everything from tractor-pulling competitions to country-western dancing; the Arts and Crafts Show on the first Saturday in August; and the Orleans County Fair, which runs from the third Wednesday in August through the following Sunday. For more information, contact the Barton Chamber of Commerce, Barton, VT 05822 (802-525-1137).

28.6 At the stop sign in Barton, turn right onto US 5 South.

Since there are no stores for the next 15 miles, make certain you have what you want before leaving Barton.

If you're ready for a swim or just a great picnic spot, ride just 0.25 mile on US 5 South and then turn left onto VT 16 North toward Crystal Lake State Park. The entrance to the park will be on your right in 250 yards. There are picnic tables and a swimming beach. Admission is charged.

35.3 One-quarter mile beyond Bean Pond on your left, bear right off US 5 onto the unsigned road. Look carefully for this turn; it is easy to miss.

As soon as you turn, you pass beneath a railroad trestle and begin to climb a formidable hill. Six-tenths of a mile up you can refill your water bottle at a mountain spring on your right. The grade of the hill tapers off a short way past the spring and remains gradual for another 2 miles. On the top you cycle for roughly a mile along a plateau, from which the views eastward are superb. Then you glide downhill into Sutton.

40.7 Just beyond the Sutton Elementary School on your right, turn left at the triangular grass traffic island onto the unsigned road. You will be going downhill when you reach this turn. Try to approach it slowly, for it too is easy to miss.

The road goes downhill for half a mile, up for three-quarters, and then down the rest of the way to West Burke. It offers exceptional views of Burke Mountain to your right, but keep your eye on the road during the final descent, for it is fast and suddenly curves 90 degrees to the left.

43.6 At the T after crossing the railroad tracks, turn left onto the unsigned road.

43.8 At the stop sign in West Burke, turn right onto US 5 South, go just past the K&G Market on your left, and then turn left onto VT 5A North.

43.9 As soon as you cross the bridge, turn right off VT 5A onto the unsigned road toward Burke Hollow and East Burke. Thereafter, follow the main road and signs for East Burke.

The ride from West Burke through Burke Hollow can be arduous after all the cycling you have done. You must climb a gradual 0.75-mile hill in the first 2 miles and then a very steep hill of the same length just beyond Burke Hollow. The second climb ends by a cemetery and gives way to an easy, occasionally downhill, ride into East Burke.

The Union Meeting House, which sends its delicate spire high above the rooftops of Burke Hollow, remains unaltered, save for fresh white paint, since its construction in 1825. It is worth stopping—either now or tomorrow when you come by again—to see the old box pews, each with its own door, and the high barrel pulpit.

48.9 At the yield sign on the edge of East Burke, turn left onto the unsigned road and ride across the bridge.

49.0 At the stop sign in East Burke, turn left onto VT 114 North.

49.3 At the sign for Burke Mountain Resort, turn right onto the road to the Old Cutter Inn and Burke Mountain Campground.

As you may recall, this hill is unrelenting, but the grade is moderate to gentle most of the way.

51.5 You are back at your starting point.

Day 2

Old Cutter Inn–Seymour Lake Lodge: *moderate terrain; 50.6 miles*
Burke Mountain Campground–Char-Bo Campground: *easy-to-moderate terrain; 31.6 miles or moderate terrain; 59.7 miles.*

0.0 From either the Old Cutter Inn or Burke Mountain Campground, follow the Burke Mountain Resort road downhill to East Burke.

Before you start bicycling, find a vantage point with an unobstructed view to the north. There, slightly to the west of north, you can see the prominent, hummocklike peaks of Mounts Hor and Pisgah. They define the glacial canyon within which lies Lake Willoughby and through which you will soon be riding.

2.2 At the stop sign in East Burke, turn left onto VT 114 South, which is unsigned here.

Buy some food for snacks and a picnic lunch; you'll have little other chance for the next 25 miles. If you are planning to take the 31.6-mile route to Char-Bo Campground, consider buying your dinner too.

2.6 Turn right toward Burke Hollow and West Burke. Ride 75 yards across the bridge and then turn right toward Burke Hollow.

You are leaving East Burke by the roads you returned on yesterday.

For the first 1.5 miles, you climb a gentle grade. Then, from the cemetery on your right, you descend quickly 0.75 mile into Burke Hollow.

5.4 *Just beyond the Union Meeting House (on your right) in Burke Hollow, bear left and then immediately bear right to follow the main road to West Burke.*

Yesterday's climb is now a descent that makes the 2 miles to West Burke easy.

7.6 *At the stop sign in West Burke, turn right onto VT 5A North.*

If you still need food or supplies, turn left at this stop sign and ride 0.1 mile to the West Burke General Store. VT 5A stays relatively flat until it passes the northern end of Lake Willoughby.

Set directly between the rocky faces of Mounts Hor (elevation 2751 feet) and Pisgah (elevation 2646 feet), Lake Willoughby measures 6 miles from north to south and 600 feet deep. Its strikingly clear waters make excellent swimming as well as fishing and can be reached most easily from the beaches at its northern and southern ends. The largest fish known to be caught in Vermont waters by rod and reel came from Lake Willoughby. Caught on May 2, 1981, it was a 34-pound lake trout with a girth of 27 inches and a length of 43.

16.3 *The Willoughby State Forest Trail Head is on the right side of Route 5A.*

This is where the Mount Pisgah Trail begins. It is 1.7 miles to the summit.

By a quirk of nature, rare, delicate arctic plants grow on the cliffs of Mount Pisgah. Mostly calcicoles, which take the calcium they need from the rocks they cling to, these relics of the Ice Age find the moist, protected ledges of Pisgah hospitable.

19.1 *At the intersection with VT 16, continue straight on VT 5A North.*

VT 5A now goes up a moderately steep hill for 1 mile.

20.4 *At the intersection with VT 58, continue straight on VT 5A North.*

VT 5A continues to go up for another mile and then turns downhill for 2 miles.

24.3 Continue straight to stay on Route 5A North; do not turn right toward East Charleston and Island Pond.

27.4 At the stop sign, turn left onto VT 105 West toward West Charleston and Derby Center.

The West Charleston Country Store—on your left in 1 mile—is the last place to shop on the 31.6-mile route to Char-Bo Campground.

31.1 To go to Char-Bo Campground, turn right onto Hayward Road and ride a half mile.

If you are taking the 59.7-mile route, you might want to stop at Char-Bo to unload your heavier gear. The next 28 miles pose a greater challenge than the first 31.

34.0 At the intersection with VT 111 East, continue straight on VT 105 West.

34.5 At the intersection in Derby Center, where VT 105 turns left, go straight onto US 5 North.

35.2 Turn left onto Beebe Road toward Beebe Plain.

37.7 Turn right onto Elm Street, which is the first paved road you reach.

Immediately after turning, you must climb a steep hill 0.75 mile long.

39.6 At the stop sign beside the town park on your left, on the outskirts of Derby Line, turn left onto US 5 North, which is unsigned here.

39.8 At the blinking light in Derby Line, bear right toward I-91.

If you would like to cross the border into Canada, this is the most convenient place to do so. It would be wise to stop first at US Customs to verify your identification. US Customs was on your left just 50 yards before you reached this blinking light. To cross the border, simply go straight from the blinking light 100 yards into Quebec.

Back on the route, in 0.1 mile you reach the Haskell Free Library and Opera House, built in Queen Anne revival style, on your left. It exemplifies the casual view often taken of the international border in this part of the country. The books in the library and the stage of the opera house lie in one country while the checkout desk and the

The Haskell Free Library and Opera House sits on the US-Canada border at Derby Line.

audience remain in the other. As the plaque outside reads: "This structure is doubly unusual: it not only straddles the Canada—United States boundary, but also contains the rare combination of a library and a theater. Built between 1901 and 1904 as a gift of the Haskell Family of Vermont, it testifies to the late Victorian belief in the intellectual and moral benefits of education and the arts." The ornate, second-story opera house seats 500 people.

Be sure you have all the food you want for the final 11.5 miles, for not a single store sits along your route between Derby Line and Morgan Center, and the ride is not easy. From Derby Line to the crossroad that marks Holland, you climb 400 feet along roads that roll more up than down over moderately steep, short hills.

40.3 *Do not turn onto Maple Street. Continue straight on the unsigned road so you ride across the overpass above I-91.*

45.8 *At the T, 0.75 mile beyond the Holland Elementary School on* *your left, turn right onto Valley Road, which is unsigned here.*

After 1.5 miles of relatively flat terrain, you ride mostly downhill to Seymour Lake.

50.6 *At the stop sign in Morgan Center, you are facing Seymour Lake. Immediately to your left is the Seymour Lake Lodge, where you end the day's ride unless you are camping. If you are following the 59.7-mile route to Char-Bo Campground, turn right at this stop sign onto VT 111 West.*

VT 111 looks in profile like the teeth of a ripsaw. For 4 miles the road rolls relentlessly up and down short, steep hills.

54.6 *At the second intersection with a paved road on the left, which comes 2 miles beyond the Morgan Store on your left, turn left onto the unsigned road.*

The Morgan Store stocks an excellent supply of fresh meats and groceries, some produce, beer, and wine—plenty to fill your panniers for dinner and breakfast at the campground. In a half mile, the road to West Charleston becomes unpaved for a half mile, but the surface is smooth and firm and, like the rest of this road, slopes gently downward.

56.5 *At the stop sign in West Charleston, turn right onto VT 105 West, which is unsigned here.*

59.2 *Turn right onto Hayward Road and ride a half mile to Char-Bo Campground.*

Day 3

Seymour Lake Lodge–Old Cutter: *easy-to-moderate terrain; 35.0 miles*

Char-Bo Campground–Burke Mountain Campground: *East Burke: easy-to-moderate terrain; 41.1 miles*

0.0 *From Seymour Lake Lodge, turn left onto VT 111 East. Thereafter do not turn onto the side roads.*

Most of the first 1.5 miles goes gently uphill. Thereafter, the terrain is easy for 4.5 miles and then dramatically downhill for 1.25 miles.

0.0 *From Char-Bo Campground, turn left onto VT 105 East and follow*

it 15.7 miles all the way to the stop sign in Island Pond. There, turn right to continue on VT 105 East and ride 1.6 miles farther and then continue from Mile 11.2 below. You will have ridden about 17.3 miles when you reach the Mile 11.2 instruction.

Remember that Island Pond is the last place for supplies until East Burke.

6.7 At the stop sign, turn right onto VT 114 South toward Island Pond and Lyndonville.

The terrain continues to be easy.

9.6 At the stop sign in Island Pond, turn left onto VT 105 East.

Before leaving town, be certain you have all the food you want for the balance of the day; there is nowhere else to shop until you reach East Burke.

11.2 Just 0.1 mile beyond the sign on your right for Brighton State Park, turn right onto the unsigned road. This road is difficult to see, for it drops downhill away from VT 105. Go slowly; in 150 yards, while you are going downhill, you must cross a treacherous set of railroad tracks.

In 1.25 miles you reach the Brighton State Park beach on Island Pond on your right. It is a wonderful place to swim and picnic. The park supplies changing rooms, toilets, picnic tables, and a lifeguard; admission is charged. Island Pond takes its name from the 22-acre island in its center. After stopping, continue bicycling in the direction you were headed.

14.4 At the stop sign, turn left onto VT 114 South and VT 105 West.

16.2 Turn left to continue on VT 114 South toward East Haven and East Burke.

You start immediately up a climb of 0.8 mile. Then, after an easier mile and a half, you climb again for 1 mile. From there, you go rollicking downhill for more than 2 miles and then ride over easy terrain all the way to East Burke. Just beware of moose.

32.8 At the sign for Burke Mountain Resort, which will be difficult to see because it faces away from you and is on your left, turn left onto the road to the Old Cutter Inn and Burke Mountain Campground.

You know this road well: a climb the whole way.

35.0 *You are back where you began your tour. As you now look out over Willoughby Gap, perhaps you sense a little of the mystique of Vermont's Northeast Kingdom.*

For general information on lodging, restaurants, attractions, and special events, contact the Barton Chamber of Commerce, Barton, VT 05822 (802-525-1137); Island Pond Chamber of Commerce, PO Box 255, Island Pond, VT 05846 (802-723-6507); Lyndon Area Chamber of Commerce, PO Box 886, Lyndonville, VT 05851 (802-626-9696); or Vermont's North Country Chamber of Commerce, The Causeway, Newport, VT 05855 (802-334-7782).

Where to Stay

Old Cutter Inn, RD 1, Box 62, East Burke, VT 05832 (802-626-5152), is a red clapboard inn with white trim and window boxes brimming with petunias. Innkeepers Fritz and Marti Walther have been attentively caring for the inn and its guests since 1977. My favorite rooms are #1, which has lots of afternoon sunshine and a bath down the hall, and #7, which faces Mounts Hor and Pisgah and has its own bathroom and outdoor deck. Dining is a priority at the Old Cutter. Fritz is a fine, Swisstrained chef, and he personally prepares outstanding continental dinners as well as breakfast. The inn's sparkling pool sits in a secluded spot looking out to the mountains.

Das German Haus, PO Box 180, East Burke, VT 05832 (802-626-8568), is just a half mile from the Old Cutter. It is a cheerful B&B with splendid views and three pleasing accommodations. I would choose either the king-bedded guest room facing Willoughby Gap or the apartment downstairs with its king-sized bed, sauna, and kitchen. Innkeepers Meta and Jim Buswell are good hosts.

Seymour Lake Lodge, Box 61, Morgan, VT 05853 (802-895-2752), is a cozy hunting and fishing lodge with lots of history. The walls and bookcases are filled with photographs and books about fishing and hunting in the North Country. You can relax either on the wide porch overlooking the inn's gardens and Seymour Lake—the swimming is outstanding—or in the overstuffed chairs in the living room. I especially like the balcony room, which has a great view of the lake. Innkeepers Dave and Sue Benware are perfect for the place. Dave is a professional guide, specializing in fly-fishing; Sue oversees the chef, who prepares a fine Sunday brunch as well as dinner and breakfast.

Burke Mountain Campground, East Burke, VT 05832 (802-626-1204), opens the Friday preceding Memorial Day and closes in mid-October. The park provides 18 tent sites and 8 lean-tos. There are fireplaces, picnic tables, hot showers, toilets, and a horseshoe pit. There are no hookups, though trailers up to 24 feet can be accommodated.

Char-Bo Campground, Box 54, Derby, VT 05829 (802-766-8807), is a private campground and member of VAPCOO. It opens May 15 and closes September 30. Owners Robert and Charlotte Knowles welcome reservations for a single night. Char-Bo offers swimming in Lake Salem as well as in a pool, 42 campsites with picnic tables and fire rings, hookups, toilets, hot showers, and laundry facilities.

Bicycle Repair Services

East Burke Sports, East Burke, VT (802-626-3215)

Great Outdoors Trading Company, 73 Main Street, Newport, VT (802-334-2831)

Village Sport Shop, US 5, Lyndonville, VT (802-626-8448)

Village Bike Shop, Newport Road, Derby, VT (802-766-8009)

Western Auto Associate Store, 34 Depot Street, Lyndonville, VT (802-626-5035)

CAMBRIDGE
UNIVERSITY PRESS

University Printing House, Cambridge CB2 8BS, United Kingdom

Cambridge University Press is part of the University of Cambridge.

It furthers the University's mission by disseminating knowledge in the pursuit of education, learning and research at the highest international levels of excellence.

www.cambridge.org
Information on this title: www.cambridge.org/9780521169752

© Cambridge University Press 2011

First published 2011
Reprinted 2016

Printed in the United Kingdom by Hobbs the Printers Ltd

A catalogue record of this publication is available from the British Library

ISBN 978-0-521-16975-2 Paperback

Map artwork by Malcolm Barnes
Cover image: Thinkstock

Also from The Countryman Press and Backcountry Publications

The Countryman Press and Backcountry Publications, long known for their fine book on the outdoors, offer a range of practical and readable manuals on hiking, fishing, and canoeing.

More Biking Guides

In New England and New York
25 Bicycle Tours in Maine: Coastal & Inland Rides from Kittery to Caribou
The Bicyclist's Guide to the Southern Berkshires
25 Mountain Bike Tours in Massachusetts: From the Connecticut River to the Atlantic Coast
25 Mountain Bike Tours in Vermont: Scenic Tours Along Dirt Roads, Forest Trails, and Forgotten Byways
30 Bicycle Tours in New Hampshire: A Guide to Selected Backcountry Roads throughout the Granite State
20 Bicycle Tours in and around New York City
25 Bicycle Tours in the Hudson Valley, Second Edition
25 Bicycle Tours in the Adirondacks: Road Adventures in the East's Largest Wilderness
25 Mountain Bike Tours in the Hudson Valley

In the Mid-Atlantic States
25 Bicycle Tours in Maryland: From the Allegheny Mountains to the Atlantic Ocean
25 Bicycle Tours on Delmarva: Cycling the Chesapeake Bay Country, Second Edition (now with 28 tours)
25 Bicycle Tours in Eastern Pennsylvania: Day Trips and Overnights from Philadelphia to the Highlands
25 Bicycle Tours in New Jersey: Over 900 Miles of Scenic Pleasures and Historic Treasures
25 Bicycle Tours in and around Washington, D.C.: From the Capitol Steps to Country Roads

Farther South, Farther West
25 Bicycle Tours in Ohio's Western Reserve: Historic Northeast Ohio from the Lake Erie Islands to the Pennsylvania Border
25 Bicycle Tours in Southern Indiana: Scenic and Historic Rides through Hoosier Country
30 Bicycle Tours in Wisconsin: Lakes, Forests, and Glacier-Carved Countryside
25 Bicycle Tours in Coastal Georgia and the Carolina Low Country: Savannah, Hilton Head, and Outlying Areas
25 Bicycle Tours in the Texas Hill Country and West Texas: Adventure Rides for Road and Mountain Bikes

Our books are available at bookstores, or they may be ordered directly from the publisher. For ordering information or for a complete catalog, please contact: The Countryman Press, c/o W.W. Norton & Company, Inc., 800 Keystone Industrial Park, Scranton, PA 18512; http://web.wwnorton.com.

Cambridge E........................

L

Series edito

D0598126

No Place to Hide

Alan Battersby

CAMBRIDGE
UNIVERSITY PRESS

Contents

Characters

Nat Marley: a New York private investigator
Stella Delgado: Nat Marley's personal assistant
Patrick O'Neill: an accountant at Ocean Star Finance
Joyce O'Neill: Patrick O'Neill's wife
Julia O'Neill: Patrick and Joyce O'Neill's daughter
Ronald Steinmann: Patrick O'Neill's head of department
Lorraine Houston: the president of Ocean Star Finance
Ed Winchester: a reporter on the *Daily News*
Brett Johnson: a financial reporter on the *Daily News*
Captain Oldenberg: a detective with the New York Police Department (NYPD)
Joe Blaney: a colleague of Nat Marley, ex-NYPD
Frank Van Zandt: the owner of Frankie's Cocktail Lounge
Gina: a receptionist at the Metro Hotel

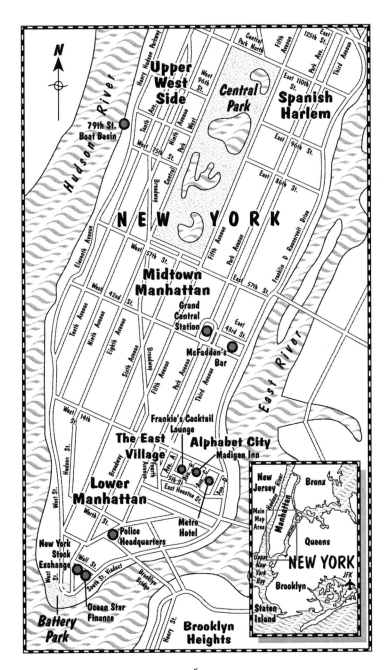

Upper West Side

West Hudson Parkway
Central Park North
Fifth Avenue
125th St.
East Ave.
Third Avenue

West 96th St.
Central Park
East 110th St.
Park Avenue

Spanish Harlem

Hudson River

79th St. Boat Basin

Tenth Ave.
Ninth Ave.
West Ave.
Park Ave.
West 75th St.
Broadway
Central
East 96th St.

East 86th St.

N E W   Y O R K

Eleventh Avenue
West 57th St.
Fifth Avenue
Park Avenue
Franklin D. Roosevelt Drive

Midtown Manhattan

West 42nd St.
Tenth Avenue
Ninth Avenue
Eighth Avenue
Broadway
Sixth Avenue
Fifth Avenue
Park Avenue
Third Avenue
East 57th St.

Grand Central Station
East 43rd St.

McFadden's Bar

East River

West 14th

Frankie's Cocktail Lounge

The East Village
Alphabet City
Madigan Inn

Hudson St.
West St.
Broadway
Ave. A
Ave. B
Ave. C
Ave. D
5th St.
East Houston St.

Lower Manhattan

Worth St.
Police Headquarters
Metro Hotel

New York Stock Exchange
Wall St.
South St. Viaduct
Brooklyn Bridge

Ocean Star Finance
Harry St.

Battery Park
Brooklyn Heights

New Jersey
Bronx
Hudson River
Main Map Area
Manhattan
East River
Queens
Upper New York Bay
NEW YORK
JFK
Brooklyn
Staten Island

5

Chapter 1 *New York City in fall*

Monday, October 4th. A cool, clear morning with the promise of a fine day ahead. Fall is my favorite season in this city – the break between summer heat and winter cold. It's a time when you're not trying to escape the worst of New York's weather. In the city parks, leaves on the trees were just beginning to turn red and gold.

The name's Nat Marley, licensed private investigator. Before I became an investigator, I used to be a police officer – a cop with the NYPD, the New York Police Department. Since then, I've worked for myself. So what does "private investigator" make you think of? A cool handsome guy with an exciting, sometimes dangerous, job? Think again. Some of the time I'm looking for missing persons. Or maybe I'm watching a husband to find out if he's seeing another woman. And when I look in the mirror, I see an ordinary guy in his forties who's losing his hair.

As usual, I caught the number seven subway train from my home in Flushing Main Street, Queens, to Midtown Manhattan.

Through Queens, the subway runs above the streets. Below you can see different areas, each home to people from around the world – Flushing: Chinese and Koreans, Corona Heights: Central and South Americans. At Grand Central Station I picked up two coffees. Crowds of New Yorkers were hurrying out onto 42nd Street. Then, like any other day, I walked the couple of blocks to my office at 220, East 43rd Street.

My personal assistant, Stella Delgado, was already at her desk opening the mail. She's a smart, good-looking Puerto Rican who understands everything about computers. She's been with me for most of the time I've been a private investigator. Stella comes from Spanish Harlem, on the Upper East Side of Manhattan – a part of the city where tourists don't go. On the streets there you'll hear more Spanish than English. She never finished school, but later, as an adult, went to night school. She's worked hard for what she has now – a job, comfortable home and loving family.

"How are you doing, Stella?" I asked. "I got coffee for you."

"Thanks. I'm fine," she replied. "Could you leave it on the desk?"

A knock at the door. Two women entered. One, a lady in her middle fifties, dressed in a dark green suit. The suit looked expensive, but she looked worried. The other, a young woman in her twenties. I compared their faces – they had to be mother and daughter.

"Do I have the right place?" said the mother. "This is the Marley Detective Agency?"

"That's correct, ma'am. The name's Nat Marley. What can I do for you?" I asked.

"Well, it's kind of difficult ..." she started.

"Come through to my office and take a seat," I said. "Your names, please?"

"I'm Joyce O'Neill and this is my daughter, Julia," said the mother. "It's about my husband, Patrick. He's disappeared

7

and I really need to find him. It doesn't matter how much it costs."

"I'm very sorry to hear that, ma'am," I said. "Let's take it slowly, from the beginning."

She looked at me with large sad eyes. "I haven't seen him since Saturday night. When I woke up Sunday morning, he was gone. He left this message on the kitchen table." She took a postcard from her purse and read to me:

"My dear Joyce. Don't worry. I'm safe, but I can't come home. The thing is, I know something which puts me and maybe you in danger. Don't phone me, or my office or the NYPD. If anyone asks for me, say I'm out of town. Trust me. Stay at Julia's place and wait for my call. All my love. Patrick."

"I have an apartment in Hamilton Heights, near Columbia University," Julia explained. "Mom has been staying with me there since Sunday."

"Mr. Marley, I'm worried sick," Joyce O'Neill continued. "Patrick's never done anything like this before."

I knew it could be bad news when someone disappears. But I didn't want to make her any more worried than she was already.

"There can be many reasons why someone disappears," I said. "Let's not expect the worst. Did your husband call?"

She nodded. "He's OK, but said he had to hide while he decided what to do. He wouldn't tell me what was happening. He just said the less I knew, the safer I would be. I just don't know what to do."

"It sounds like he's in immediate danger," I said. "It would be useful to know as much as possible about your husband."

I learned that Patrick O'Neill worked as an accountant. His employer was a firm on Wall Street called Ocean Star Finance. He had worked there for over ten years. His home address was Henry Street, Brooklyn Heights. His photograph showed a tall, gray-haired guy with black metal glasses, but there was nothing special about him. He had been married for twenty-three years. He was just an ordinary family man, with a daughter studying for her MBA at Columbia University.

"There must be a good reason why your husband asked you not to call his office. So tell me some more about his work," I said.

"Patrick's the second highest person in his department," Joyce O'Neill answered. "The head of department is Ronald Steinmann."

"What kind of guy is this Steinmann?" I asked.

"He's good at his job – excellent in fact, though he's not well liked. Patrick and Steinmann aren't the best of friends."

"A few more questions, if you don't mind," I continued. "Has your husband been acting strangely or differently in any way?"

She thought carefully before answering. "I can't say he has. His work's really important to him. He often has to work late, and he sometimes brings work home – that's normal."

"I'm afraid I have to ask this. Could there be another woman?" I asked her.

She looked at me angrily, then said, "Sorry. I guess it's your job to ask. My husband has never even looked at another woman."

"One final question," I said. "It's useful to know how carefully a missing person has planned to disappear. Has your husband taken anything with him? Did he pack clothes? Did he take the car?"

"The car's gone, and he took a travel bag with a change of clothes and some books," she replied.

"Thanks, ma'am. You've been really helpful," I said. "I'll do everything possible to find out what's happened. I'll need to visit you at your home later to look at your husband's papers and computer. That might give me some ideas. Could you meet me there at three o'clock?"

After Mrs O'Neill and her daughter had left, I looked out of the window. The sun was trying to make the gray buildings of East 43rd Street look beautiful. It would need to try harder. So a normal, hard-working guy had suddenly disappeared. He could be in serious trouble. I had thought this was going to be another ordinary day. My mistake.

Chapter 2 *Wall Street*

I told Stella what I'd learned so far. As I talked, her fingers flew over the computer keyboard.

"Take a look, Nat," she said. "The latest information from the Ocean Star Finance website."

It was an investment firm on Wall Street, the financial center of America. "Investment" meant lending out its clients' money on international money markets to make more money. So their already rich clients became even richer. Also, it seemed to be one of the best firms – a favorite of many famous New Yorkers. Year after year Ocean Star had returned excellent money to its clients. It was like a money-making machine.

The head of the firm was Lorraine Houston. She was well known to the public through TV talk shows and magazine stories about her homes on Long Island and in New England. Her clothes only came from the best stores. She'd lived the American Dream – the daughter of a poor New Jersey family who had become the president of Ocean Star.

I decided to call O'Neill's office and spoke with his personal assistant. I let her think I had some money to invest. Of course, it wasn't the truth – I've never had enough money to save much. But after fifteen years in the NYPD, I'd learned how to tell a good lie.

"This is Mr. Marley," I told her. "I'd like to meet with Mr. O'Neill this afternoon. I just wanted to check if he could see me at three thirty."

11

"I'm sorry," said the personal assistant. "Mr. O'Neill called this morning to say he was sick."

"Really? In that case, I'll have to speak to the head of department," I said.

"I'm afraid that's not possible," she replied. "You see, Mr. Steinmann doesn't work here anymore. He left the firm on Friday."

"Left the firm?" I asked. "Why? Did he find another job?"

"I couldn't say, sir," replied the personal assistant.

"Whose decision was this?" I asked.

"I don't know," she said.

"Do you mean you don't know or you're not allowed to tell me?" I asked.

"As I said before, sir, I really couldn't say," she said.

Something felt wrong. Both the head guys in the department had gone? Working at Ocean Star didn't seem too good for your health. Was it Steinmann's decision to leave? You know what they say when someone suddenly leaves a job? "Did he jump or was he pushed?"

Stella was going through the mail. I picked up the phone bill.

"Ouch! That's going to hurt my wallet!" I said. "Did we really make that many calls? Well, we'd better find Patrick O'Neill quickly and make ourselves some money. Come on, Stella. We're going to visit Wall Street. Let's see if we can find out anything more on Ocean Star."

Some investigators take cabs everywhere. Not me. If possible, I take public transportation, the New York subway. It's cheap, fast and much safer than it used to be when I was a cop. We took a train from Grand Central Station to Wall Street. While traveling downtown, I described a plan to

12

Stella. It was, of course, going to mean telling some more lies.

"When we get to Ocean Star, we check in with reception and let them think we're millionaires with money to invest. We'll tell them we need financial advice and ask to meet with one of their advisors immediately. Let's see what they can offer us. We'll act all unsure, and ask for promises that our investment will be completely safe. I'll do most of the talking and you watch the advisor."

From the subway station, we walked east, past the New York Stock Exchange. Outside the building, tourists were busy taking pictures. Ahead of us we could see the full height of the New Century Building. Thirty floors of glass and metal, a wall of silver in the sunshine. Ocean Star Finance used the top four floors.

At the reception desk, you could almost smell money in the air. The black office furniture looked expensive and the carpets were deep and soft. A meeting was soon organized. Yes, they wanted to talk to the millionaires. It's true what people say – money does open doors. The advisor gave complete answers to my questions and seemed to be sure of herself. Finally I asked, "So you can promise us a return of up to fifteen per cent on our investment by this time next year? No problem?"

"None at all," she said immediately. "You don't need to worry. We offer the best service on Wall Street."

Afterwards, I asked Stella for her thoughts. "You know, Nat, it was like listening to an actor who'd learned her lines well," she said. "She was giving the usual message: 'Don't worry. What could possibly go wrong?' But you know and I know that's not always the case in the world of finance."

I told Stella I was going to take an early lunch at McFadden's Bar to talk with the people from the *Daily News*.

The information I needed to know about Ocean Star couldn't be found on the internet. I wanted the inside information. McFadden's, on the corner of East 42nd Street and Second Avenue, was the second home of *Daily News* reporters. These guys often knew much more than they could write about in their newspaper – the kind of news that could be dangerous.

Inside the bar, the lunchtime crowd was beginning to come in. I looked around and saw a tall man with white hair among a group of younger reporters. He was Ed Winchester, a reporter who had been with the *Daily News* longer than I could remember. He had helped me several times in the past.

"Nat! Over here. And while you're at the bar, get me another drink," he called, waving an empty glass.

I knew that the price of information from Ed would be a beer, but that was cheap enough. I ordered two beers and went over to Ed. He had moved to an empty table and pushed a chair toward me.

"Well, Nat, what brings you here?" he asked. "You got that 'I need to know something' look on your face."

I described what had happened during the morning and what I already knew. "It seems kind of strange to me. One of the two head guys in the department has suddenly left and the other has disappeared on sick leave."

Ed thought carefully. "Finance isn't my field, but there's a young friend of mine who might be able to help." He went over to the reporters and returned with a guy in his twenties. "Nat, I'd like to introduce Brett Johnson, a financial reporter on the Wall Street page. Brett, Mr. Marley needs anything you might have on Ocean Star Finance."

"OK, Mr. Marley," Brett began. "There are two sides to the story. Each year, Ocean Star makes excellent money for its clients. How can they do it? Is it just luck? Or is Lorraine Houston really a financial superwoman?

"Second, if Ocean Star can make such good money, then why aren't all the other firms on Wall Street doing the same thing? However, I don't have all of the facts, so that's why you haven't read about it."

"Thanks, Brett. You've given me something to think about," I said.

Chapter 3 *Brooklyn Heights*

After lunch I met Stella at Grand Central Station by the information desk, under the big clock. We were going to see Joyce O'Neill at her home on Henry Street, Brooklyn Heights. As usual, we took the subway.

Henry Street is just one block away from the subway station. On either side of Henry Street are lines of old brownstone houses, built in the nineteenth century. We walked in the sunshine to the house.

The O'Neills opened the door before I could knock. Joyce O'Neill looked terrible – she was crying and her eyes were red. Julia was holding her mother's hand. "Please come in," said Mrs. O'Neill.

As she was speaking, the phone rang. She picked it up and said, "Joyce O'Neill speaking." Then she slowly put it down.

"Nobody there. That's the third time today," she told me.

"I'll check that number if I may?" I asked. I called the service to find out who last phoned. As I expected, it refused to give me a number. I didn't want to make Mrs. O'Neill any more worried. "No luck. It wouldn't tell me anything – maybe just a wrong number. But if it happens again, tell me. Now, this morning I called your husband's office at Ocean Star – I let them think I was a client. I was told he was on sick leave. And another thing. Steinmann has left the firm. I couldn't find out why."

"Really?" said Mrs. O'Neill. "What on earth's going on?"

"I wish I knew," I said. "While we're here, we'd like to find out more about your husband – his interests, what kind of person he is. You never know, any little thing could be important. Does he have a home office?"

"Sure, it's through here," said Mrs. O'Neill.

The room looked out onto the street. On either side of the window were pictures of old New York. Under the window was a desk with nine drawers and on the desk sat a computer. On the other walls were bookshelves.

"Ms. Delgado will look through your husband's computer files, if that's OK with you," I told her.

Stella turned on the computer, but of course, we needed the password.

Julia spelled it for Stella: "It's J-U-L-I-E. That's what my father always calls me."

While Stella continued with the computer, I began my search through the books. They were of little interest to us. Then I continued with the drawers of the desk. Again, I discovered nothing that might help us until I tried to open the final drawer – it was locked. But a minute's work with a small knife was enough to open it. It was full of books about card games, mainly poker. I read the titles: *Ninety-nine Ways to Win at Poker*, *Poker – Use Your Intelligence and Win*, *The Complete Poker Player* and so on.

O'Neill had read every book carefully. On most pages there were notes in pencil – the sort of notes that only a serious student of the game would make. Was he hiding the books from his wife? I showed them to Mrs. O'Neill.

"Could you tell me if this is your husband's handwriting?" I asked.

"Yes, that's Patrick's," she replied.

"Did you realize that your husband was interested in card games?" I asked her.

"I had no idea. It's a complete surprise. That's something he never talked about. And I thought I knew everything about him," she said sadly.

Stella opened O'Neill's email and I waited patiently as she checked through all the information. Finally, she was ready.

"Most of what I've opened here seems to be quite normal," said Stella. "Work letters mainly. But there's something here – the last email to Steinmann, sent on Friday afternoon. It reads, 'I didn't think you could be so stupid. I can't believe what you've done.'"

"Do you have any idea what this could be about?" I asked Mrs. O'Neill.

"It could be some kind of disagreement," she replied.

Stella needed Mrs. O'Neill's help to get into the family bank accounts. She entered the numbers and soon the information came up on the screen. There was a joint account in the names of Patrick and Joyce O'Neill, and also an account in Joyce O'Neill's name. The joint account seemed normal, as did Mrs. O'Neill's account. But we needed another password to open Patrick O'Neill's account.

Mrs. O'Neill went straight to the kitchen and returned with a little notebook. "Patrick said I should keep this in a safe place. If anything happened to him, I'd be able to find the information on the computer." She passed the book to Stella, who searched through it to find the necessary numbers. New information came on the screen and Stella now looked more serious.

"Mrs. O'Neill, do you know someone called F. Van Zandt?" she asked.

"I've never heard the name," she answered. "Why?"

"Well, if you look here, there have been several large payments to this Van Zandt over the last six months," Stella explained.

Mrs. O'Neill looked at the screen and put her hand to her mouth. "I just don't understand," she said. "This last payment is $15,000! And look here. Patrick took out $10,000 this morning."

"There's more," said Stella. "Two large payments to Steinmann during the past three months. Over $25,000."

"I really can't understand it," said Mrs. O'Neill.

"There must be a good reason," I said. "Van Zandt's an unusual name, so I hope it won't be too much trouble to find him – or her."

I had a good idea what was going on. O'Neill could be a secret poker player. Those payments could mean that he'd lost heavily at poker and was paying back the winner month by month. But why had he paid all that money to Steinmann?

Chapter 4   *A voice from the past*

Tuesday, October 5th. Stella and I were at East 43rd Street early. Now we had another person to find.

"Stella, see if you can find a phone number for this Van Zandt," I asked. "I'll look for a number for Steinmann."

My search was much faster than Stella's. It was all there in the phone book – the number and an address on West 75th Street, on the Upper West Side near Central Park. You needed serious money to live in that part of town.

I made the call. "Good morning. May I speak with Mr. Steinmann?" I asked.

"Who are you and what's your business with Mr. Steinmann?" answered a loud voice. A voice I knew very well – Captain Oldenberg of the NYPD. What was he doing there? I wondered.

"Oldenberg! Great to hear your voice again!" I said. "Remember me? Nat Marley. Why, it only seems like yesterday when we used to be cops together."

Oldenberg didn't want to talk about old times. "Just answer the question, Marley!" he shouted.

"OK, OK. I'm making the call for a client. Mr. Steinmann is the head of her husband's department. It's important that I speak with him."

"Very interesting," replied Oldenberg. "That's going to be kind of difficult. You see, Steinmann has disappeared. Nobody's seen him since Friday. How about you tell me what's going on?"

I knew I might need Oldenberg's help. I told myself to be patient. "My client's husband is in some kind of trouble," I said. "I thought his boss could help with a few questions."

"I get the picture," said Oldenberg. "As usual, you can't tell me the full story. But let me tell you this, Marley. Don't try hiding information that could help my investigation, or else I'll have you at Police Headquarters for questioning."

Message received and understood. Oldenberg was a good cop and was doing his job. But, as I knew from the old days with the NYPD, he was neither the friendliest nor the easiest guy to work with.

As soon as I put the phone down, it rang. It was Mrs. O'Neill. She had returned home to Henry Street to pick up a change of clothes and she had found the front door wide open. Someone had broken into the house. I remembered the calls that Mrs. O'Neill had received yesterday. Now I knew that someone was checking to see when the house was empty.

"Is anything missing?" I asked.

"I really don't know. Please come quickly. I'm so afraid they'll come back," she said.

"Don't touch anything," I told her. "Can you wait with a neighbor? … Good. I'm on my way."

I left Stella looking for phone numbers for Van Zandts. I took another subway ride to Brooklyn Heights. With the number of traffic lights between Midtown Manhattan and Brooklyn, the subway was always faster. I called Mrs. O'Neill's cellphone five minutes before I arrived. She was standing by the front door, her hands shaking.

"Mr. Marley, this is just horrible. It must be something to do with my poor Patrick," she cried.

She led me into the house. Someone had made a complete mess of the home office. All the books were off the shelves, with their pages open. Empty desk drawers were lying on the carpet. The computer was still there, but when I felt around the back of the machine, it was open. The hard drive was missing.

"Look here," I said. "That's what they were looking for – information on the hard drive. But if they don't find what they're looking for on the hard drive they could return and you'll be in serious danger. So I don't want you to return to this house again."

"I'll stay at Julia's until this is over," Mrs O'Neill said sadly.

"OK. We have to make sure this house is safe before you leave," I said. "I'll call a twenty-four hour lock service. You'll need new, stronger locks. I'll stay here while we wait."

I would probably have a couple of hours to wait with Mrs. O'Neill. It was a chance to ask a few more questions and get a better picture of her husband. I didn't think she realized how much danger she could be in. When would she agree to call the NYPD?

"Mrs. O'Neill, what can you tell me about your husband's boss, Steinmann?" I started. "Yesterday you said they weren't the best of friends."

"A couple of years ago, Patrick had the chance to become the department head. He was the right person for the job and he was well liked. Unfortunately, he didn't get the job, though that wasn't his fault. Lorraine Houston, the president, wanted someone fresh and new from outside. She preferred the kind of guy who didn't care if he wasn't liked. So Steinmann got the job. Patrick continued with his work as best as he could, but there was no friendship between him and Steinmann."

"Thanks. That's useful to know. Has your husband always lived in Brooklyn?" I went on.

"No. We moved here when Julia was just a kid. Patrick's family are Irish-American. His grandparents arrived in the U.S. from Dublin in the 1920s. They more or less got off the ship and moved straight to the East Village. Patrick grew up in Alphabet City, on 10th Street."

Alphabet City is the part of the East Village which gets its name from Avenues A, B, C and D, which cut across it. It didn't use to be a safe area. In fact, it was a center for drugs and crime. But now things have changed. Today you can find cool cafés, bars and stores in the area.

"So he didn't come from a rich family?" I asked.

"Not at all. Patrick's parents had a hard life. They never lived the American Dream. It wasn't easy for Patrick, either. He's the youngest of six children, so there was no question of the family paying for college. Patrick did it the hard way and paid for everything by working nights at a 24/7 store. He never had the advantages that I had."

"Where do you think he might hide to escape from somebody?" I asked. "Where would he feel safest in this city?"

"I couldn't say for sure. But the area he knows best of all is the East Village," she replied.

"Right. Now, Mrs. O'Neill, I don't want to worry you more than necessary, but I think you're in real danger. The people that broke into your house could come back. I think we should call the NYPD."

Mrs. O'Neill got up from her armchair, walked over to the window and looked out into the street.

At last she spoke: "Mr. Marley, I know you're offering the best advice. But you remember what Patrick said in his message: 'Don't call the NYPD.' Those are his wishes, and I have to follow them."

Chapter 5 *Death by the Hudson River*

It was midday before I got back to East 43rd Street. I picked up a snack at Grand Central Station before returning to the office. It hadn't taken Stella long to find phone numbers for Van Zandts. There were over fifty in all of New York City.

"OK, Stella. We can share this job," I said. "I'll take the first phone book and you can start on the second. Say you're an old friend of O'Neill's and that you're trying to find him."

It was slow and boring work, but I felt it would be worth it in the end. "Good afternoon. Is this Mr. Van Zandt? If I could have a minute of your time? … You see, I'm trying to find an old friend of mine, Patrick O'Neill … Would you know him? … No? OK. Thanks for your time."

As the calls continued, I wasn't feeling too hopeful. Then I got an answering machine. I listened to the message: "I'm sorry I can't get to the phone right now. Leave a message or phone 212-555-01230."

I called the number. The phone was answered after a couple of rings. First the sound of jazz music, then a voice: "Frankie's Cocktail Lounge."

"Good afternoon. Is that Mr. Van Zandt?" I asked.

"Hold on …" I heard the guy shout above the noise, "Frank! Call for you."

Could this finally be the right Van Zandt? I waited patiently.

"Frank Van Zandt speaking."

"If I could have a moment of your time, Mr. Van Zandt," I began. "I've lost the phone number and address of an old friend, Patrick O'Neill. Would you know how I could find him?"

"Oh yeah? I might. Who's asking?" replied Van Zandt.

Not very welcoming, I thought. Time to tell another lie.

"The name's Marley. I'm an old college friend. Patrick and I were at accounting school together."

"If you're so clever, mister, look in the phone book. And don't call again," he added, then put the phone down.

The line went dead – clearly this guy didn't like me asking after O'Neill. This time I felt I was in luck. Perhaps I should visit Frankie's Cocktail Lounge. Before I could organize anything, the phone rang. I picked it up and heard that voice from the past again – Captain Oldenberg.

"Marley!" he shouted. "Your line's been busy for ages. Could I have a minute of your valuable time?"

"Sure. Go ahead." I replied, holding the phone away from my ear.

"Get yourself to the 79th Street Boat Basin. I got something to show you." He laughed.

When Oldenberg laughs, it usually means bad news.

"OK. But why? What's going on?" I asked.

"It's a surprise. But I want you here now," Oldenberg ordered.

I told Stella what was happening. She gave me a smile and said, "Don't get mad at Oldenberg. Remember, we may need his help."

I was back on the subway again, this time to West 79th Street. I walked the two blocks from the subway station west toward the Hudson River, and crossed the Riverside

Park to the boat basin. From here you could see across the river to New Jersey. The temperature had dropped and the sky was full of heavy gray clouds. A cold wind started to blow from the west.

All around the boat basin were houseboats. I've heard it's the cheapest way to live in this city. Ahead I could see NYPD cars in a parking lot near the river. As I got closer, an NYPD cop stopped me and said, "Sorry, sir. You can't enter."

"The name's Marley. Captain Oldenberg's expecting me," I replied.

"OK. Come with me and we'll find the captain," said the cop.

Oldenberg was standing in the parking lot behind a Chevrolet Impala. He was smiling, which always made me feel uncomfortable.

"Take a look at this," said Oldenberg, waving at the car.

Oldenberg moved to the back of the car and opened the trunk. Inside was a dead man.

Oldenberg called to the police doctor. "Could you show me his face again, Doc?" he asked. "OK, Marley, time for your surprise!"

The NYPD doctor was wearing a suit of white material over her clothes, and white plastic gloves and shoes. She carefully took the dead man's head in her hands and moved it round so we could see the face. His skin was gray and his mouth was open. Between his eyes was a hole.

"Marley, meet Ronald Steinmann. Doc, would you tell Mr. Marley what you know?" said Oldenberg.

"I'd say he's been dead about two or three days. A single shot to the head. You see these cuts around his face? This guy was hit hard a number of times before he died. Can't tell you much more just now," the police doctor told me.

Heavy rain began to fall. I was feeling sick. Although I've seen dead bodies before, I still get that same horrible feeling.

"I just checked the license plate. This car belongs to Mr. Patrick O'Neill, Henry Street, Brooklyn. We need to talk, Marley," said Oldenberg. "And I guess you need a drink. Let's go somewhere warmer."

Oldenberg took me to the Boat Basin Café, where he ordered me a double Scotch. The drink was just the right medicine.

"Marley, I got an idea and I think I may be right. Your client could be Patrick O'Neill, an accountant with Ocean Star Finance? Or one of his family?" he asked.

I nodded. The safest thing was to listen and see what Oldenberg wanted.

"Steinmann disappeared some time on Friday afternoon. I've been asking questions at Ocean Star. On Friday morning, people heard Steinmann and O'Neill arguing. This was no conversation between friends. People said it was more like a fight. It was behind closed doors so they couldn't say what they were arguing about. Today Steinmann is found in O'Neill's car, murdered. At the same time nobody seems to know where O'Neill is. You see where this is leading?"

I understood very well. The sick feeling in my stomach started to get stronger.

"I'm talking murder, Marley. I want to question Patrick O'Neill about the murder of Ronald Steinmann. I want to know why O'Neill was paying money into Steinmann's account. Also, the reason why O'Neill had sent him an angry email. It began, 'I didn't think you could be so stupid.' That means I have to find him and I believe you know where he is. You used to be a cop, Marley, so you know the way the police work. If you refuse to tell me, that's a crime."

I held my head in my hands. I could only tell Oldenberg the truth. That wouldn't be what he wanted to hear.

"Believe me, Oldenberg, I'm being completely straight with you. I have no idea where O'Neill is. Yes, my client is his wife. All she knows is that her husband is hiding somewhere."

"OK. Another thing, Marley. I have to question Mrs. O'Neill, but I can't find her. I just get the answering machine every time I call. I need your help," said Oldenberg.

"OK, Oldenberg. I'll see what I can do," I replied.

On the journey back to East 43rd Street, I thought about the information I already knew. I took a fresh page in my notebook and wrote down the facts I knew for sure and the questions that needed answers.

I knew O'Neill had disappeared sometime between Saturday night and Sunday morning. He didn't like his boss, Steinmann, and on Friday he'd argued with him. Also, he had sent an angry email to Steinmann. O'Neill had made large payments to Steinmann and Van Zandt. He was interested in poker. Someone had broken into his house and stolen the hard drive of his computer. Now the police had found Steinmann dead in the trunk of O'Neill's car.

What was I less sure about? What did O'Neill know which put him in danger? Had Steinmann known the same thing? Had O'Neill lost heavily at poker? Was Ocean Star in difficulties? What could explain those payments to Steinmann and Van Zandt? And finally, could a guy like O'Neill kill? The more I thought about it, Ocean Star had to be the key to all the questions.

I called Mrs. O'Neill at her daughter's apartment. "You said that your husband took his car when he disappeared," I said.

"That's right. It's not parked in the street," she replied.

"I'm afraid I have some terrible news. This morning, Steinmann's body was found in the trunk of your husband's car."

I heard a scream over the phone, then nothing.

"Are you still there?" I asked.

"Yes," she replied quietly. "This is just awful. I can't believe it. So what happens now?"

"The police are now looking for your husband," I explained. "I'm sorry, but you'll have to talk to the police."

"I realize I don't have any choice," replied Mrs. O'Neill. "But there's one condition. The meeting should be at your office on East 43rd Street."

Chapter 6   *Questions and answers*

Wednesday, October 6th. Captain Oldenberg and Mrs. O'Neill were in my office at nine o'clock. Mrs. O'Neill was wearing a very fashionable black jacket and skirt with a white blouse. Maybe she did her shopping on Fifth Avenue. Oldenberg was dressed in an ugly brown suit with an orange tie – clothes that had been in fashion sometime during the last century.

Before Oldenberg started questioning Mrs. O'Neill, I told him what I knew about Patrick O'Neill. I was trying to show the captain that O'Neill was just a good ordinary guy, not a murderer.

"As I see it, Patrick O'Neill could be in the middle of something very dangerous," I began. "So far, we have no clear idea of what that might be. We can't be sure if the key to this case is Ocean Star or something that happened between O'Neill and Steinmann – or both.

"Let's move on to O'Neill, the person. We have a happily-married family man who's worked for the same employer for over ten years. In that time he's risen to be second in his department. He's given years of his life to the firm. Also, he has no criminal history."

Oldenberg started to question Mrs. O'Neill. As I thought, his main interest was the argument between O'Neill and Steinmann.

"Mrs. O'Neill," said Oldenberg, "I was told at Ocean Star that your husband and Steinmann argued on Friday before they both disappeared. We don't know what it was about, but people heard Mr. O'Neill shouting. Would you say they worked well together?"

"It was never easy for Patrick," she replied. "Steinmann pushed people hard. Second best was never good enough for him. I can't say Patrick liked him, but he did his work as well as he could."

"Two years ago, your husband had the chance to become the department head. But Lorraine Houston brought in Steinmann. How did your husband feel about this?" asked Oldenberg.

"At the time he was angry, but he learned to accept what had happened. Life has to go on," Mrs. O'Neill replied.

"Could you think of anybody who would want to kill Steinmann?" Oldenberg asked her.

"No," she replied. "OK, so he's not the nicest of guys, but that's no reason for murder."

"Your husband was paying money to Steinmann. Do you have any idea why?" Oldenberg went on.

"None at all," Mrs. O'Neill replied.

Oldenberg continued with questions about the angry email, which Mrs. O'Neill answered patiently. At last, he said, "One more thing, Mrs. O'Neill. Would you agree to a search of your house?"

"I guess I have to," she replied, and handed him her keys. "Go ahead and do it."

"Thanks," he said. "If I'm going to get any further with this case, I must find him. Will you call him?"

Mrs. O'Neill looked him straight in the eyes and said, "That's impossible. Patrick only calls me from pay phones."

"Patrick O'Neill is wanted for murder," Oldenberg said. "And if you, Marley, or you, Mrs. O'Neill, know where he is, and refuse to tell me, that's a crime. You could both find yourselves in jail."

Mrs. O'Neill looked angrily at Oldenberg. If looks could kill, he would be a dead man.

After Oldenberg had left the building, Mrs. O'Neill started to cry.

"I'm sure Patrick has nothing to do with Steinmann's murder," she said. "But what if the police don't believe me? And what if the people who killed Steinmann go after Patrick next?"

"I will find him, I promise you," I said. "But you must be careful. When you get back to Julia's apartment, stay inside, OK? Stella, could you call a cab for Mrs. O'Neill?"

When Mrs. O'Neill had left, I organized some help from an old friend who used to be a policeman like myself. A guy who was as useful as ten NYPD officers – Joe Blaney. He'd taught me more about staying alive on the streets of Manhattan than you could ever learn at Police Academy. He's the sort of person you needed if there was going to be trouble and he knew how to use a gun. I last carried a gun when I was a New York cop. I haven't carried one since and haven't wanted to – but there are times when one is necessary.

I picked up the phone. "Joe, I have work for you. It could be dangerous, so bring a gun. A missing person's in danger, and we're going to find him. Come to East 43rd Street with your car, as soon as you can."

Chapter 7   *Frankie's Cocktail Lounge*

The plan was that Joe and I would pay a visit to Van Zandt and see if he could lead us to O'Neill. Meanwhile, Mrs. O'Neill would come back to the office that afternoon and stay with Stella.

Joe Blaney arrived in his car soon after midday. He's in his middle-sixties, but he's tall and slim with a full head of white hair. Although he's probably twenty years older than me, I'd say he looks younger. Some guys have all the luck.

In the car, Joe pulled his jacket to one side to show me the gun. "Let's hope we don't have to use this, boss," he said. We drove downtown on Second Avenue toward 4th Street. The traffic wasn't too heavy and we soon arrived in the East Village. We went straight along 4th Street to Avenue A. Frankie's Cocktail Lounge was on 5th Street, between Avenues A and B.

Joe stopped the car. Above the double doors, I could read the words: "Frankie's – Cold Drinks, Warm People, Hot Sounds".

"Let's do it," I said.

We went into Frankie's and sat at a table. At first, it seemed almost dark, but soon I could see better. It was a comfortable room with armchairs, sofas, red carpets and the sound of jazz guitar music. We needed clear heads so we ordered two coffees, not the Cocktail Specials. There were no customers at the bar, so I had a look at who was working behind it. A couple of bartenders and someone who I guessed must be the boss. He was medium height with a short black beard, but without a single hair on his head.

"I think we've found Van Zandt," I said, looking toward the bar. "We'll try and have a little talk."

I walked over to the bar with Joe. Van Zandt looked up from some papers he was checking.

"Would you be Mr. Van Zandt?" I asked.

"That's me," he replied. "What can I do for you?"

"Could I talk to you about Patrick O'Neill?" I asked.

"Who are you?" Van Zandt asked carefully and gave me a cold, hard look.

"Nat Marley, licensed private investigator," I said. "I spoke to you on the phone yesterday. I believe you know O'Neill. His wife's very worried about him and I think you could help."

"I don't have to talk to you!" he said angrily.

Suddenly a big strong bartender was standing in front of me.

"You got a problem, boss?" he asked Van Zandt.

"It's OK," I said quietly. "We're not looking for trouble. Look, take my cellphone and press 'Call'. You'll get my office. Ask to talk with O'Neill's wife."

Van Zandt did as I said and spent a couple of minutes checking facts with Mrs. O'Neill. After a while he returned the cellphone and said, "OK. What do you want?" He waved the bartender away and led us to a room behind the bar. Inside, the air didn't smell too fresh – old cigarette smoke. Van Zandt found chairs and sat us at a round table. I introduced Joe, then began questioning Van Zandt.

"I believe that O'Neill has paid you a lot of money?" I asked. "You're not stealing from him, I hope."

"It's not robbery," replied Van Zandt. "That's what I won fairly in a poker game. It works both ways. Patrick's an excellent player and I've paid him thousands when I lost. We're old friends. I've known him since we were both kids, working nights at a 24/7 store."

"So explain this," I continued. "Why does a Wall Street accountant come to a back room in the East Village to play poker?"

"I've met several guys like Patrick – hard-working family men who earn good money. But they want a little more from life. Maybe they're just bored so I give them a good time. I know organizing back-room poker games is a crime, but I'm not hurting anybody. These guys have the money – like Patrick's boss, Steinmann. I'm just offering them a service."

"So O'Neill brought Steinmann here?" I asked Van Zandt in surprise.

"Yeah. Once or twice. I don't think Patrick really wanted to, but I guess he couldn't refuse. One night we all lost heavily to Steinmann. He played like poker was his second profession. I had to ask Patrick not to bring him again. It would hurt my bank account too much."

Van Zandt had answered two questions – why O'Neill had made payments to both himself and Steinmann.

"OK. Let's forget the money," I said. "I'm really interested in finding O'Neill. You know he's in some kind of trouble?"

"After reading about Steinmann's murder in the morning papers, I had a good idea what the trouble could be," replied Van Zandt. "Patrick got here soon after midnight, Sunday morning. He said he was in danger, but he wouldn't talk about it. He needed to hide someplace for a few days and was going to check into a hotel around here. He also told me to keep quiet if anyone came asking questions. And one last thing – he told me to expect a letter from his firm. He said it was really important and I should keep it for him."

"If it's arrived, could we take a look?" I asked.

"I guess I could show you," he said.

It was a thick envelope with the address written in O'Neill's handwriting. I took out my pocket knife and cut it open. Inside, I found some papers – probably about twenty pages. At the top of each page I could see the words "Ocean Star Finance" in red and gold letters. On every page, there were lines of numbers.

"You know what this is?" asked Van Zandt.

"I guess some sort of accounts from Ocean Star," I said. "Another guess – this information may have something to do with Steinmann's murder. Mr. Van Zandt, I'd like to thank you for your help. We may be able to reach O'Neill in time. I don't think anyone else knows these papers are here, so could you keep them in a safe place?"

Before Joe and I started searching the East Village, I called Stella to tell her what we'd discovered so far. When I'd finished, Stella said, "Mrs. O'Neill wants to speak with you."

"Mr. Marley, thank you," said Mrs. O'Neill. "You're getting close to Patrick, I can feel it. Please find him and make the police believe that my husband is no killer."

Chapter 8 *The East Village*

Our search area was wide – everything between Fourth Avenue and Avenue D, then everything between East Houston Street and East 14th Street. Within that area are fourteen streets and eight avenues. Now do the math – that makes around eighty blocks. The good news was that if O'Neill was staying in a hotel in the area, like Van Zandt said, we didn't have too many places to check. Most of the hotels are either along Third Avenue or the streets off it.

There were two problems. First, what sort of hotel would O'Neill choose? Somewhere busy, on a crowded street where he wouldn't be noticed? Or would he prefer somewhere quieter and more basic, with less activity? A place where it would be easier to watch and listen. Second, how would we find out if he was staying there? Would he check in under his own name and how could we get the hotel receptionist to tell us if he was there? Hotel receptionists don't give information about their guests to complete strangers.

So we had a plan – I'd say I had a business meeting with O'Neill. To help receptionists believe the story, I'd asked Stella to produce some company information for "Patrick O'Neill Accounting". There was a photo of O'Neill on the front, which I'd hold so the receptionist could see his face.

Time after time at hotels I introduced myself and spoke to the receptionists. "Excuse me, the name's Marley. I have a meeting with Patrick O'Neill. Would you call his room to tell him I'm at reception?"

We had no luck at the more expensive places, which were full of tourists and business people. After asking at a few, we knew what sort of answers to expect: "I'm sorry, sir. Do you have the correct hotel? … I wish I could help you, but …"

Hour after hour, our search area grew wider. We had moved away from Third Avenue, deeper into the center of the East Village, toward Alphabet City.

At some of the cheaper places, the receptionists were less patient: "We got nobody by that name staying here, mister … Look, mister, I just work here. It's not my job to remember faces."

We continued until early evening. It was six thirty, not long before sunset, and the sky in the west was growing pink. We just had one or two more places to check in Alphabet City. The next hotel, the Madigan Inn on Avenue B, looked like an ugly, dirty place, but the receptionist was helpful.

I asked the usual questions and made sure that she could see O'Neill's photo. Then the surprise – I could see from the look on her face that she knew something. "Sure I know the guy," she said. "But not by the name of O'Neill. I don't know if I'm allowed to say …"

I showed her my investigator's license and said, "The truth is, this guy's life is in danger. I'm working for his family and we need to find him quickly, before someone else does."

She believed me and turned to check the computer. "Yeah, there he is," she said. "He stayed for one night and checked out yesterday. The name he gave was Brendan Touhey."

"Can you tell me anything more?" I asked. "Did he have any visitors? How did he spend his time?"

"Well, he asked for a room on the street. That seemed to be important. He didn't have any visitors and spent most of the time in his room. I think he was watching the street. Or that's what I thought when I looked up at his window."

"Thanks," I said. "You've been really helpful."

"You could ask at our other hotel," she said. "I could phone ahead to tell them to expect you. It's the Metro, on Avenue C between 4th and 3rd."

"Please. If you would," I replied.

As we left, I said to Joe, "At last we're getting somewhere. I think I know what he's doing. Just staying a night at one place, then moving on."

Joe suddenly stopped in front of the door to the street. "Nat, you see that car just across the street?"

"The black one?" I asked.

"That's it. I think I've seen it before. Outside your office, but I couldn't be too sure," Joe went on.

I studied the car carefully. A Lexus, which costs serious money. Three guys with dark glasses were inside. It was starting to get dark and I've never liked guys who wear sunglasses at night. I had a horrible feeling that those people meant trouble.

Then the driver looked toward us and the car quickly moved along the avenue. In the poor light, I couldn't read the license plate.

"What do you think, boss?" asked Joe. "Are they following us?"

The streetlights had now come on. Under their yellow light I could see the answer to Joe's question. On the road beside Joe's car was a knife. There was no air in two of the tires so it was impossible to drive.

Now I realized what was happening. Those guys had followed us, hoping we would lead them to O'Neill. They knew we were checking hotels, and the Metro was the last one in the area. They wanted to make sure they got there first.

We ran across to Avenue C, but we were losing valuable time. The Metro, like the last hotel, looked as if nobody cared for it. The receptionist, though, was friendly and welcomed us with a smile.

"Hi, I'm Gina," she said. "You guys didn't need to hurry. We got—"

I stopped her and said, "The receptionist at the Madigan just phoned ahead and told you to expect us. We're looking for Patrick O'Neill. He's in danger and might be using a different name. Has anyone asked for him?" I showed her O'Neill's photograph.

"Oh yes," said Gina. "He's staying here, but under the name of Bernard Delaney. Nice, quiet guy. He stays in his room most of the time. There's something I don't understand. You're the second group of people asking about him. The others went up to his room five minutes ago, but they just left."

"What others?" I shouted.

"Three guys in black suits and dark glasses," she replied. "I thought they were the ones I was expecting."

"Did O'Neill leave with them?" I asked.

"No," Gina replied.

"Oh my God! Give me the room number quick!" I shouted. "I hope we're not too late!"

Chapter 9   *The Metro, Avenue C*

"Second floor, Room 219," said Gina.

No time to lose. Joe and I ran upstairs to the room. The door was open and the lock was broken. Inside, we could see that someone had quickly searched the room. An empty travel bag was lying on the floor. The blankets had been pulled off the bed, and clothes thrown around the room.

"O'Neill's not here, but those other guys won't be far away," I said. "I don't like this one bit. Let's get back to the lobby."

At the desk, I made a 911 call for the police, described the three guys and their car, and said, "I believe they're looking for Patrick O'Neill, who's staying at this hotel."

We walked out onto the street to wait for the police, who I knew ought to be here in minutes. But things now happened very quickly. A guy in dark glasses was standing opposite us, across the road. He laughed and said, "I guess you ain't going no place fast."

Then he began to cross the street, like he didn't need to hurry. He spoke again: "You guys. Just tell me where O'Neill is. Then you can go home and forget you ever saw me."

He wanted O'Neill, but we had no idea where he might be. I looked left and right along the street. On either side of us was a guy in a black suit walking slowly toward us. Both of them were carrying guns. We had no place to run, no place to hide.

Luckily, Joe was thinking more quickly than me. "Back inside the hotel, now!" he shouted and pushed me toward the entrance.

We turned and ran inside. Behind us I could hear the sound of running feet as they chased after us. "On the floor, behind the desk, now!" said Joe.

There was no time to say "If you please, ma'am" as I threw Gina to the ground. The front door opened with a crash, but Joe was ready for them. I heard two shots, followed by a scream, then everything was quiet. There was a cloud of smoke from the shots in the air. Joe was now at the desk.

"I think I hit one, but they'll be back," said Joe. "We have to hurry. Gina, you got to help us! Is there a back entrance?"

"Through here," replied Gina. "Follow me."

She led us through a door behind the desk, then down some steps. Behind us I heard a crash as the men in black returned. We were now hurrying through the hotel kitchen. I heard shouts and feet on the stairs. They were getting close.

"Turn off any lights and lock doors behind us if you can," I told Gina.

I decided to make things more difficult for the guys following us. I pulled glasses and bottles to the floor. We reached the back door just as we heard the men coming into the kitchen. There was a shot, which left a hole in the wall beside me. That was much too close. A second later, the room was in complete darkness as Gina turned off the lights. There were shouts as one of the guys fell over.

"Up these steps. Hurry!" said Gina.

We were now outside in the cold night air. We went up a few more steps, then out into a narrow street behind the hotel. In the darkness, I could just see back entrances to buildings along Avenue C. We had passed a few doors when Gina suddenly stopped. "I don't know what to do!" she screamed.

"Through this door, quickly," I ordered. "And get down!"

We hit the ground behind some boxes. It didn't smell too clean down there, but this wasn't the time to worry about the dry cleaner's bill. Gina had started to cry, so I put my hand over her mouth to keep her quiet.

"Don't make a sound,' Joe whispered. "With luck, the NYPD should arrive before they find us."

As we hid there in the darkness, we heard feet running to the left and right along the narrow street. Then we heard the steps returning more slowly, and voices.

"They got to be here someplace," said one. "They can't have gotten far."

"Start with these doors," said another. "Let's see where they're hiding."

There was crash after crash as the doors were opened. More shots. Well, that's one way to unlock a door if you don't have the key. The noise was now getting closer. I kept my hand over Gina's mouth. Her body was shaking. Finally, above the crashes and shots, a new but very welcome sound. The scream of a police car.

"It's the cops. Let's get out of here!" shouted a voice on the other side of the door.

We heard them running back toward the hotel. Then all went quiet. After waiting a few minutes, I decided it was safe to come out.

Back inside the hotel kitchen, it looked like the morning after a wild party. We walked carefully around the broken glasses and bottles on the floor. In the hotel lobby, two guys in black suits were lying on the floor. Above them stood two NYPD cops.

"Am I pleased to see you!" I said. "I'm Nat Marley, licensed private investigator. Did you catch all three of them?"

"Yes, sir. The other one is outside with the sergeant. He'll need an ambulance," said one of the cops.

"We got here just in time," said the other. "Captain Oldenberg's on his way. He'll need to question you."

Gina was feeling better. Her suit was black with dirt and oil. Mine didn't look much cleaner, though. Now I started to shake. It's always the same. It never hits me at the time, but later, when I realize I'm lucky to be alive.

"I guess I could make everyone coffee," said Gina.

"That'd be great." But then I had a sudden thought and shouted, "Joe, upstairs now!"

We ran back up to Room 219. The door was closed and when I knocked there was no reply. I put my ear to the door and listened. Somebody was moving around in the room. I tried to open the door, but there was something against it on the other side. However, it wasn't strong enough for Joe's boot and flew open. Inside we saw a man holding the travel bag.

He threw the bag into Joe's face and tried to push past me. But I was able to catch his coat and pull him to the floor. I looked at him closely – a middle-aged guy with gray hair and black metal glasses – Patrick O'Neill.

"Don't be afraid!" I said. "I'm Nat Marley, private investigator. I'm working for your wife, Joyce. You're going be safe. It's time to stop running."

Chapter 10   *Time to fight back*

There was a hopeless look in O'Neill's eyes. His lips moved, but he couldn't speak. I shook his shoulders and made him look straight at me. "Listen, we're the good guys. You're out of danger. Your wife sent us to find you."

He still seemed to be unsure, so I pulled him to his feet and tried again. "Here's my cellphone. It's calling my office number. As soon as my personal assistant answers, ask to speak to Joyce."

We waited while he spoke to his wife. He sat down on the bed as he talked. Now he looked tired and weak, like a lost child.

"If you don't mind, Mr. O'Neill, I need to talk to my personal assistant now," I said. He returned my cellphone.

"Stella, listen carefully," I said. "Call a cab, and take Mrs. O'Neill to Frankie's Cocktail Lounge on 5th Street. We're going to meet you there as soon as possible. We need to make Oldenberg believe that O'Neill is not Steinmann's killer."

Now O'Neill was beginning to look more normal. "I guess I should say sorry," he said. "How did you know where to find me?"

"I can explain that," I replied. "Through information in your bank accounts, we learned that you'd made payments to a Van Zandt. That's how we found your old friend Frank."

"So you know about the poker games," said O'Neill. "When I told Joyce I was working late, I was actually—"

"It doesn't matter now," I said. "Van Zandt told us that you'd checked into a hotel somewhere in the East Village. You heard about Steinmann's murder? The police think you did it, but I didn't think that could be true. So I thought you might be in danger too. But how did you get away from the guys in black suits?"

"I was watching the street from my window," began O'Neill. "I saw them arrive and thought they had to be bad news. I ran up to the top floor and hid in a blanket cupboard. I'd been up there for about ten minutes when I heard the shots. So I stayed there until I heard the police car arrive and came down to my floor. When I looked out of my window again, I could see the sergeant outside with one of them. Finally, I thought it was safe enough to escape."

"That letter you sent to Van Zandt. What do all those numbers mean?" I asked.

"They're the reason why Steinmann was murdered," replied O'Neill.

Suddenly, there was someone at the door. It was Captain Oldenberg. He looked around, shook his head and asked in a tired voice, "Would you mind telling me what's going on, Marley?"

"Oldenberg, let me introduce Mr. Patrick O'Neill. Mr. O'Neill was almost murdered here tonight. Thanks to the sergeant and his team, we're all still alive. Mr. O'Neill has a story to tell you. I believe that once you know all the facts, it will be clear that he can't be Steinmann's killer."

"I'm listening, Marley," said Oldenberg. "But whether he's the killer is for the police to decide, not you."

"Mr. O'Neill can show you all the information you need," I continued. "If you agree, it means a quick journey to Frankie's Cocktail Lounge on 5th Street. Everything's there."

"Agreed," said Oldenberg. "But for the moment, O'Neill, you're still wanted for murder, and that means you're my prisoner. Anyway, I guess Police Headquarters will be rather safer than this hotel."

We all went downstairs, back to reception, where Oldenberg organized everyone. "Sergeant, you're coming with me and O'Neill. Have your men take away the other two prisoners and one officer should stay with the guy who was shot."

Joe had to leave and get some help with his car. Oldenberg drove us through the East Village back to 5th Street. Frankie's Cocktail Lounge was now noisy with the evening crowd. A jazz band was getting ready to play. I saw Stella and Mrs. O'Neill sitting at a corner table, waiting for us to arrive.

"Your husband's outside, Mrs. O'Neill," I told her. "If you could be patient for a few more minutes, I'll find somewhere less public to talk."

I went over to the bar and shouted above the noise to the bartender. "I need to speak to Frank. Where can I find him?"

"In the back room," answered the bartender. "Just go straight through."

I coughed as I entered because the air was heavy with cigarette smoke. "O'Neill's outside with the police," I said. "Could we meet in here? Oh, and we'll need that envelope."

"Sure. Let's get some fresh air in here," said Van Zandt as he threw open a window. Oldenberg brought O'Neill into the room, and Stella followed with Mrs. O'Neill.

As soon as everybody was inside the office, O'Neill took his wife in his arms. "It's wonderful to see you again, Joyce," he said. "I'm going to stop hiding. Now it's time to fight back."

"Patrick, I've been so worried for you," she said. "What's been happening? Why all these secrets?"

"There's so much to explain," replied O'Neill. "I'll tell you everything, I promise. But first, I have to make the captain understand that I'm not to blame for Steinmann's death."

O'Neill turned to Oldenberg and opened the envelope. He took out the papers and laid them on the table. He said, "These are secret papers from the Ocean Star president's office. There's enough information here to send Lorraine Houston to jail."

"If you could keep it short," said Oldenberg.

"OK. Ocean Star is an investment firm. Its business is making money for its clients," continued O'Neill. "How do they do this? By investing clients' money in the international money markets – or that's what should happen. Look at this page. It's organized in two halves, so let's compare the two sides. On the left the numbers show money that was paid to clients – often a fifteen per cent return. On the right we see what the firm actually made from investments. Surprise, surprise! These numbers are far less. You realize what this means?"

"Go on, tell me," said Oldenberg. "You're the accountant."

"Ocean Star can't possibly earn enough from its investments to pay big money to the clients and millions to the president. It's using the money from new clients to pay the old clients. As long as it continues to get large numbers of new clients, this can work, and people think it's the smartest firm on Wall Street. However, it's a serious crime. I believe that's why Steinmann was murdered. He knew about it too after I showed him these accounts, and he talked to Houston. I want to make all this public, and now I don't care if it destroys Ocean Star at the same time. Is that clear, Captain?"

"More or less," replied Oldenberg. "If I could take those papers … Thanks. But there are a lot more questions which I want answered. We'll continue at Police Headquarters. Mr. O'Neill, you're still my prisoner."

Chapter 11   *O'Neill's story*

At Police Headquarters, Oldenberg led us up to his office. I'd sent Stella home – at least one of us should try and get a good night's sleep. Mrs. O'Neill wouldn't leave her husband.

Inside Oldenberg's office, it couldn't be more different from the offices I'd seen at Ocean Star. The walls were a dirty green color and there was no carpeting on the floor. "Basic" was the best word to describe it. Oldenberg had ordered coffee and sandwiches for everybody. At least the NYPD coffee tasted better than it used to when I was a cop.

"You have a story to tell us, Mr. O'Neill," said Oldenberg. "I want to know everything about you, Steinmann and Ocean Star."

"OK. Two years ago, the old department head moved to another firm," began O'Neill. "I'd worked at Ocean Star for over eight years and I thought I had a good chance of getting the job. I was wrong – the president, Lorraine Houston, had decided to bring in someone new. Someone who didn't care who he hurt.

"So I went on with my work and did what was necessary. With Steinmann as head of department, the firm was making even more money than before. Houston thought he was wonderful, but people who were working with me thought the opposite. Steinmann loved to push people hard.

"A year ago, I asked Steinmann how the firm could continue paying so much money to its clients. The money our department made from clients' investments wasn't that high. I did the math again and still didn't understand. Where was the money coming from? I was worried, but Steinmann promised me that there were no problems. He said, 'Just do your job and don't ask too many questions. She knows what she's doing on the top floor.'

"The 'top floor' is where Lorraine Houston has her offices. Steinmann hoped to get his own office there some day. It seemed impossible to talk to him, so I kept my mouth shut. Time passed and Ocean Star went on paying out big money to its clients. Then, on Friday morning last week, I received the information that could destroy the firm and send Lorraine Houston to jail.

"It happened by chance. I got a letter from Houston's office. At first I didn't understand why I'd been sent a hard copy of the accounts – usually everything like that is sent through office email. I soon realized that it had been a mistake. Houston's personal assistant had sent me an envelope which was meant to go to the vice-president.

"I knew I shouldn't, but I continued reading. As I read, I was more and more surprised. Now I understood that the public accounts weren't the truth. These were secret accounts, which weren't on computer. They showed that Ocean Star was using the money from its new clients to pay the old ones. Now I understood how Houston had so much to spend on her cars, homes, clothes and vacations.

"I didn't like the idea, but I thought I should talk with Steinmann. I knew I had to be careful, so I made a copy of the accounts to show him. What about the ones I'd received? How could I get the information out of the building safely? I had an idea – I put the accounts in an envelope and addressed it to my old friend Frank Van Zandt. Then I left the building for five minutes and dropped the envelope in the nearest mailbox.

"Later that morning, I spoke with Steinmann, and gave him the copy of the accounts. He was immediately very interested. He laughed and said, 'So that's how she does it. You've done the right thing. I'll go straight upstairs and talk with Houston. With this information, I could make a lot of money. Maybe I'll share some with you.'

"His plan was to ask Houston to pay him to keep quiet. I became really angry with him and tried to make him change his mind. But he refused. He wouldn't listen to me and went up to the top floor. Now I knew that I could be in real trouble because Steinmann had gotten the accounts from me. I wasn't sure what to do, but my first move was to get out of the office quick.

"I told my personal assistant that I'd had an awful headache all day and had to go home. Back home, I waited a couple of hours, then made some phone calls. First I called Steinmann's personal assistant. She told me that Steinmann's desk was empty and his computer was gone, but she couldn't tell me anything more. I sent Steinmann an angry email to his home computer. I wrote something like, 'I didn't think you could be so stupid. I can't believe what you've done.'

"The next day, I felt bad about what I'd said in the email, so I tried to phone Steinmann. His wife answered and told me that he hadn't come home, and she was very worried. That night, I stayed up late thinking about what I should do. Just before midnight I got a call. Someone said, 'You have information which belongs to the firm. Return this information to Ms. Houston by midday tomorrow if you want to stay alive.'

"How could I return the accounts? They were in the U.S. Mail. So I thought the safest thing to do was to hide. I wrote a note for Joyce and left in the middle of the night. Looking back, maybe it wasn't the most intelligent decision. I packed a bag, left by the back entrance, took a cab to Frank Van Zandt's place. I can promise you I left my car on Henry Street. I told Frank to expect the letter with the accounts, then I checked into a hotel. On Monday morning I took out $10,000 from the bank so I wouldn't need to use any credit cards. I think you know the rest of the story."

"Thanks, Mr. O'Neill," said Oldenberg. "That's very helpful."

Oldenberg led me to another office. He thought for a few moments, then said, "Marley, I need some advice. My problem is this – if I accept that Houston ordered Steinmann's murder, how can I show that it's true?"

"If you'll allow me, Captain," I said. "I got an idea that just might work."

Chapter 12 *If the price is right*

What if nobody knew that O'Neill was at Police Headquarters? That would give us the chance to tell some clever lies – lies that might give us the advantage. I shared my ideas with the captain.

"We don't know for sure, but let's say Lorraine Houston planned Steinmann's murder," I began. "She's killed one person and she wants O'Neill badly enough to kill again. Why don't we try out this plan? Give the news of what happened at the Metro Hotel tonight to the newspapers, TV and radio stations. Some of it can be true, but a few things can be changed. We tell them that O'Neill escaped and is believed to be somewhere in the East Village area. Houston will be very afraid. She has a lot to lose if she doesn't find O'Neill first and stop him from talking."

"OK, Marley. So far, so good. What next?" asked Oldenberg.

"If you agree, I could speak with her. I'll tell her I have something to sell – the secret accounts."

"Go on," said Oldenberg. "I'm interested. But why you? Why couldn't an NYPD officer do it?"

"I'll tell her I've found O'Neill and am keeping him someplace safe – where she'll never find him. I'll also tell her I have the accounts, which I'll offer to sell if the price is right. I'll make her an offer which she can't refuse. For $100,000 I'll return the accounts to her and give O'Neill to the police. Houston will think she has won. The secret accounts will be safe and O'Neill will be in jail for Steinmann's murder. I'll meet with her, then try and get her to talk."

"Come on, Marley. Get real!" said Oldenberg. "You think a hard businesswoman like Houston is just going to say, 'Oh, by the way, I ordered Steinmann's murder.'"

"I'll let her think I'm the same sort of person as her," I continued. "A businessman who doesn't care how he earns his money or who he hurts. If she feels comfortable with me, then we might get the truth."

"This had better work, Marley. I hope you're a good enough actor," said Oldenberg.

"Believe me, Oldenberg, on a good day I could win Oscars," I told him.

"All right. We'll do it," replied Oldenberg. "This could be dangerous. You know that as well as I do. You'll need a full NYPD team behind you. I'll organize that as soon as you and Houston have a time and a place to meet. So now I'll talk to the newspapers and Houston will think that O'Neill is still in hiding."

"OK. And one more thing," I said. "Mrs. O'Neill and her daughter Julia could be in real danger. Could you move them to an NYPD safe house?"

"Consider it done," said Oldenberg.

* * *

Wednesday had been a very long day. I got home at three o'clock in the morning and I was so tired that I felt like a dead man walking. I fell into bed and slept well.

The next morning I woke up late, feeling much better. After quickly getting dressed, I ran down to the nearest newsstand and picked up the morning newspapers. I took the papers into Slim Pete's Diner on Main Street to read more carefully. The name "Slim" is a joke. Actually, he has a serious weight problem.

"What'll it be, Mr. Marley?" asked Pete with a big smile.

"Eggs, pancakes and bacon," I answered. "And make that coffee strong, will you?"

"You got it. So what's the famous Mr. Marley doing today?" asked Pete. "Helping New York's Finest win the war against crime?"

"Something like that," I replied.

"New York's Finest" – that's what people call the NYPD. I never thought of myself as one of the "Finest" when I was a cop and I never thought I was fighting a war. I was just doing my job. If there was a little less crime on the streets by the end of the day, that was good enough for me.

I read through the newspapers. Oldenberg had done an excellent job. The O'Neill story was on all the front pages. The headline of the *Daily News* read, "NYPD's MOST WANTED ESCAPES". The *New York Post* headline made me smile: "KILLER ACCOUNTANT ON THE RUN". There was some truth, but the rest of the story sounded like something from the movies: "This man is both intelligent and dangerous," said Captain Oldenberg. This wasn't the O'Neill that I knew.

While I ate my breakfast, I watched the TV news. Their reporter said, "This is Cindy Lu outside the Metro Hotel on Avenue C. Here, last night, NYPD officers almost caught Patrick O'Neill, the man wanted for the murder of Ronald Steinmann …"

"Well done, Oldenberg," I thought. Now Houston would get a clear message. Neither her people nor the NYPD had found O'Neill, so she still had a real problem on her hands. I hoped she was one very worried woman.

I got to the office by ten o'clock. Stella had already been there a couple of hours. "That was quite a day, yesterday. You feeling OK, now?" she asked.

"A lot better," I replied. "And thank you for taking care of Mrs. O'Neill all day. With luck, we're going to send Lorraine Houston to jail."

During the morning I agreed on a plan with Oldenberg. I would meet with Houston in a public area, the kind of place where it would be easy for an NYPD team to watch and wait. Our choice was Battery Park, at the foot of Manhattan, with its tall trees and green grass. This is where New York meets the ocean. From here you can look across Upper New York Bay to the Statue of Liberty and Staten Island.

I tried to get through to Houston on my cellphone, but her personal assistant wouldn't allow me to speak with her. "I'm sorry, sir, but Ms. Houston isn't taking any calls," she said.

I wasn't going to take "no" for an answer. "Listen carefully and just do what I say. Your boss lost something of great importance. Tell her I've found it and want to return it to her. I'll call back in ten minutes and expect to speak with her in person. Understood?"

"Careful, now," I told myself. "No mistakes." I waited a full fifteen minutes before calling back. People think less clearly when they get impatient. This time I got ahold of Houston immediately.

"Who are you and what do you want?" she asked crossly.

"The name's Marley. I was working for Mr. O'Neill. He found some interesting papers of yours, which he gave me to look after. Now I'm working for myself and I thought that you might like to have those papers back. I'll make this offer even more generous. The police will be very interested when I tell them where O'Neill is. The price is $100,000. Wait in your office for my call at eight o'clock tomorrow morning."

"What?" began Houston.

"That's it, lady!" I shouted. "Be ready in your office, eight o'clock tomorrow with $100,000, OK? And don't think of doing anything clever or every newspaper in this city will know the truth about Ocean Star's accounts."

With that, I ended the call. I felt very pleased with myself. Would I still feel so pleased tomorrow?

Chapter 13 *Battery Park*

Friday, October 8th, 7:00 a.m. I was on my way from Grand Central Station to Bowling Green on a number five train. This subway station is just north of Battery Park, which was where I was going to meet Lorraine Houston.

Battery Park is a public area where it would be easier for the NYPD team to watch and wait. I thought that Houston would feel uncomfortable away from the deep carpets and expensive furniture of her offices.

From the subway station, it was just a few minutes' walk to Battery Park. I walked across to the Sphere, a famous piece of public art at the north end of the park – a large gold metal ball, as tall as a house. Oldenberg's team was already waiting there with hidden cameras, though you wouldn't know they were police officers. Two young guys talking on a seat. A couple standing under an umbrella. Their orders were to watch and wait. But if I waved my hat, they would immediately help me.

The sky was full of black clouds and it was starting to rain. I put up my umbrella and looked at my watch. It was eight o'clock, time to call Houston.

"Ms. Houston? I'm waiting for you," I said. "Bring the money and come alone. If there's any trouble, my personal assistant has a copy of your accounts ready to email to every newspaper in New York. If all goes to plan, she'll destroy that copy."

"OK. That's understood," she replied. "How do I know you're telling the truth?"

"Ask yourself this question: What will happen if you don't believe me? I'll need your cellphone number … Thanks. Now, leave the building and wait outside the front entrance."

I let her wait a few minutes in the cold. I wanted her to feel angry and impatient by the time she arrived at Battery Park. Now for my next call.

"So sorry to keep you waiting," I lied. "You see a tall white-haired guy in a dark green overcoat, carrying a copy of the *Wall Street Journal*? He should be opposite you, standing by a cab." Houston said she could see him.

"That's my assistant, Mr. Blaney. Go and talk with him," I continued. "He has a cab waiting for you."

We had to make sure that Houston arrived alone. Joe Blaney's job was to make sure that she took our cab – a cab with an NYPD driver. Houston was going to be taken on a little tour of Lower Manhattan. We were going to take our time and make sure she was in a very bad mood by the time she met me.

Thirty minutes later I called Houston again.

"Tell the driver to drop you at the north entrance to Battery Park, opposite Bowling Green. Then walk south to the Sphere. You'll see me holding a blue and white golf umbrella. By the way, you don't need to pay the driver. Hope you enjoyed your sightseeing."

I wouldn't like to repeat Houston's reply – such bad language! The rain was beginning to fall more heavily as I saw her. She was tall and slim and was wearing a red suit with a short skirt that showed a lot of leg. She really wasn't dressed for the weather. I turned on my little secret recorder. I waved to her and sat on a park seat under the trees opposite the Sphere.

"This had better be good, Marley," she said. "Do you have my papers?"

"Not so fast," I replied. "Do you have my money?"

She put her case on her knees and opened it. Inside, it was packed with hundred-dollar bills.

"Count it if you like," she said.

"Don't you think the park looks lovely in fall?" I asked.

"I don't have all day. Hurry up and give me the papers," she said impatiently.

I slowly reached into my case and took out an envelope, which I gave to her. Then I reached into my coat pocket for my cellphone.

Houston took a single piece of paper out of the envelope and looked at me like a dog which was about to bite.

"Give me the rest of the accounts, Marley, or you're dead meat!" She had taken a small gun out of her purse and was pressing it into my side.

"Not very intelligent, Ms. Houston," I said. "Remember, if anything happens to me, my personal assistant will email your accounts to every newspaper in this city. If I press 'Send', my personal assistant gets that message. Also, shooting people in public isn't a good idea. You'll get the rest of the papers. Just be patient. Like any good businessman, I like to count my money first."

She gave me a cold, hard look through narrow eyes, then put the gun back in her purse. Now she was beginning to shake with the cold.

"Here, take my overcoat," I said.

She took the coat and put it over her shoulders. She smiled for the first time and thanked me. Now I felt I might have the advantage.

I quickly checked the money, then took a second envelope from my case and held it in front of her.

"There must be some very important information here. You're one smart businesswoman, Ms. Houston, and a good employer. I like the way you find answers to problems with your people. Like sending Steinmann on his final drive in O'Neill's car. Good work. The police think that O'Neill is the killer. That way you can be completely sure it's the end of your trouble with those two. As soon as I tell the police where O'Neill is, you're safe."

She smiled again. "You're a smart guy. I'm sorry about Steinmann. He was good at his job, until he started to think he was smarter than me. I couldn't let him tell me what to do. I had to get rid of him."

At last I had it, and everything was on the recorder. I passed her the second envelope. She opened it quickly, took out the papers and counted them.

"Looks like it's all here. It's been good doing business with you," she said, and returned my overcoat. "Now just make sure the police get ahold of O'Neill."

As she walked away, I called to her, "Actually, Ms. Houston, I got a message from O'Neill. He'd like to tell you, 'Smile! You're on a police camera!'"

I waved my hat in the air. Houston screamed and pulled out her gun, but in seconds the NYPD team was all around her. She dropped the gun and fell to the ground.

A minute ago she had been the president of Ocean Star Finance and a very rich woman. Now she was going to spend many years in jail.

I called Oldenberg to tell him the news. "Good work, Marley!" he said. "O'Neill will soon be a free man."

The rain had stopped and the sun had begun to break through the heavy clouds. In the sunshine, leaves were dropping from the trees and turning in the wind. The air from the ocean smelled fresh and clean. It felt good to be alive. I should spend more time in this city's parks.